MAN'S CONCERN
WITH DEATH

MAN'S CONCERN WITH DEATH

Arnold Toynbee, A. Keith Mant, Ninian Smart,
John Hinton, Simon Yudkin, Eric Rhode,
Rosalind Heywood, H. H. Price

McGRAW-HILL BOOK COMPANY
St. Louis   New York   San Francisco

Library of Congress Catalog Card Number: 69-17873
First UNITED STATES Edition published by McGraw-Hill Book Company, 1969
65126

Originally published by Hodder and Stoughton Ltd., London, 1968

Contributors

Arnold Toynbee, C.H., Litt.D., D.C.L., F.B.A., Membre de l'Institut de France, Professor Emeritus of International History in the University of London and former Director of Studies in the Royal Institute of International Affairs.

A. Keith Mant, M.D., F.C.Path., Reader in Forensic Medicine, University of London at Guy's Hospital, London; author of *Forensic Medicine—Observation and Interpretation*.

Ninian Smart, M.A., B.Phil., Professor of Religious Studies, University of Lancaster.

John Hinton, M.D., M.R.C.P., D.P.M., Professor of Psychiatry, Middlesex Hospital Medical School, London.

The late Simon Yudkin, Ph.D., M.B., F R.C.P., former Consultant Paediatrician, University College Hospital and Whittington Hospital, London.

Eric Rhode, broadcaster and journalist; author of *Tower of Babel*.

Rosalind Heywood, Member of Council of the Society for Psychical Research; author of *The Sixth Sense* and *The Infinite Hive*, contributor to *Science and E.S.P.*

H. H. Price, LL.D., D. Litt., F.B.A., Professor Emeritus, University of Oxford and former President of the Society for Psychical Research.

ACKNOWLEDGEMENTS

The authors and publishers are grateful to the following for permission to include quoted extracts:

Chatto and Windus Ltd. for "Ignorance of Death" from *Collected Poems* by William Empson; "Dead Man's Dump" from the *Collected Poems* of Isaac Rosenberg.

Faber & Faber Ltd. for "Vergissmeinnicht" from the *Collected Poems* of Keith Douglas; *Four Quartets* and *The Waste Land* by T. S. Eliot; "Nothing to be Said" from *The Whitsun Wedding* by Philip Larkin; *Rosencrantz and Guildenstern are Dead* by Tom Stoppard.

Faber & Faber Ltd. and Alfred A. Knopf Inc. for "The Emperor of Ice-Cream" from the *Collected Poems* of Wallace Stevens.

Victor Gollancz Ltd. for *Language, Truth and Logic* by A. J. Ayer; *A Drug Taker's Notes* by R. H. Ward.

Hamish Hamilton Ltd. and Alfred A. Knopf Inc. for *The Plague* by Albert Camus, transl. Stuart Gilbert.

Hughes, Massie Ltd. for lines from St. John of the Cross, transl. Roy Campbell, published by the Harvill Press Ltd.

Macmillan & Co. Ltd., the Trustees of the Hardy Estate and The Macmillan Company of Canada Ltd. for "The Walk" and "The Twain" by Thomas Hardy.

Routledge & Kegan Paul Ltd. for "Corposant" from *The Nature of Cold Weather* by Peter Redgrove; "Psychology and Parapsychology" by Sir Cyril Burt from *Science and E.S.P.* edited by J. R. Smythies.

The Scottish Medical Journal for "A Voice from the Grandstand" by Lord Geddes, quoted from the *Edinburgh Medical Journal,* vol. 44, 1937.

Sidgwick & Jackson Ltd. for *Zoar* by W. H. Salter.

The Society of Authors and Jonathan Cape Ltd. for *The Dead* by James Joyce.

Tavistock Publications Ltd. for "A Psychoanalytic Approach to Aesthetics" by Hannah Segal, taken from the book *New Directions in Psycho-Analysis* by M. Klein, P. Heimann and R. Money-Kyrle.

Lines from "Death of a Ball-Turret Gunner" from *Selected Poems* of Randall Jarrell are reprinted by permission of Faber & Faber Ltd.

The extract from *The Invisible Writing* by Arthur Koestler, published by Hamish Hamilton Ltd. is reprinted by permission of A. D. Peters & Co.

The chapter "What Kind of Next World?" by H. H. Price is reprinted here from an article in *Tomorrow,* Autumn 1956, by permission of the Parapsychology Foundation, Inc., New York.

The British and American Societies for Psychical Research, for permission to quote from their records.

Additional permissions for the American edition:

Schocken Books, Inc. for "Dead Man's Dump" from *Collected Poems* by Isaac Rosenberg. Copyright © 1949 by Schocken Books, Inc.

Chilmark Press, Inc. for "Vergissmeinnicht" from *Collected Poems* by Keith Douglas. Copyright © 1966 by Marie J. Douglas.

Harcourt, Brace & World, Inc. for *Four Quarters* and *The Waste Land* by T. S. Eliot; "Ignorance of Death" from Collected Poems by William Empson.

Grove Press, Inc. for *Rosencrantz and Guildenstern are Dead* by Tom Stoppard. Copyright © 1967 by Tom Stoppard.

The Macmillan Company, New York, for "The Twain" and "The Walk" from *Collected Poems* by Thomas Hardy. Copyright © 1925 by The Macmillan Company.

Dufour Editions, Inc. for "Corposant" from *The Nature of Cold Weather* by Peter Redgrove.

Humanities Press, Inc. for "Psychology and Parapsychology" by Sir Cyril Burt from *Science and E.S.P.,* edited by J. R. Smythies.

The Viking Press, Inc. for "The Dead" from *Dubliners* by James Joyce.

Random House, Inc. for excerpt from *Ulysses* by James Joyce.

Mrs. Randall Jarrell for "The Death of a Ball Turret Gunner" from *Selected Poems* of Randall Jarrell.

which make necessary reference to bodily activities, etc., then "my" survival in the next life becomes very thin, and leaves aside so much of what constitutes me as an individual person that it might be doubtful whether it is even appropriate to speak any more of "me".

But although such questions about the conceivability or meaningfulness of an after-life are important, they do not bear directly on the concept of death itself. Here there has been rather a dearth of concern to be clear about what is meant. It is true that at a practical level there has been a necessary interest in "defining" death from a legal and moral point of view, since it is vitally important for doctors to define the conditions in which an act of theirs does not constitute the taking of life. It remains useful, however, to consider the idea of death from a philosophical angle, and to analyse its meaning. I shall here attempt this task, before proceeding to consider some existentialist and related theological motifs.

Death as distinguished from dying

A first point to note is that though it may be plausible to regard death as an event, dying is not. We say, for instance, that a person died slowly and, perhaps, painfully. But if one can die quickly or slowly, dying is a process rather than an event. As will be seen, this conclusion is over-simplified, though it has an important substance. Part of the explanation of why our language treats dying as a process can be gleaned from the fact that "to die" is an active verb. This does not mean that a person is in the ordinary way active in his dying: but it implies that somehow the source of dying is in the person rather than outside him. This is where there is a difference between dying and being killed. A person can be killed by lightning or by a murderer or by a bus; it is a metaphor to speak of his being killed by a tumour or by grief. Built into language, then, is a distinction between what lies "within" a person and what lies "outside" him, and dying is predicated of the person himself as though it is a process, as it were, originating in him.

This does not mean that its ultimate cause lies in him. The point is that we look upon the events and processes of a person's existence from a continually shifting perspective. One man is mortally wounded by another, and is carried to hospital. From the perspective of what happened after the shooting, we can say that he was obviously dying. He was, that is, in a state where he was going to die, unless some remarkable interference in the process were to take place. When he dies, we can well say that the cause of his death was his being shot: here we revert to an earlier perspective, and account for his getting into a state where he was going to die.

In these distinctions, we rely upon a rough sense of what is normal, natural and foreseeable. He would not have died, had it not been for the shooting. This was an event interfering with the foreseeable on-going of the man's life. That is why we pick it out as *the* cause of his death. It might seem that from a more rigorous and expanded point of view the cause of his death was the total state of himself and of his environment; but in fact we are interested for practical and other reasons in significant interferences with what could otherwise normally be expected.

This comes out in the concept of the process of dying. When we say of a person that he is dying, we do not absolutely mean that he will die. "Can't you see the man is dying? For God's sake do something about it!" Such an imperative is not incoherent or contradictory. In himself, so to say, the man may well be dying, but there remain possibilities of interfering dramatically, and rescuing him from impending death. It is not surprising that the ordinary-language concept of dying should be increasingly hard to apply in hospital situations, where the resources for dramatic interference in the normal sequences of disease are so vastly multiplied.

It should be noted that the idea of what can normally be expected, given a person's present condition, does not preclude one's being wrong in saying that a person is dying. Dying is not a matter of symptoms, but of actually being in process of dying. One might normally expect from given symptoms that a person's condition is such that he will die; but the symptoms might be highly misleading and the man might not really be dying at all. What we are concerned with in saying that someone is dying is his actual condition, which normally issues in death, not with the symptoms or other evidence which might lead us to think that he is in that actual condition. We are speaking of his condition, not of the evidence which leads us to speak in this way about his condition.

If dying, in one sense, is a process, how long can it last? If a man is badly injured, he can be said to be dying now and in a minute or two he may be dead. It can last a very short time; but in many circum-stances, of course, dying takes a long time. But if our present analysis is correct, it would be paradoxical and rhetorical to say that a healthy child of five is dying, on the ground that he will sooner or later die of something or other. Death indeed is inevitable, but before we can say that someone is dying we must have an idea of some rather specific condition or conditions *of* which he is dying. It is true that some-times we may know that a person is dying, but be unable to fix on the condition which is bringing this about; yet we certainly believe that there is some specific malaise which is responsible (or some combination of malaises). Normally, however, it is known both that a person is dying and of what in particular he is dying.

This is brought out by the way in which we regard dying of old age. We certainly often say that a person died of old age; but there is something grossly unsatisfactory in a diagnosis where it is said "He is dying." "And of what?" "Just old age." Rather, the point about old age is that certain malaises can be expected—for instance, the heart begins to wear out. We can certainly say that an old person is dying because of some such specific condition.

Thus the process of dying may be a long one, but it is tied conceptually not just to a normal expectation of what will happen given a person's present condition, but also specifically to that given condition. Dying, in this sense, is dying *of*.

But if dying is a process, death is an event. About the process we may ask: "How long did he take to die?" About the event, we may ask: "And when did he die?" The latter can in principle be timed to the minute or second. (It is true that some of the criteria of what constitutes death have somewhat vague or even contradictory applications—the brain may function even when the heart has stopped, etc.;[1] but we are not in doubt that King Charles I died very close to the instant when the executioner's axe severed his neck.) The distinction between the process of dying and the event of death is underlined by the fact that a person can die even if it was not previously true that he was dying. A child of five in good health is not dying, but he can meet an instantaneous death under the wheels of a bus. A person can die of some internal condition also without its having been true that he was dying. A healthy man who has bits of shrapnel left in his body may have the disastrous bad luck of a fragment's entering his heart via the blood stream. We would not say that he was dying all these years since Normandy. Again, a person might burst a crucial blood vessel by sneezing, and might drop down dead, but we would not say that he had been dying.

Most typically such cases of death where the person was not previously dying are cases of sudden death, either from internal or external causes. It is possible for a case of sudden death to supervene upon a process of dying, but this is sudden death *per accidens*. For instance, a man dying of cancer is killed in a car smash: this is sudden death—but it is *per accidens* in the sense that the cause of death is not what the person was dying *of*.

Emotions experienced when facing death

Sudden death involves that a person is not aware, or is only briefly aware, of the occasion and nature of his death. This reminds us of a further distinction which has to be made, namely between dying with awareness of dying and dying without such awareness. With instantaneous death, there may be, as we have just said, some fleeting awareness. But this can hardly suffice to allow us to qualify dying by such adverbs as "bravely", "resignedly", "cheerfully", "fearfully", "gracefully" and so forth. These adverbs bring out the attitudes of

[1] See Dr. Mant above, "The Medical Definition of Death", p. 22.

those who die in the knowledge that they are dying or about to die.

Before exploring these attitudes, let us note briefly that dying and being about to die are not the same concepts. If I am condemned to hanging in five hours' time, I can be said to be about to die, but i would be wrong to say that I am dying (unless again, *per accidens*— might be dying of cancer and condemned to death by hanging). But being about to die and dying are frequently accompanied by knowledge that this is so, and may thus call forth similar emotions and responses.

To display courage or fear in dying or being about to die, in such a way that one can say "he died heroically" or "he died a coward' death", a person's courage, etc., has to be related to his death or his mode of death. Suppose a person is lying mortally ill during an air-raid he might be facing his own death and suffering serenely, and yet be full of fear and trembling at the explosions. Would it here be right to say that he did not die, in a certain sense, courageously? We might hesitate to answer, for there is the feeling that dying is a matter, so to say, for the whole man, and lack of courage in one respect could not allow us to ascribe courage in dying. We might qualify, and say "Basically a courageous end, but . . ."—just as with ascriptions of happiness (in its most important sense, ascribable to the "whole" man): if I say that a friend of mine is happy, though his marriage is unhappy, I feel inclined to interpolate "basically" before "happy". Nevertheless, the point remains, that a courageous death is one where the courage comes out in relation to the awareness that one is dying, and possibly painfully It is thus not possible to speak of a person's being courageous in the process of dying (in the sense of dying courageously) where there is no awareness that he is dying.

The adverbs, then, typically have to do with facing death and the process of dying. From a practical point of view, the concept of the process of dying with awareness is most important; for it is hardly possible to prepare to meet a sudden end, except in so far as one might prepare for dangerous situations where a sudden end is quite likely Here again is a distinction that can be made. If death can appear to us in the guise of a certainty, given that we know that we are dying within a determinate period, it can also appear in the guise of proba bility. A soldier in battle can thus be said to die heroically, even i there was no time at which he was (in the process of) dying. It is no that his being blown up by a mortar-bomb was characterised by heroism—there is scarcely a style in such things. Rather it is that his previous actions, say in storming an enemy position at vast risk to his life, etc., was heroic, and met its probable outcome, namely death. H was aware of all this, and thus faced death, though he need not have seen himself as certain to die or being about to die, but only as very liable to die. This kind of courage can perhaps be prepared for too (in

---

[1] For a discussion of practical issues involved in facing death, see below, John Hinton "The Dying and the Doctor", pp. 43-5.

is thought in the army that the virtues of courage and resource can be inculcated by training). But though *this* facing of death can be prepared for, so that one can have hope of displaying courage, serenity, etc., there can be no such preparation for an unfaced sudden end. One can write one's will and so forth. But there is no question of heroism or cowardice or serenity in being instantaneously killed by a car on a dark night.

The adverbs, then, characterise behaviour in the known face of death (either in being in process of dying, or in being about to die, or in being in danger of death). But how does this tie up with attitudes that one might have just now, when one is not facing death in any of these ways? Can I be said to look on my own death serenely or with equanimity or with apprehension? The discussion so far would indicate that I cannot properly be said to look on my own death thus, for I am not genuinely facing it. Does not death have to be known to be rather imminent or likely before we can speak of "facing" it?

It is here useful to revert to a point made in passing earlier on: the inevitability of death has to be distinguished from its certainty as imminent. If I am dying it is virtually certain that I shall die within a given period (virtually—we remember the caveat that medical practice may be able unexpectedly to intervene); if I am about to die, likewise there is virtual certainty. But certainty here is coupled roughly to dates. What matters in being about to die is that I am due to die in five hours' time or whenever, whereas I could otherwise expect to live a good bit longer. The inevitability of death is not thus coupled to dates, save in the most expansive way. Thus I am certain that I shall not be alive in 2066 A.D., but I cannot now know at roughly what age I shall die or how or of what. And I cannot claim heroism because I live my life in the knowledge that I shall inevitably die, and live it without overt signs of cowardice, fear, etc.

Facing death in the strict sense involves knowing roughly the timing and mode of my death (or the probability of a certain mode and timing). What, then, should be said about attitudes to my death as simply inevitable, though its timing and mode is not known? Here there is room for a practical and a rather speculative approach.

At the practical level, it could be said that at least I can face up to the fact that there is a strong chance that one day I shall face death, and so should order my life so that this facing of death will not prove a bitter experience. This is a prudent way of looking at it: but it may link up with a more outward-looking moral attitude—for facing death is facing the dissolution of the projects that I may have devoted myself to and the plans and joys that I cherish, and will show me a limit to selfish pursuits. I may in fact be better able to face death if already I am relatively selfless. *Memento mori* has its ethical uses.

Asymmetry of our attitudes to birth and death

More speculatively, the contemplation of death may raise some questions about human values and existence. Some of these will be treated a little later, in relation to existentialism. But in the meantime we can note a certain asymmetry in our attitudes to birth and death. We are more inclined to think that death makes a mockery of our achievements, for in the end it looks as though we are nothing, than to think of birth or conception as mocking us, even though they indicate a previous time when we were nothing. Future non-existence seems to be more disturbing than past non-existence. This is not just a reflection of traditional Christian (and some other) doctrine, promising a judgment after death. This no doubt solemnises death. It perhaps more importantly reflects the structure of practical action. A great deal of human activity is directed to further ends. It is true that playing cricket, making music and love and the like are typically treated as ends in themselves; but many activities are undertaken because they are instrumental to further ends, which of necessity lie in the future. And even with many activities undertaken for their own sake, there is a sense of anticipation of future variations. Cricketers do not regard cricket history as closed, but look for new excitements and styles still waiting in the future; and so with music, the arts, etc. Family life also does not rest quite content with those now living, but reaches in anticipation towards a future generation. There is something sad in a tradition that becomes closed.

Thus over a vast range of human concerns, there is an orientation towards the future, and the future sometimes is brought in explicitly as providing a kind of justification for the present. But a person who is solely concerned in promoting his own welfare and ambitions cannot look too far into the future, for anything beyond his own death can have no force in justifying and making sense of his present activities. It is not surprising, then, if the contemplation of death raises some wider questions about the point and value of human activities. The matter becomes even more forcible if we contemplate the possibility of the destruction of the whole race.

The asymmetry between our attitudes to death and birth is a reason for the attractions of myths of the future consummation of history, whether through the coming of the kingdom, or through establishment of communism, or through the reaching of the omega-point.

Though the facing of death in the strict sense is not the destiny of everyone (for some are struck down without warning, and others do not know that they are dying even though they are), it is clearly an important phase of human existence, and itself can be a mode of the expression of a person's character. This is no doubt why it sometimes takes on the character of a kind of achievement. The process of dying can meet with admiration, if a man compasses it with dignity and serenity

The assumption that in facing death one is facing something unpleasant encourages us to think of a death well met as being courageous. But it is hard to see on what grounds death considered in itself is unpleasant. For instance, it is surely not obvious that it is somehow a disaster that a person has to die at some time or other. This is where the present analysis of what it means to face death (i.e. where one is dying or about to die or in great danger of dying) is relevant: what is here sometimes at least disastrous about death is that it is occurring earlier than might have been expected—a man is cut off, so we say, in his prime. But in addition to this we must take account of the *mode* of death: this itself may be painful and frightening. In this case, it is appropriate to think of facing death not just as facing the fact of imminent death, but as facing the process of dying. A person who is aware that he is dying is aware of the way in which he is dying.

To sum up so far on the analysis of the concepts of death and dying. First, dying is a process, death an event. Second, one may or not be aware of the process of dying. Third, if one is aware of it, then this is one case where one is facing death (other cases are where one is about to die or in great danger of death). Fourth, not everyone is dying, though everyone will die. Fifth, not everyone is in a position of having to face death. Sixth, we may all, however, reflect about death, and be realistic or the reverse about the chance that one will in fact have to face death. Seventh, to die courageously, etc., is to face the process of dying (or the situation of being about to die) in a certain style. But it may be that such an analysis of concepts of death and dying is in a sense banal. It leaves aside some of the more important poetic and mythic ideas associated with death.

Mythic interpretations of death

Here it is convenient to move to existentialist and theological approaches to the concept of death. For instance, Christian theologians in recent years have been intensely concerned with the rediscovery of biblical ideas made possible by modern historical researches into the Old and New Testaments. But ideas of death in the Bible have a mythic ambiguity typical of the thought-forms of the day: thus for Paul, the wages of sin is death, and there is in Genesis also a connection made between sin and dying. It is too crude to look upon the connection simply as a causal one, as though sinning is the cause of dying. The mythic thinking of the biblical writers is not translatable into the language of contemporary English, precisely because in modern times we make distinctions which were not made in biblical times. One could put the point crudely by saying that death was then seen as a symbol of the disastrous alienation between men and God, due to sin. Conversely, right relationship to the divine being was conceived as being eternal life, realisable here and now. It is thus possible to approach the meaning of death from a "positive" point of view, namely by trying to elucidate the opposite of death, that is—life. But just as death has mythic and poetic overtones, so its opposite, life, is not just a matter of biology, of breathing and in other ways continuing as a viable organism; but of quality of life.

In view of this, it is not altogether surprising that modern Protestant theologians (and to some extent Catholics) have tried to reinterpret the mythology of death as expressed in the Bible by recourse to modern existentialism, for the latter is concerned rather markedly by a certain sort of quality of life in relation to death, itself viewed as a symbol of human finitude.

Living in the light of death

Thus there has been a particular appeal in Heidegger's account of authentic existence. To live "authentically" is to accept one's finitude, and thus to avoid running away from one's responsibility through absorption in instrumental concerns. For men, the world is not just present to them, but is open to manipulation; yet our possibilities of changing the world are themselves conditioned in ways not of our choosing. In this sense, we are "thrown" into the world, and the most marked instance of this "thrownness" is death itself, which is the limiting condition of our possibilities. The way to meet this authentically is to live in the light of death. Once we fully and realistically accept it, then it will no longer be something which happens to us (coming upon us, as it were, externally and as a meaningless destruction of our endeavours). Use is made of these existentialist ideas, but within a Christian framework, by Rudolf Bultmann, for instance (for him, authentic freedom is a gift of Christ) and by Karl Rahner (for him, the acceptance of death is found in the sharing of Christ's death sacramentally)—notable representatives of modern Protestant and Catholic theology respectively.

Superficially, it seems as if Sartre takes quite a different view of death. Death is not something which can be treated positively, in the way indicated by Heidegger: it is the destruction of the individual's capacity to create values and is the closing off of freedom. Nevertheless, the very absurdity of death aligns it with man's real situation; by the acceptance of the absurd a proper freedom and authenticity is conferred on the individual.

These views of death are not, correctly speaking, definitions of it, and only in a partial way analyses of the concept. But they are of interest in bringing out, in modern guise, the symbolic and mythic overtones of the idea of death. They may tell us, further, something about the concept which the earlier analysis overlooked. An attempt to combine something of the existentialist approach to death with the concerns of linguistic analysis has recently been made in an interesting article of

W. H. Poteat.[1] In this essay, entitled "I will die", Poteat makes use of the elusive remark of Wittgenstein, in the *Tractatus Logico-Philosophicus:* "As in death, too, the world does not change, but ceases. Death is not an event in life."

Poteat argues that the idea of *my own* death is logically peculiar, in that in thinking of my own death I am not merely contemplating an event in the world, but rather the cessation of my world. It is possible to argue from this that a mythic representation of death in relation to my existence—for instance the Christian myth of the resurrection of the body—is natural, for where one reaches, so to say, the limits of the world, the language which we ordinarily use to describe events *in* the world has to be stretched: mythic language is what occurs when one's language is put under this sort of logical pressure.

It is not altogether clear that Poteat's account is a plausible diagnosis of the actual basis and origin of mythic language, and there can be little doubt that many religious people have not used language about survival and heaven in a consciously mythic way, and so have accepted some of the literal implications of traditional teachings about immortality.

In general, one can say that the existentialist approach to death places the emphasis upon "this world": it is authentic existence here and now which essentially is offered as a possibility for those who have accepted the finitude implied by death.

Some allusion has been made earlier to problems about survival of death from a philosophical point of view. These turn mainly on problems of personal identity and how it can be preserved in a trans-mortal state. These may not be insoluble; but they may remind us that in so far as motives for belief in existence beyond death may be intimately bound up with personal concerns requiring bodily expression, a merely psychic survival will not be satisfying.[2] Thus some of the existentialist emphasis upon coming to terms with death is relevant, in that people may be impelled not merely to contemplate death, but to ask themselves what their motives are (if any) for wishing to survive beyond the grave.

---

[1] Now reprinted in D. Z. Phillips *Religion and Understanding*, Oxford, 1967.
[2] See below, Rosalind Heywood, "Death and Physical Research", p. 219 ff; H. H. Price, What Kind of Next World? p. 251 ff.

3. The Dying and the Doctor

by JOHN HINTON

UNLESS a man's death comes upon him with unexpected suddenness, he will have some cause to suspect when he is dying. His doctor will, most likely, have already seen evidence that his patient is fatally ill. Both then have to cope with the growing realisation that the illness is likely to kill, with the doctor usually knowing it a little earlier than the patient. They wish it were not so, but the inevitable progress affects, amongst other things, their way of regarding each other. To the dying person his doctor, however much he is trusted and regarded as a source of treatment, is no longer one with the power to cure; to the doctor, the patient has become one whose death, despite every possible effort, he is impotent to prevent. This gives rise to problems in the special professional relationship which often develops between a patient and his doctor, and besides that they have the difficulties that face any two people trying to adjust to the fact that one of them is shortly going to die.

Since it is often asserted that many fatally ill people have little awareness of the fact that they are dying, and indeed, they often refer to their recovery or their future, is it misleading to consider their overt or covert awareness of the real situation as an important basis of our insight into their feelings? No one can say with certainty the extent to which dying people know, because they themselves are often uncertain or may have unpleasant suspicions which lead to their avoiding the topic rather than discussing it openly. Nevertheless, in some enquiries where the dying have felt free to talk, a very large proportion have acknowledged the possibility or the certainty that their life would soon end. Sufficient clues arise sooner or later during the course of the terminal illness for a person to suspect that his disease is incurable. He can ignore the evidence or regard it in an optimistic light, but usually it is there. The warning may come as ominous symptoms, for example widespread tumours or breathlessness so severe that it seems to take him to the threshold of dying; it may be the manner of his treatment, such as radiotherapy which is not always successful in the treatment of cancers; it may be the steady deterioration in health so that serious new symptoms are added to those that previous treatment has failed to relieve; it may be the attitude of his friends, relatives and doctor that can reveal that he has no remediable disease; or it may occasionally be a deliberate statement by the doctor to confirm the fatal nature of the illness, although more often this is inferred from chance remarks—not always directed to the patient. The evidence usually grows so that a dying man could know that recovery may not or cannot come about. How does he react to evidence of his fatal condition?

A very common way of coping, illogical though it may appear, is for him to act as if the situation did not exist. It is quite normal for painful thoughts or distressing memories not to reach consciousness. The thought of his own death can easily be too distressful for a patient to bear and so the knowledge of dying is repressed. Sometimes such ideas are more deliberately suppressed so that a fatally ill person half-believes, half-acts as though his life will go on with little change once his illness is over.

While the patient consciously or unconsciously deceives himself, the doctor, usually colludes and often positively encourages the pretence. There are many good and charitable reasons for him to do so; but they are diluted by rationalisations originating in the doctor's own need to be spared distress at his patient's dying. Being human, the doctor can be hurt when forced to acknowledge that his patient is going to die. Perhaps as his medical experience lengthens he is less aware of the hurt he first felt earlier in his career when his patients died; but although the situation becomes bearable it can still perturb. He must admit to the person most concerned that he is now impotent to do what is desired so much, to save his patient's life. The doctor's ability to cure and bring relief usually sustain him in his work—and in his own self-esteem. He can feel very threatened at having to admit failure to a person who is depending on him. He may dread having to admit outright to his patient, whom he may know very well, that he is not going to survive.

When both patient and doctor join in a tacit conspiracy that recovery will take place, it is often to their mutual advantage. The doctor applies his treatments as though they were remedies, and reassures the patient as to his progress. The patient faces his illness with apparent courage and equanimity. He evades, unconsciously or subconsciously, the emotional distress that dying can bring. He need not fear the terrors so often associated with dying and death, nor does he have to prepare sadly to part from life and loved people. He focusses his attention on a theoretical cure, relying on the natural healing and medical skills that have been successful in previous illnesses.

The patient's self-deception combined with the doctor's deception can often be carried out with considerable success for a long period. Acting as if the patient were not mortally ill does, in many ways, make it easier for the doctor to maintain his usual professional front. He need not question too deeply the ethics of his deceit if this deception is one that his patient wants and finds comforting. He can reinforce his patient's denial, and help banish distressing doubts. The authority and dignity of the doctor remain intact and the patient relies on him. An authority that needs buttressing by the assumption of impossible therapeutic powers is inherently imperfect however, and certainly a doctor does not need to claim omnipotence to retain his patient's confidence. Perhaps a doctor's pretence to healing powers that he does not possess is culpable, but it is usually less hurtful than a retreat from failure into cynicism, apparent indifference or the actual avoidance of dying patients.

Although many doctors have by practice become skilled and accustomed to their part in the masquerade of eventual cure, their unease may well grow as the deception falters. Amongst other things, the doctor knows that eventually the well-intended charade must fail, the patient will die although he has been leading him to believe otherwise. Moreover there is a lack of honesty between patient and doctor that is discordant. Many doctors are reticent with their patients, sparing in the information they divulge, but what they do tell their patients should always be in good faith. Hence the doctor, however well-intentioned when contributing to a deception, is apt to feel a nagging sense of failed trust. He is not in a good position to give the understanding which is needed so much if his dying patient becomes apprehensive or depressed. The doctor's unease at the situation may lead him to avoid his patient, cut short his visits, or, at least, avoid mentioning any topic which could lead to making a choice between disquieting truth and lies. This situation is apt to lead to the doctor "managing" the patient as an adult "manages" a child who is thought to lack the capacity to understand. Although some ill people may want the doctor to take over completely, others may find such "managing" adds to the sense of desolation that they, as dying people, are beginning to experience; they may protest that they are not children, nor are they senile, they want a say in things that concern them—*what is going on?*

This is one way in which the collusion between patient and doctor is strained and may break down altogether. The façade is bound to be tested further as the dying person's health deteriorates, because then the hopes and the desperate pretence of the patient may not parallel the more deliberate false optimism of the doctor. A patient who believes or needs to believe that he will recover will expect any new symptoms to be given full attention. A doctor who recognises the further symptoms as part of the inevitable disease process may appear to the patient to be viewing new developments in a cursory manner, dismissing of the symptoms and so, seemingly, of the patient. This reaction can cause a dying person to seek feverishly for further help which may result in sound advice but invites ineffective, expensive treatments that lead to eventual disappointment. If, on the other hand, the doctor plays his fore-doomed role of healer too vigorously, if he loses insight into the fact that he is playing a role, or if he himself cannot accept clear evidence that his patient will not recover, the patient may for a while have to endure uncomfortable investigations and treatments that might sustain a fluctuating hope but offer no material benefit.

The dying man cannot easily believe in recovery when he is aware of deterioration. His façade of unreasonable hope tends to crack, and although he may make frequent attempts at patching, the pretence will sometimes crumble or be abandoned. The cracks may appear as periods of fear and misery which, to the dying man, seem strangely causeless because he denies that his illness is fatal. He may often find false reasons for his emotional distress if he cannot yet admit that it originates from the fact that he is dying. In this situation, for example, he may become unduly preoccupied by some physical symptom or some relatively minor worry. He seems to be fussing over the trivial or exaggerating his discomfort. This may cause his friends and relatives or his nurses and doctor to become intolerant of his complaints, but it is safer for him to displace his anxieties and preoccupations on to problems potentially less devastating than distress over his approaching death.

As an ill man feels hope beginning to dissolve he may try to strengthen it by asking questions of his doctor in a way that makes it very likely that he will get reassuring answers. It is very difficult for a sympathetic doctor to give anything but encouraging, even if untrue, answers to such questions as "I haven't got cancer, have I doctor?" or "Will you get me better, doctor?" Many doctors have been prepared to be fairly frank with a patient and yet found themselves manoeuvred into dishonest optimistic opinions or useless treatments which they never intended to give.

Although many patients, together with their doctors, find solace in an innocent charade of anticipating cure, others do not wish to shelter continuously behind false hopes. However sombre the outlook, some people want to know the essential truth about their prospects as soon as their illness is recognised. Most surveys of medical practice show that doctors usually do not make it clear to a patient early on in his fatal illness that there is no chance of recovery. In fact, the patient is often told the opposite. There are some individual physicians who are much more frank and some medical centres, commoner in the United States than in Britain, where it is the practice to be open about the patients' condition. The frequent custom of the doctors who are prepared to be relatively frank is to keep pace with their patient's growing realisation that recovery will not come. The dying patient then has his suspicions fully confirmed by others when the disease has entered its last stages.

The majority of those patients who are quite prepared to be told if they have little time to live are apt, despite their preparedness, to be met only by words which do not have the ring of truth. If such a patient then asks straightforward questions about his disease and prognosis his confidence may be more shaken by indirect answers than sombre truth. Then he may begin to test his doctor's optimistic outlook or question what is behind his professional reticence. Dissatisfied with soft answers, he may repeat his enquiries in an oblique manner, perhaps asking his doctor if he should go ahead with some future plans. He may ask his questions of many others, relatives, nurses, orderlies, fellow patients— anyone who might give an honest, revealing answer which could shine its cold light through the clouds of insubstantial promises and wisps of optimism.

Reasons for reticence

What justification is there for not taking the questions of mortally ill patients about their condition as a simple cue for telling them of the illness and the outlook? There are some good reasons for caution. Many a patient would like to learn good news, or could take a certain amount of disappointment but is not yet prepared to face an illness without any hope of recovery. The doctor may start on a course of honesty which can become a slope into more painful truths as the further questions of an increasingly troubled patient finally produce an unwanted avalanche of distressing news. A physician who has felt that he has lost control in such situations and witnessed his patients' resultant hurt emotions, may well regret what he considers to be his own professional misjudgment. Present medical custom gives more support to a doctor when he speaks with cautious reassurance, revealing only enough to minimise uncertainty and encourage co-operation in treatment.

There are cautionary tales of individuals who have reacted disastrously to finding out that they would never recover. Not infrequently, however, such distress has been extreme owing to the unfortunate way in which they have obtained the knowledge. An accidental revelation of previously concealed fatal illness, or an abrupt dismissal after an unsympathetic announcement of incurable disease are bound to cause distress. Reticence is also encouraged because some patients have asked insistently to be told what is wrong with them and when told the diagnosis and prognosis they have found it unbearable and even gone to another who will provide half-truths and unlikely promises. Other patients, having become aware that they are dying, can neither accept it nor put it out of their minds and so their remaining life has been little but anguish. Such examples reinforce people's dislike of telling patients that they will not recover, so that if there is any indication that a patient's question seeks for reassurance, the answer will nearly always be encouraging. "It's not cancer, is it, doctor?" is usually answered "No" and "Will I be all right?" is answered "Yes." So patients and doctors use words as a screen to hide the fact that death is near. The doctor may assure the dying patient that he will get better, because he believes it better to sacrifice honesty for the charity of an optimistic lie. In addition, quite often he is asked by relatives not to let the patient know that he is dying.

If it appears better to avoid the hurtful truth with some mortally ill people, it can be done in a way that encourages the patients' conscious thoughts not to dwell on the outcome. Often this is carried out by speaking optimistically of the intentions of treatment rather than the forlorn expectations. If a patient poses a number of doubts and questions, the answers are often restricted to the innocuous matters that were raised. Sometimes a doctor will take refuge in his professional position, indicating with some justification that the patient could not really appreciate the medical intricacies of the situation and must be content to know the best is being done. He may avoid any sincere conversation by professional hurry. He may well restrict his own comments to topics that deal with the limited matters of the past or the controllable aspects of the troubling future. If the future is mentioned in more than general terms the doctor can give it a little reassuring structure, even if it is only to put out little flags of survival—"See you next week." It all adds up to a masquerade of hopeful treatment which makes it easy for a patient to think he will get better and difficult to burst rudely through with a demand to be told what the doctor really thinks.

If the patient is in hospital, all the staff will probably collude in the clinging to optimism. To difficult questions they may plead ignorance or refer the matter to the consultant. They may give plausible mis-interpretations to explain the new symptoms, the lack of response to treatment, or even misleading reasons for transferring a patient to a hospital for terminal care. By these means the masquerade of curative treatment can be maintained. At best it succeeds at stilling the doubts which arise—doubts concerning death that are often adjudged so painful that they must be doused. By avoiding the unpalatable truth, the dying person can cling to hopes, find comfort in promises of im-provement and feel that there are still opportunities for success and times to enjoy. Many who care for the dying are skilled at maintaining their patient's comforting hopes and supporting them in their struggles against disease, a fight which some patients could only exchange for defeat as they always regard death as the enemy and never the friend.

Are there personal reasons for doctors to contribute so readily to a pretence of recovery? Their attitude is unlikely to be solely due to their wish to be rid of an unpleasant task; after all they do make a practice of telling close relatives the real situation and that is far from easy. It does seem that in addition to the justifiable wish to spare patients distress, it is probable that many doctors have an inherent bias which causes them to prefer to "reassure" the dying patient. The influence of personal feelings is bound to be suspected when doctors express complete unwillingness to vary a policy of professional reticence or when they say that they would like to be told if they themselves were dying but do not speak the truth to their patients, even to those who are medically qualified. What are the personal consequences that might make a doctor reluctant to tell his patient that he would not recover?

To some extent a doctor often identifies himself with his patients and feel how explicit words about dying would cause them to suffer. To say plainly to a person that he will soon die tends to give the doctor an additional feeling of responsibility for curtailing his patient's life; this may not be logical but it is understandable, in so far as his words, his failure, may mark a change from a person anticipating further life and enjoyment to one who faces regretfully the approach of death. To recognise openly the unwelcome truth may mean abandoning a professional optimism which a doctor often uses to encourage his patients and sustain himself throughout the vicissitudes of medical practice. He frequently feels the need to give his dying patients hope, especially if he has to support them through a long fluctuating terminal illness, and he would be lost without having recourse to optimism. Moreover, the alternative of admitting to a patient that he is likely to die entails more than the immediately harrowing duty. If the doctor is conscientious, he knows it means that he should then be prepared to spend a good deal of time with his patient helping him to assimilate the growing awareness of dying and its many implications. Many doctors feel that they are not capable of doing this.

Both patient and doctor can therefore gain comfort through avoiding the unpleasant truth, and abandoning optimism for stark reality may find both ill-prepared. Nevertheless, misunderstanding, mistakes and misery are apt to lurk in this silence. The dying person often continues to be distressed in spite of the doctor's attempts to reassure. He may still feel uncertain and perhaps, added to his anxiety over his disease, is a sense that he is being deceived by those he relies on for his medical care. Some of his fears have been made light of and he may feel dismissed at a time when he craves understanding. The suspicion that his condition is incurable and the fear that he may suffer pain and helplessness may grow and yet apparently no one will talk seriously about it, even those in whom he has, willy-nilly, to put his trust.

Fear of suffering

It is a partially accepted convention that patients do not expect to hear their physician say that they are about to die. Are the implications of this white lie so bland? If the patient believes he is going to die but hears the benign but unconvincing words of others that he will recover, what trust can he place in promises that he will not experience physical suffering? In this chapter we have been considering how the dying person and his doctor may view the concept of death. But many people who are fatally ill have greater concern over the manner of their dying. The present discussion has deliberately, if artificially, excluded many aspects of the symptoms of incurable disease and the care of dying patients; but the thoughts of the mortally ill will often focus upon the fearful anticipation of pain, upon encroaching or disfiguring tumours, upon mutilation or upon helpless invalidism and possible neglect. They wonder if the "reassuring" words that they will not suffer and that their future care will be quite adequate mean no more than the false talk of recovery.

Many doctors are unable to escape from this impasse, or, at least, see no reasonable alternative but to continue to assert to the patient that he will be all right and he is not to worry. At the same time the doctor will be uneasy because his stratagem is failing. He is dissatisfied with his failure to give comfort, and with his own deceit which is now looking more like an unsuccessful lie. Rightly or wrongly he may sense that his patient is criticising his efforts, and this will further tempt him to avoid visits as far as he is able. A barrier of silence and unease can grow, untouched by the commonplaces that pass between them.

Accepting the prospect of death

Can only exceptional people openly admit the truth when death approaches? There is certainly no universal need to join the conspiracy of denial or for patient and physician to impose artificiality upon one another. Many have found greater equanimity in an open acknowledgment that the disease may be fatal. It is probably better that both the dying person and the doctor have not previously relied on too emphatic a denying so that mutual awareness and acceptance can steadily grow. The realisation can come very gently—perhaps only an exchange of glances, or certain intonations, which tell them that they both know what the other knows. It can stay covert, perhaps not even interrupting the outward pretence of cure, but now supports this with a shared tacit understanding. Open acknowledgment may be brought about by the obvious means of the doctor meeting his patient's questions with cautious honesty. Many doctors will do this when they feel the patient can accept the truth. Sometimes it needs a third person, such as one of the clergy, to disentangle the web of denial spun by patient and doctor. Occasionally a dying patient will share his awareness with one person and is helped by this, but equally although differently sustained by the attitude of others who keep up the pretence that all will be well.

When people first learn or acknowledge that their life will shortly come to an end, they usually experience some initial distress. It would take remarkable equanimity to remain unmoved, except for those where a mental numbness wipes out all reaction. The common attitude to personal death, which is so often to shun all thought of it, frequently leaves people poorly prepared to die. Even though death is recognised as inevitable and even if age, infirmity and loneliness have shrivelled the prospects of happiness, there still comes a sense of loss and sadness when it is clear that life really will be over soon. For people who have formerly clung too firmly to the comforting belief that their death must be a long way off, or for those to whom the realisation of dying has come too unexpectedly, abruptly or harshly, this awareness may come as a great shock. If it is too much to bear, the mind often takes refuge in denial once again. The patient may have no memory of the episode or he will dismiss it as a mistake or protest that something will turn up.

Even the most acceptant and courageous do not want to spend all their remaining days constantly thinking that this is the end; they toy with future plans and pretend they will be present for future occasions—a game to dilute some of the harshness of the situation.

Many people will feel much grief when they realise that soon there will be no more life to be enjoyed and personal existence will cease. There may be the intense hurt of parting from loved people, who will be distressed by one's own death. Dying people who are going to leave behind young children may find the situation almost intolerable. There can be a deeper disappointment contributing to depression. Many people desire to live better lives, have greater success and be nicer persons, and always they have had the hope that this may yet come about. Imminent death means they must now judge themselves for what they are and as they have been and, judging themselves uncharitably, they can be self-blaming and depressed.

Although many feel sorrow when they are aware of dying, it is not infrequent for people to experience very little distress at the realisation that their life's end is approaching. More commonly, people go through a day or two of sadness or anxiety and then adjust to the prospect. In fact, they often find it easier to adjust once the uncertainty has been removed. Many become completely acceptant. Others may need to draw on courage, but can do so once they know what they have to face —and they do not have to abandon hope totally. If franker speaking has come about, they can learn what is likely to happen to them—they can now ask if they are likely to have much pain, if they will be bed-ridden for a long time, who will look after them if they are helpless and so on. These anxieties need no longer remain as personal unshared fears because no one will talk in factual terms about their outlook. They can frame more candid questions and place more reliance on answers given in a setting of greater honesty.

If the physician feels himself in harmony with the patient who is adapting to the progress of his disease, he will find that caring for the dying can be a rewarding experience rather than a confession of failure. He can use his medical knowledge and skill to prevent physical discomfort and so relieve his patient of one frequent cause of fear. The doctor will also note the comments of the dying person, listen sympathetically and learn to what extent his patient has gone towards accepting the end. He may need to do no more than listen or he may see that a little more help is needed. Understanding and intuition will guide when the need arises for encouragement, for reassurance over ill-founded fears, for changes of treatment, for help with the relatives, or for no more nor less than human companionship.

The dying often find the settling of various practical matters concerning family life, property and work responsibility a satisfying task. They can get a sense of completion. They can take pleasure in ensuring that their dependents will be grateful for their forethought. Sometimes, those who are aware that their existence is to be curtailed, may get a little more from life by advancing their plans, even a proposed marriage, and so have further shared pleasures, bitter-sweet though they may be. It is not uncommon for dying people to get more pleasure out of their remaining days than others would believe possible. Couples who have married in spite of knowing that one of them was to die, may be very sad when the death does draw near and others grieve for them; but they are usually quite sure that they were right to take advantage of the life that could be enjoyed. They rightly feel no need to give up life because they are going to die. Other people, when dying, will not want to *do* things but can quite pleasurably review their life, on the whole satisfied with its achievements and satisfactions. Some, knowing the situation, will wish to prepare themselves spiritually for their anticipated eternal existence.

A great proportion of people, especially the elderly, reach a perfect willingness to die before they finally lose consciousness. Some attain this unaided, some sustained by their religious faith and some helped by the open understanding of those who care for them. The minister may be the appropriate person to lead the way to acceptance. If the doctor can enter this open relationship, it not only removes deception and the artificial limits imposed on their talk by avoiding the most important features of the situation, but the morale of the dying person is sustained by knowing that he will be cared for with understanding. The doctor will need to give a little of himself to his patient and may be saddened. He may also be rewarded by playing his needed part in helping while his patient reaches a peaceful acceptance of dying, and there are times when the quality of content and acceptance that the dying man attains is a help to those about him.

4. Death and the Young

by SIMON YUDKIN

WE are supposed to understand our children now, to accept their angry outbursts, the violent expressions of their loves and hates; we are supposed to take their interest in biological phenomena for granted and to answer their questions about these things as if they were asking about the weather. But although it is true that we are ready—even eager—to explain how babies grow, to let our children feel the baby in "mummy's tummy" and even to explain how the seeds got together, death is not on the list of approved subjects. It was not always so; indeed, the change is quite recent.

Of course, until quite recently, the death not only of grownups but also of friends and of brothers and sisters was an experience within the lot of most children, even whilst they were quite young. Until two centuries ago the death of a newborn baby was an accepted hazard of childbirth and the survival of a child beyond the first few years of life was regarded as something of a phenomenon. Rousseau, writing about the education of children in *Emile* (1762) could say "Of all the children who are born, scarcely one half reach adolescence, and it is very likely your pupil will not live to be a man."[1] And Edward Gibbon, the historian, describes how his father kept naming successive children Edward so that at least one child would survive to perpetuate this name in the family.[2]

The frequency with which infants and young children died meant that custom and cultural patterns had perforce to come to terms with this phenomenon. "Perforce" may be too strong a word. Death did come frequently but as inevitably and as incomprehensibly as storms in winter. Custom made some allowance for grief, but planned to inure everybody to inevitable loss and must have been at least moderately successful. In the Middle Ages the death of an infant or of a young child seems to have been accepted with some equanimity. For example Ariès quotes how a neighbour calmed the fears of a woman who had just given birth to her sixth "brat"; "Before they are old enough to bother you, you will have lost half of them, or perhaps all of them",[3] and Montaigne could write "I have lost two or three children in their infancy, not without regret, but without great sorrow."[4] Such attitudes may well have been very common.

[1] Rousseau, J. J. (1762) *Emile*, Everyman Library, (1963), p. 42.
[2] Gibbon, E., quoted by Illingworth, R. S. and Illingworth, C. M., *Lessons from Childhood*, Livingstone, 1966.
[3] Ariès, P., *Centuries of Childhood*, Jonathan Cape, 1962, p. 38.
[4] Montaigne, M. de, quoted by Ariès, *loc. cit*, p. 39.

Although in any age of history a parent might grieve inconsolably for the death of a child, the depth of a parent's grief must surely bear some relationship to the age of the child, the chances of it dying and the closeness of the relationship between the child and its parents. These factors themselves must be interrelated. It takes time for parents to form attachments to their children and to develop memories and hopes and the ties of intertwined lives. Even today most parents show sadness, rather than grief, for the baby who dies in childbirth or a day or two after it is born. And when the death of five or six children out of ten was usual, parents must surely have developed a less intense tie, have entertained less extravagant hopes, than now in this country when almost every child that is born will survive to adult life. Yet, even as recently as the 1930s, I can remember mothers of large families who talked with some stoicism of having "buried two or three children". Familiarity with the death of infants and children must have bred acquiescence, variously translated, perhaps, as "the will of the gods", "submission to God's will" or simply as a natural phenomenon like life itself and, in early times, nearly as common. But by the 18th century, sadness and grief for the loss of a child was already accepted behaviour amongst those whose intimate lives we know something about. Joseph Addison could write ". . . when I meet with the grief of parents upon a tombstone, my heart melts with compassion . . ."[1] and as early as 1647 Mary Verney, having lost her little baby Ralph and their daughter Peg almost at the same time, wrote to her husband affirming "My trust is in my good God, for He gave them to me and He took them from me," but continued, "I hope and trust He will in His good time deliver me of all my troubles and give my mind some quiett, and bring me to thee, for untill I am with thee I cannot take any comfort in anything in this world."[2]

The demographic fact of the almost certain survival of children born today in our country has made possible the development of intense and intimate ties between parents and children, which we now stress as psychologically important. But the repeated severance of such intertwined relationships would leave raw and sensitive wounds which would be intolerable if the death of children were as common now as it was two centuries ago.

Today the death of a child seems an obscenity, a burden which parents should not be expected to bear and from which they suffer for years whilst relatives and friends, their immediate sympathy over, retreat into a defensive conspiracy of silence.

In earlier times children too were not excluded from problems of life and death. From an early age children were part of an adult society, a

---

[1] Addison, J., "Thoughts in Westminster Abbey", *Essays of Addison* (J. R. Green, Editor), Macmillan, 1965, p. 377.

[2] Verney, M., quoted by King-Hall, M. *The Story of the Nursery*, Routledge & Kegan Paul, 1958, p. 81.

society in which violence, disease and death at all ages was common-place. Children were involved, almost as a result of the sheer unaware-ness of the adult world. They might see, or be taken to see, the hanging of a criminal; violent and drunken fights ending in murder were not uncommon. In the less salubrious parts of most towns, swarming with children anyway, a child might come upon an abandoned baby, perhaps still alive, in the gutter or on a dung heap. In the crowded back streets such events could not be hidden from children, but even in country mansions death was too common to be ignored or hidden. Some at least of a child's own brothers or sisters were very likely to die whilst young and the child himself, in each illness, might be at death's door.

Death in children's literature

Literature, representing or interpreting daily experience, also incor-porated death as part of that experience. The death of a child from illness, disease or violence and the participation of other children in the event was an integral part of literature and offered a dramatic and credible, yet important, turn to a plot. In today's literature, only wars, epidemics or other major calamities can provide a credible circumstance in which a child might die.

Even in the 18th and 19th centuries, when children began to be given a world of their own, with their own games, their own style of clothes, their own literature, death amongst children continued to be commonplace and children's literature and customs continued to reflect this reality. In books and poems children died, slowly and painfully from disease, violently from drowning in wells or in the sea, caught in burning houses, falling off roof-tops or bridges or under horses.

The attitude of these times towards children was compounded of several moods, authoritarian, sentimental and even the beginning of a real appreciation of children's own interests. For each of these moods death provided examples and illustrations. The authoritarian attitude was straightforward and predictable. Death stood as a warning. Death would result from disobedience, from warnings disregarded, from carelessness, or from any one of the thousand daily sins the Victorian child was taught to abjure. The ease with which children were disposed of in stories for the young was quite remarkable. In *Dangerous Sports, A Tale Addressed To Children Warning Them Against Wanton, Careless, Or Mischievous Exposure To Situations From Which Alarming Injuries So Often Proceed* published in 1808,[1] almost every activity of daily life might apparently end in death or severe injury (the two are used almost interchangeably). Sometimes a child's carelessness could result in the death of a brother or sister, sacrificed to teach the careless one a lesson.

In the latter part of the 19th century warnings became less frequent

[1] Quoted by Avery, G., *Nineteenth-Century Children*, Hodder and Stoughton, 1965, p. 213.

and childish innocence became a popular theme for adult and children's literature. Children's deaths, still frequent, became an occasion for an almost sickening sentimentality. William Carlyle's death in *East Lynne* is one of the better known examples of the genre.

"I wonder how it will be?" pondered he, aloud. "There will be the beautiful city, with its gates of pearl, and its shining precious stones, and its streets of gold ... Madame Vane [his mother] will Jesus come for me? ... It will be so pleasant to be there; never to be tired or ill again ... Don't cry papa" whispered William, raising his feeble hand caressingly, to his father's cheek. "I am not afraid to go. Jesus is coming for me."[1]

The all pervasive influence of religion showed itself both in the authoritarian and in the sentimental moods about children. Religion offered little comfort for the Victorian child constantly being taught that obedience to parents was as important—even the same—as obedience to God. Warnings of death were underlined by descriptions of the horrors that were to follow in the hell where all sinners went.

The Lord delights in them that speak
The word of truth, but every liar
Must have his portion in the lake
That burns with brimstone and with fire.[2]

This poem, embroidered on a sampler, was fairly typical. Much earlier Isaac Watts offered this future for a disobedient child:

The ravens shall pick out his eyes
And eagles eat the same.[3]

There may have been more comfort for a sick child, as there un-doubtedly was for parents, in a description of Heaven as a haven of peace, free from pain and sorrow and joyful in the loving care of Jesus. But credibility and even comfort must sometimes have been stretched to its limits. Here is a passage describing the death of a boy from the convulsions of hydrophobia after being bitten by a mad dog:

"Dreadful to witness were the struggles of the body; yet the soul seemed in perfect peace, and as if the body was enabled to bear its abounding sufferings by the abounding mercies of an indwelling Christ.

"Again he exclaimed, 'O Elijah! O my God!' His father assured him, 'You will soon be happy, and at rest, Johnny!' He replied, 'Oh yes, very happy!' "[4]

[1] Mrs. Henry Wood, quoted by Coveney, P., *The Image of Childhood*, Penguin Books, 1967, p. 183.
[2] Quoted by King-Hall, loc. cit., p. 158.
[3] Watts, Isaac, *Divine and Moral Songs for Children*, King-Hall, loc. cit., p. 157.
[4] de Vries, L., *Little Wide-Awake*, Arthur Barker, 1967, p. 35.

D

But it is the ever present threat of death that strikes the modern reader in the tales for adults and children of the 18th and 19th centuries. Can we imagine anyone today composing this *Hymn for Infant Minds*?

CHILD

Tell me, mamma, if I must die
One day, as little baby died;
And look so very pale, and lie
Down in the pit-hole by his side?

MAMMA

'Tis true, my love, that you must die;
The God who made you says you must;
And every one of us shall lie,
Like the dear baby, in the dust.

These hands, and feet, and busy head,
Shall waste and crumble right away;
But though your body shall be dead,
There is a part which can't decay.[1]

It is difficult to be sure just how these admonitions and these stories affected most of their readers. Probably a number of the warnings of drowning, burning, broken limbs and perhaps of death were real enough and would be underlined from the child's own experience and some at least of the stories pointed morals which no child could escape. The tales of the happiness and joy in heaven may have seemed quite real to many children. On the whole, however, it seems likely that a good deal of what was intoned or recited in the stories and poems would have as little meaning as a nursery rhyme to a modern child.

Not only are we ignorant of the effect of much of the literature that children read or were taught. We know even less about how the death of a brother or sister or friend or parent or other close relative was felt and appreciated by the children, although the literature would suggest that any death would be used as an opportunity either to issue appropriate warnings or to press home a belief in the good life that awaited the pure in heart when they died.

A child's understanding of death

Today we know a little more about how children's minds and thoughts develop, but we still know very little about how they think of death. Our attitude now has simply been to try to ban the subject altogether. Partly, of course, the banishment has reflected the real near banishment, in a country like ours, of death in childhood. Few

[1] *Ibid.*, p. 95.

children now die; few children now have lost a brother or sister and relatively few, whilst still children, a father or mother. How do children think of death? The death of others or the possible death of themselves? There has been very little real study. Children are not born understanding growth and development, life and death, relationships with other people. These understandings come gradually from experience and from what we are taught. The biological reality of death, its final severance of a relationship, are difficult enough for adults to comprehend.

The very young child knows nothing of all this. Once a baby becomes aware of the existence of other people as individuals distinct from himself and distinct from objects which feed him and comfort him, he begins to be aware of loss, of the sense of absence. His idea of time is small and he cannot distinguish between short term separation or long term separation. But the realities of disappearance and reappearance are learned quickly. The game of "peek-a-boo", which seems to be almost universal with young children, may be one way that parents help children to learn the difference. The fearful expectancy and explosive relief of a child playing "peek-a-boo" shows how real is the anxiety at possible loss. But children seem to learn very quickly to distinguish a long separation from a short one, and by the end of the first year or so, a child has often learned to tolerate short separations with relative equanimity. His experience and his gradual appreciation of time sequence has helped. At this age too, a child faced with a long term separation of a person to whom he is attached seems to experience at least some of the features of grief and mourning shown by adults,[1] though of course without the depth that memories and expectations bring.

From the time that a child is about two or three, fantasy joins hands with experience, and death takes on new dimensions of curiosity, anxiety and fear. In a country like ours, a child's first experience of death is likely to be in relation to his pets. A child's experience, moreover, comes to him in the context of the feelings and reactions of the adults around him to the same subject. A child who sees a dead bird, rabbit or pet is interested in the difference between "live" and "dead". He soon learns to appreciate that "dead" things have different characteristics from "live" ones. His emotional involvement is often very small and his parents may accept this, since their own emotional involvement is also small. Sometimes, however, parents may be shocked by their child's questions even about the death of a pet.

The death of a grandparent or, more rarely, of a parent or other loved relative and, more rarely still, of one of his own generation is quite a different matter; and, although parents may hope that his experience of the death of pets may help a child to understand the

[1] Bowlby, J., *Grief and Mourning in Infancy and Early Childhood. Psychoanalytic Study of the Child*, Vol. XV, p. 9, 1960.

death of a real person, it is very unlikely to do so. If a relative or friend of the family dies, a child is very unlikely to see the body and he is quite likely to be told, not that the person is dead, but only that he has "gone on a journey" or "gone away" or, possibly, "gone up to heaven". But of course a child can see that something special has happened because of the emotional upset of his family, the furtive whispering, the avoidance of direct talk. Even if he is told that the person has died, our embarrassment and concern when he talks of the death of someone he doesn't know very well in the same rather detached and curious way that he talks of the death of his pet must be very confusing and disturbing to him.

But the child of between three and seven is not only learning facts and experiencing social attitudes about death; he also has many fantasies. Fantasy mingles with facts and with adult attitudes and adds terror to the fantasy. A child knows what it is like to hold his breath and knows what it is like to be alone. He can imagine what it might be like to be put in a box deep in the ground. To be dead might be to wake up and find you are in a box under the ground, or not to be able to breathe when you are bursting with holding your breath. It might mean being alone for ever.

Death for young children may also be personified. Death is what is done to you by others or by God for being bad or wicked or by an enemy who is fighting you or hates you, and it might be violent like death on the television screen or cinema. Most children everywhere seem to play games in which they kill each other or die violently. "Bang! Bang! You're dead!" accompanied by the certainty that the shot one isn't dead, seems to be an important way of dealing with the fear.

Influence of adult attitudes

When we consider the fantasies of a child's world and his relatively poor understanding of the complexities of our own cultural patterns of forbidden and acceptable subjects, we can perhaps begin to appreciate how our own behaviour can contribute to the fantasies and the fears. We may recoil now at the way that children in the 18th and 19th centuries were so frequently confronted with death and so constantly threatened with death and hell-fire, but our own secretiveness has its failings too, probably leaving our children just as defenceless in the presence of their own fantasies. The Victorians may well have terrified children with their realistic descriptions of dying and death and with their details of God and of hell and heaven. We allow them to be terrified by our secrecy and by our private and often furtive misery. The Victorians dwelt on children's departure from this world and the subject of their origin was prohibited from polite conversation. We have reversed the process. But we have not banished our children's fantasies about death and our clumsy attempts to protect them from reality simply allow their fantasies to grow.

Grief and mourning

Children can mourn and grieve at the death of a loved one and, given an opportunity, will do so unashamedly. Their immediate grief may be shortlived and they may be more upset by the plainly unusual and deep emotion shown by their parents than by their actual loss but, as the immediacy passes, a child may begin to miss the reality of the person he knew and loved, his visits perhaps, or his play or other aspects of his relationship and he may then grieve and mourn for a long time. He may feel guilty for the bad thoughts he has sometimes entertained about the dead, or the death of one adult may light up his anxieties about the possible death of his own parents. His parents, if they are sensitive, may understand what is happening and give him an opportunity to show his sadness. More often the child is aware that the subject is not a welcome one and he keeps it to himself. Only his quietness or occasional unexplained temper, or perhaps his restlessness and sleeplessness at night, indicates his concern, not only at the missing person, but at his inability to talk about what he feels so deeply.

For such children, then, the sadness of death as well as the fantasy, whether of God, the devil or of punishment or guilt is real enough and is usually fearful. But their fantasies make their understanding different from ours, and we need to be sensitive both to the simplicity of their thought and the possible variety of their fantasies if we are to talk with them about death.

The older child gradually develops a more realistic understanding of death. Some of the fantasy may recede and grief and mourning about the death of a loved one takes on a more adult aspect. His attitudes now are becoming similar to those of the rest of his own family and his own culture.

The child's attitude to his own death

Although children of two to three years are aware of death and afraid of it, fear of death for themselves seems rare and, when it exists, it is usually a fear of death by accident or by other violent means and is probably just one aspect of the fantasy of death as a punishment. Children who are ill, even acutely ill, hardly ever seem to conceive that they will die or even to think about it at all. Of course, this behaviour refers to Britain where almost all ill children do in fact recover. It may not be true in countries of Asia or Africa where children who are ill often do die. Certainly it was not true in Britain in earlier times when children were aware that others died and that they too might die.

"How can we tell that we shall ever live to grow up? Many children die much younger than us; and if we do not think of preparing for death, what will become of us?"

Thus speaks a child in Mrs. Cameron's *History of Margaret Whyte, or the Life and Death of a Good Child*[1] and even real children often apparently realised that they were dying and accepted this fact. The story of John Evelyn's little boy Richard, who asked if he "should offend God by using His Holy Name so often calling for ease"[2] when he was dying at the age of five must have been matched by those of other children, although perhaps not so piously.

Even now in Britain, however, there are some exceptions. Some children are afraid that they are going to die and suffer a great deal. This happens not infrequently around puberty when children often have morbid anxieties about their health, mostly without good reason. A few palpitations, a pain, a small swelling; these may be seen as signs of impending disaster so real that one dare not even whisper the fear. Other children may be ill with, for example, a disease of the kidney or heart or lung which they vaguely know to be essential for life, but about which they entertain only the ordinary lay and popular notions. These children can be and often are reassured very easily if they are allowed and encouraged to talk about their fears. Otherwise they will keep them to themselves, showing only angry resentment or sadness or depression as an indication that something is deeply worrying them.

On the whole, however, even children who are very ill do not seem to think that they might be dying. This is true even when they have a disease with a fatal outcome. Mercifully the majority of children who die from an illness in this country are infants and are much too young to realise what is happening to them. Others are so ill that they are not properly conscious. But there are a few children, even in this country, who have a fatal disease and may be old enough to understand what is happening. Even these often don't seem to realise, though they may be puzzled by the behaviour of their parents or of others who know that they are dying, by the unaccustomed granting of every wish, by inexplicable tears and extra manifestations of love and affection. A few children who have a fatal disease probably do understand that they are dying or at least think about it, but mostly they are not allowed even to mention their fears and everyone around maintains silence, comforting themselves with the idea that children could not possibly be aware that they might die.[3]

Nothing seems to be more difficult nowadays than to talk to children

---

[1] Quoted by Avery, G., *loc. cit.*, p. 214.
[2] Quoted by King-Hall, *loc. cit.*, p. 103.
[3] I have written more extensively elsewhere about the fear of death of children in hospital where the death of a child, though still rare, excites deep emotions amongst doctors, nurses and the other children. Yudkin, S., 'Children and Death", *Lancet.*, Vol. I., 1967, p. 37.

about death, especially the possibility that they might be afraid of dying themselves. But the majority of children who are afraid of death are not dying. Moreover, we should remember that the fear of death in children—whether justified or not—is often a fear of something quite different from the fears of adults. It may be fear of loneliness or of pain or of some nameless fantasy. If we can be aware that children may be afraid of death, even more often when they are not fatally ill than when they are, we would be enormously helpful simply by allowing them to talk about their fears, and to be reassured. Even the very few who may be dying can be given the comfort of closeness and of protection from fear. But we sadly fail in this as we so sadly fail ourselves to face the fact of death.

But however difficult it may be to talk to a child about fear of his own death, at least children have the right to honesty about the death of adults; to an understanding that death, like birth, really does happen and that the death of a loved one is an event which deserves sadness, grief and mourning from the parents and from the children themselves.

PART TWO

Attitudes towards Death

1. Traditional Attitudes towards Death

by Arnold Toynbee

Are there any attitudes towards death that are innate in human nature?

THERE are, on this planet, some species of non-human social living creatures—e.g. the social insects—whose ways of behaving, and the attitudes implied in their behaviour, appear to be built into their natures and to be transmitted in stereotype, by physical procreation, from generation to generation. In human nature, too, there may be, and indeed are likely to be, built-in instincts of this kind. At the same time, it is hazardous to assume that any ways of behaving or any attitudes are instinctive in a creature that is endowed, as Man is, with consciousness, will, the power to make choices and to take decisions, and the consequent power to form habits—and to break them. In human history, we may find that attitudes and ways of behaving which date from the earliest ages of which we have any record still survive today, but this gives us no guarantee that they are going to persist throughout the coming 2000 million years or so for which it is believed that this planet will continue to be habitable. All the same, those age-old attitudes that have persisted so far, and that may conceivably be inborn in us, deserve to be considered before we pass on to other attitudes that have come and gone, however important a part these other, relatively ephemeral, attitudes may have played in human life at the times and places at which they have prevailed.

The sense of human dignity

Our oldest evidence for our human predecessors' attitudes towards death is to be found in their ways of disposing of dead human beings' bodies. Archaeological evidence seems to show that funerary rites were already being practised by Neanderthal Man—a now extinct variety of hominid which was different from, though, for all that we know, not older than, *homo sapiens*, the variety to which the present-day so-called "races" belong, all alike. Funerary rites are ceremonial practices that are intended to express reverence for the person who has died; to express grief at the loss of this now dead member of the community; and to express awe and concern in the presence of death itself, when it is the death of a human being.

The oldest, most numerous, and most imposing relics of our ancestors are funerary. At different times and places the dead bodies of human beings have been honoured in an amazing variety of ways. They have been buried in graves or in tombs or under tumuli or inside pyramids. They have been burnt on pyres, and the ashes have been preserved in urns or have been scattered to the winds. They have even been exposed to be eaten by carrion birds or by scavenging wild animals—not because they were not held in honour, but because earth, fire, and water were held in still greater honour, and these elements were thought to be defiled and dishonoured by contact with a human corpse. But, however diverse man's funerary rites have been, they have all had a common signification. They have signified that a human being has a dignity in virtue of his being human; that his dignity survives his death; and that therefore his dead body must not simply be treated as garbage and be thrown away like the carcase of a dead non-human creature, or like a human being's worn-out boots or clothes.

In our present-day society, this attitude of reverence towards the dead, and this feeling of obligation to give them "decent burial", are as lively and as compelling as ever, even among present-day people who believe, with their minds, that the idea of human dignity is an illusion and that, in terms of value, a human being is on a par with any non-human living creature and indeed with any other natural phenomenon, animate or inanimate. In practice, people who believe this still pay reverence to the dead, even though this behaviour of theirs may be in conflict with their beliefs and even with their principles.

The assertion that reverence for the dead has been a universal human attitude might seem, at first sight, to be refuted by the deliberate indignities that the members of some human societies have inflicted on the corpses of slain enemies. Head-hunting, scalping, and other forms of mutilation have been permitted. A slain enemy's skull has been adapted to serve as a drinking-cup. The dead bodies of human beings have even been used for food by other human beings, as well as by man-eating tigers and by sharks. How can such practices be compatible with a genuine feeling of reverence for the dead, and with the actual practice of disposing of one's own dead with reverent funerary rites?

The main cause of this inhuman treatment of alien dead is the age-old human habit of tribal-mindedness. Human beings have tended, so far, to regard and treat only the members of their own community as being fully human, and to feel that the alien majority of mankind is in some sense sub-human and is therefore not fully entitled to enjoy full human rights. However, both the mutilation of dead enemies and cannibalism have come to be reprobated by an increasing majority of the human race; and, even in societies in which cannibalism has been practised, the motive has not always been the sheerly utilitarian

one of satisfying physical hunger. In some cases the motive for cannibalism has been a belief that by eating a human being's dead body
one can appropriate for oneself the potency, of all kinds, that the
victim possessed while he was alive. It is true that there has also been
the same superstition about the eating of the dead bodies of physically
potent animals.

Another practice, besides cannibalism and the mutilation of the
dead, that has come to be abhorred and to be sternly prohibited is
human sacrifice. This dreadful practice, however, has not been a
cynical denial of human dignity; it has been a perverse but heartfelt assertion of it. If one believes in the efficacy and the duty of sacrifice
in the form of taking the life of a living creature as a way of honouring
and propitiating a god, then, the more precious the victim, the more
acceptable the offering will be. The most precious kind of victim will
be a human victim, if man is held to be the highest species of living
creature. The most acceptable human victim will be one's own
child—above all, one's eldest son—since the pain and grief suffered
in deliberately putting him to death will be the measure of one's
devotion to the god to whom he is being immolated. Human sacrifice,
committed on this ground, has been practised widely in the past.
According to Pausanias, it was still being practised surreptitiously, in
his time, at the altar of Zeus Lykaius in Arcadia.[1] It was rife in
Middle America in the pre-Columbian age, and in Canaan and the
Canaanite colonies in North-West Africa throughout the last millennium B.C.

Classic instances, recorded in the Old Testament, are Jephthah's
sacrifice of his daughter to his god Yahweh in fulfilment of a rash
vow[2] and King Mesha's sacrifice of his son and heir to his god Chemosh
on the city-wall of Kir-haraseth.[3] King Ahaz and King Manasseh
of Judah, too, are recorded each to have "made his son to pass through
the fire".[4] The story of Yahweh's command to Abraham to sacrifice
his only son Isaac, and of the rescinding of this command when the
sacrifice was on the point of being consummated,[5] reflects a mitigation
of this dreadful rite. The human victim was replaced by an animal,
and this substitution of vicarious animal sacrifice for human sacrifice
is attested by archaeological evidence from Carthage.

This practice of human sacrifice has been abandoned almost universally today—except in the institution of war, in which millions of
young men have been condemned to be killed and to kill in our lifetime, as human sacrifices to the deified collective human power of a
belligerent nation.[6] It is significant that a young man who has been
sacrificed in battle is honoured by his community and has, in many
cases, himself been a proud and willing victim. The human victims

---

[1] Pausanias, Book VIII, chap. 38, §. 7.   [2] Judges xi, 30-40.
[3] 2 Kings, iii, 27.   [4] 2 Kings, xvi, 3, and xxi, 6.   [5] Gen., xxii, 1-18
[6] This is discussed further in the chapter "Death in War", see below, p. 146 ff.

who were sacrificed on Aztec altars or were "made to pass through the fire" by Canaanite kings were probably, in some cases, consenting parties likewise. At any rate, it is clear that human sacrifice, horrible though it is, is a perverted assertion of human dignity, not an impious or callous denial of it.

Man's feeling that his dignity is incongruous with his being mortal

In most human societies, a human being—at any rate, a fellow tribesman—has been invested, in people's minds, with a dignity that has not been accorded to any non-human living creatures. This distinction has been made particularly sharp in societies professing one or other of the religions of the Judaic family (Judaism, Christianity, Islam). On the other hand, in Ancient Egypt some species of animals were worshipped as gods and, at death, were honoured with human funeral rites—rites that, in some cases, were of royal grandeur. Moreover, the part—a major part—of the human race that professes religions or philosophies of Indian origin today does not draw a clear-cut distinction between human beings and other sentient creatures. Believers in metempsychosis assume that they have been incarnate in non-human form in the past and that they may be reborn in non-human form after their next death. This belief prompts Hindus and Buddhists to be vegetarians; and any Westerner who has travelled in India will have been struck, not only by the self-assurance of domesticated cows, but by the fearlessness of monkeys, kites, hawks, and vultures. These wild creatures will boldly venture within close range of human beings, and will even take liberties with them, because they have learned by experience that, in this sub-continent, their human fellow-creatures are unlikely to molest them. Adherents of the Jain religion take pains to avoid killing insects, even inadvertently.

It has, however, been more common, on the whole, for human beings to draw in some degree the distinction between themselves and non-human living creatures which the adherents of the Judaic religions draw so sharply; and this distinction is enshrined in language. In modern Greek, for instance, the colloquial generic word for a horse, mule, or donkey is "alogon", meaning a creature that lacks the human faculty of reason. It is still more significant that in ancient Greek, and in some Iranian languages too, one of the commonest words used for designating human beings is "mortals".

The use of the word "mortals" as a distinctive title for human beings speaks volumes. All living creatures are mortal above the level of the amoeba, and the existence of the amoeba was unknown to the Greeks and the Iranians when they took to using the word "mortal" as a synonym for "man". Evidently the characteristic of man that they felt to be distinctive was not man's mortality; in itself it was the incongruity, in man's case, between his mortality, which he shares with all other species of life on this planet that reproduce their kind by sexual procreation, and certain other features of human nature that are truly peculiar to man. Man alone possesses self-consciousness, can make choices, and range in thought over aeons that bear no proportion to the length of a human life-time, and over galaxies with which he can hardly hope ever to be able to make bodily contact, even when he has developed a science and a technology that have enabled him not only to see these inconceivably remote heavenly bodies but to analyse their chemical ingredients. Since man first became aware of himself and of the universe in which he finds himself, it has seemed to him incongruous that a being of his intellectual stature—and of his moral stature too, sinner though he knows himself to be—should be subject to death. For death transforms a living human being into a putrefying corpse, which quickly dissolves into the inorganic matter out of which the organic molecules of the previously live body were constituted. For all sexual living creatures alike, including man, death is inevitable and inexorable, but for man it is also incongruous and humiliating. These two aspects of death, in death's dominion over human beings, are brought out poignantly in Psalm 49.

"None of them can by any means redeem his brother, nor give to God a ransom for him . . . that he should still live for ever and not see corruption . . .

"Their inward thought is that their houses shall continue for ever . . . Nevertheless man, being in honour, abideth not; he is like the beasts that perish."[1]

Well, no, he is not quite like these. It is true that man, like them, is bound to die, but it is also true that, unlike them, man has foreknowledge of his coming death while he is still alive, and, possessing this foreknowledge, has a chance, if he chooses to take it, of pondering over the strangeness of his destiny—the apparent misfit between different features in human nature that coexist, unreconciled, in every human being. This misfit in human nature is a fact, but man has at least a possibility of coping with it, since he is endowed with the capacity to think about it in advance, and, in thinking about it, to face it and to deal with it in some way that is worthy of his human dignity.

"Man that is in honour and understandeth not, is like the beasts that perish."[2]

In fact, if man stumbles into death in the animals' blind way, he is actually degrading himself to a lower spiritual level than theirs, since—possessing, as he does possess, the power of meeting and facing death with his eyes open—he will in this case have refused to make

[1] Psalm 49, verses 7, 9, 11, 12. [2] Psalm 49, verse 20.

use of his distinctively human faculties. On the other hand, if he perishes with an understanding of his human condition, he will have demonstrated that he is not like the beasts that perish, even though, like them, he too is mortal.

The humility that is required of man by the incongruousness of his condition

So far, there is no limit in sight to man's capacity for understanding in the intellectual sense, and no limit, either, to his capacity for turning this understanding to practical account by applying science to technology. Since the beginning of the deliberate application of science to technology in the western world about three hundred years ago, the rising curve of man's technological progress has soared upwards in a geometrical progression. Today we possess material power of a potency that even our recent ancestors could not have imagined to be possibly within man's reach. But, as Sophocles remarked 24 centuries ago, one thing in man's universe that has defeated man is death.[1] Since Sophocles' day, the progress of medical science has, it is true, appreciably lengthened the average expectation of life for human beings who are in a position to command first-rate medical service; above all, infant mortality has been drastically reduced, and this even in relatively backward communities (though civilian casualties in war, when we choose to make war, have now been drastically increased). However, we still die, and our failure to liberate ourselves from our continuing subjection to meeting with death sooner or later, is not, in truth, *the* one signal failure of man, as Sophocles suggests that it is. On this point, Sophocles does not have the last word. Sophocles has been dazzled by man's intellectual genius and by his practical ability in applying this to technology. Sophocles has left it to Saint Paul to bring man's spiritual infirmity and inadequacy into the foreground.

"Death is the wages of sin" (to invert the predicate and the subject of Saint Paul's lapidary sentence); and the unreduced sinfulness of man has been floodlighted by the recent vast and accelerating increase in man's material power. Our actions are not either more good or more wicked than they were when we were armed only with flint tools, instead of being armed, as we are now, with atomic war-heads carried by missiles that can be catapulted accurately from any point on this planet's surface to any other point on it. But the consequences of our actions—consequences for either good or evil—are now incomparably more potent materially than they have ever been before, owing to this feat of ours of increasing our material power by applying our science to technology; and technology is a morally neutral force; it can be used, at will, for either good or evil.

Human beings do not die only of natural causes such as assaults by non-human living creatures (a rare cause of death nowadays, though less

[1] Sophocles, *Antigone*, lines 361–2.

rare when the non-human predator is a microbe or a virus than when it is a tiger or a shark). Nor do we die only of diseases that our physicians cannot cure—diseases that can more easily prove fatal in old age, when the self-renewing power of an organism diminishes, leaving the organism more prone to succumb to disease than it has been at the prime of life. We also deliberately kill each other and, less frequently, kill ourselves. The killing of each other by private enterprise, which we call murder, has been penalised in all societies—in relatively anarchic societies by the institution of blood-feuds that can be terminated either by taking a life for a life or by paying blood-money to the murdered person's kinsmen. However, in the deliberately inflicted death that is part of the wages of sin, private enterprise has played a minor part compared to public enterprise. Up to date, the number of human beings who have been privately murdered has been very small compared to the number of those who have been killed in war; and war is an institution, governed by rules and conventions.

The institution of war cannot have become a going concern until man's intelligence, applied to food production, had released him from having to spend the whole of his working time, as a sheep, cow, or rabbit has to spend it, on finding food and eating it. A second enabling condition for committing the sin of going to war has been the acquisition of enough power of organisation, administration, and indoctrination to train numbers of men to work together as one man in trying to kill other human beings systematically, and also to condition them to trying to kill, and to risking being killed themselves, without flinching from this twofold ordeal. The two enabling conditions cannot have been obtainable before the birth of civilisation, and the oldest civilisation known to us, the Sumerian civilisation which arose in what is now Iraq, came into existence no longer than about 5,000 years ago. Since then, man has spent on making war the major part of the margin of time, energy, intelligence, and material resources left over after he has satisfied his minimum needs for keeping himself fed, clothed, and housed.

War is only one of many symptoms and consequences of man's moral failure, and his moral failure brings him face to face with another incongruity in his condition. Besides the incongruity between man's sense of his dignity and the hard fact of his mortality, there is an incongruity between his intellectual gift for mastering non-human nature by his science and technology and his moral inadequacy for dealing with his fellow human beings, with himself, and with the spiritual presence, spiritually higher than man himself, that lies behind the phenomena of the universe—by whatever images this spiritual presence may be represented in the vocabularies of different religions.

Man's moral failure gives him—if he does use the understanding with which he is endowed—a sense of his unworthiness to offset his

E

sense of dignity. If, nevertheless, pride and presumption gain the ascendancy in him over humility and awe, he is exposing himself to disaster. Pride proverbially goes before a fall, and this maxim is a reflexion of experience. According to Christian theology, pride is the deadliest of the seven deadly sins, because pride inhibits a human being from acknowledging any of his other sins, and therefore also inhibits him from repenting and reforming.

When a human being recognises the fact that he and his fellow human beings are moral failures, he will not only concede that, when they bring death on each other and on themselves, they have only themselves to blame. He may also admit that death itself, even when it has not been caused by sin, may be not an outrage, but a godsend, for a creature whose nature is what man's is. Though man's sinfulness is perennial, death does at least limit mankind's and Nature's or God's liability for the wickedness and folly of any individual specimen of our species. Hitler's mortality, for instance, was providential.

When we acknowledge our moral failure—acknowledge, that is, the ingredient in human nature that Christian theology calls "original sin"—we are implicitly admitting that man cannot be the highest spiritual presence in or behind the universe. We are admitting this, even though we may not have had the personal experience of direct encounter, and even union, with this higher spiritual power which the mystics, of many different religious faiths, believe that they have had. Man the highest form of spiritual being! The mere statement of this proposition is a *reductio* of it *ad absurdum* for any human being who does have a modicum of understanding of our human condition.

This negative reaction implies a positive belief. But, when we try to express this belief, we are trying to define the ineffable, and it is not surprising that, in different cultures and different religions, an identical ultimate reality has been conceived of in widely different forms. It has been described as a supra-personal non-personal presence: the "holy spirit" of Zoroastrianism, Judaism, and Christianity, the Brahma of Hinduism, the nirvana of Buddhism; it has also been described as a personal presence in which the divine person is pictured in the image of a human person, and in which the number of persons may be conceived of as being either singular or plural. This anthropomorphic conception of the ultimate reality is represented by the unique and omnipotent God of Judaism and Islam; by the unique but not unchallenged God of Zoroastrianism; by the triune God of Christianity (a trinity in which two of the three members are pictured anthropomorphically); by a Supreme God presiding over a pantheon (e.g. the Sumerian Enlil, the Babylonian Marduk, the Assyrian Ashur, the Theban Egyptian Amon-Re, the Hindu Brahma, the Greek Zeus, the Scandinavian Odin); or by one or other of the countless subordinate members of the many pantheons (Indra, Vishnu, Shiva, Apollo, Athena, Thor, Freya and so on).

When the Ultimate Reality is conceived of as being non-personal in the sense of being supra-personal, the question whether it could or could not be subject to death does not arise. Death, in our experience of it, is a phenomenon that is characteristic of, and is confined to, those species of live organisms, inhabiting this planet, that perpetuate themselves by the process of sexual reproduction. Man is one of these, and, as such, he is subject to death, though in some other respects he may be unlike any of his other fellow mortal creatures. Accordingly, when the ultimate spiritual presence behind the universe is conceived of anthropomorphically, the question does arise whether the gods are, or God is, mortal like the divine person's prototype, man himself.

Man's usual answer has been that one of the ways—indeed the most distinctive way—in which a god is super-human is that a god is immortal. Man's attribution of immortality to gods is one expression of man's sense of the incongruousness and indignity of his own mortality. To be exempt from death is, in man's eyes, the prime qualification for being regarded by man as being super-human. It is also the expression of a hope, either latent or explicit, that, if such a thing as an immortal living being does exist, immortality may be attained by man too, either with or without the Immortal God's or gods' aid. At the same time, the belief that a god is not subject to death threatens to open up an unbridgeable spiritual gulf between the god and his human worshipper. If the god has not shared, and is *ex officio* exempt from sharing, with man an experience that is a human being's most formidable ordeal, how can the god enter into man's feelings in the face of death, and how can he then be "a very present help" to man in coping with the most grievous of all man's troubles? The god in whom man longs to believe, with whom he is eager to get into personal touch, and for whom he is moved to feel an extreme devotion is a god who is immortal, yet who, paradoxically, has nevertheless shared with his worshippers the human experience of death.

Of all the gods who have been worshipped by human beings, the most ardently adored have been those who have been believed to have died and come to life again, either recurrently or once for all; for instance, Tammuz, Osiris, Adonis, Attis, Persephone, Balder, Christ. Man's adoration of a god who has died and has then asserted his immortality by coming to life again rises to its acme when the god is believed to have suffered death voluntarily and deliberately. The first place in Christianity's triune godhead is attributed officially to God the Father, the person in the Trinity who is identical with Yahweh the god of Judaism and with Allah, the unique god of Islam who has no personal name because He is God himself without any fellow gods from whom he needs to be distinguished. Officially, the three members of the Christian Trinity are co-equal aspects of a godhead that is identical with the unitary and unique God of Judaism and Islam. Actually, in the thoughts and feelings of devout orthodox Christians, God the Son overshadows God the Father and God the Holy Spirit and receives the major part of a Christian's devotion and gratitude, because God the Son is believed to have been unique among the three members of the Trinity in having voluntarily suffered death for man's sake and for man's salvation. The Christian's feeling for Christ gives the full measure of man's concern with the problem and ordeal with which the fact of death confronts a human being.

The concept of a god who is immortal yet is mortal too is so paradoxical when enunciated in these abstract terms that it seems improbable that any human beings would ever have conceived of it, if they had not been familiar with it in a phenomenon that recurs annually in some of the representatives of the vegetable kingdom. There are some plants and trees that are "perennials" in the sense that they appear to die in the autumn and to remain dead during the winter but to come to life again in the spring and to bloom during the summer, repeating this cycle of dying and rising again year after year. This natural phenomenon would hardly have been taken as a clue to the nature and experience of a god in a scientifically sophisticated human society in which the vegetable kingdom is labelled "the flora" and is regarded as being a lower order of life than "the fauna", which is an order that includes man himself. The analogy was drawn in societies in which our "fauna", "flora" and "inanimate nature" were all still conceived of as being animated with divine power.

On the other hand, in a scientifically-minded society the freedom of the "lower orders" of living creatures from the phenomenon of death, to which man is subject, has been regarded as one of Nature's paradoxes, and has excited wistfulness, resentment, bitterness, irony or a mixture of some or all of these feelings. A Greek poet[1] has expressed, in six inimitable lines, the poignancy of the contrast between the destiny of frail and tender plants that die to live again and to bloom in another year, and the destiny of us human beings—"so great, so strong, so clever"—who, "when once we have died, then, sunk, unhearing, in the hollow earth, sleep a sleep that is long indeed—so exceeding long that it knows no end and no awakening".

This conclusively everlasting death which was felt by the Greeks to be a pathetic lot for human beings shocked them as a scandalous libel when it was attributed to a god. One of the reasons why the Cretans incurred their reputation for being liars was that they displayed, on Mount Iouktas, a grave that purported to be the grave of the high god Zeus.

The biologists of the Greek poet Moschus's day were ignorant of the existence of the amoeba—one of the lowest representatives of the animal kingdom, but also one that, thanks to its being so rudimentary a form of life, is exempt from the ordeal of death and will presumably preserve its lowly immortality for as long as the surface of this planet

[1] Perhaps Moschus, in the *Epitaphios Bionos*, lines 98-104.

continues to be habitable for any form of life. From man's standpoint, the immortality of the amoeba, which does not die because it perpetuates itself, not by sexual procreation, but by periodical fission, presents a more bitterly ironical contrast to man's subjectness to death than is presented by the seasonal wilting and revival of some species of plants and trees. Of all things that have come to be known by man down to our day, the immortality of the amoeba ought to make mortal man feel humble.

Various ways in which human beings have sought to reconcile themselves to the fact of death

   (a) *Hedonism.* The most obvious way of reconciling oneself to death is to make sure of enjoying life before death snatches it from us. The catchwords *"Carpe diem"*[1] and "Let us eat and drink, for tomorrow we shall die"[2] are notorious, and Herodotus[3] has preserved an Egyptian folk-tale in which the Pharaoh Mycerinus, when the gods had sentenced him to die after enjoying only six more years of life, successfully doubled the term arbitrarily allotted to him by turning night into day. This hedonistic solution of the problem of death is, of course, illusory. In reality a human being cannot stay awake, enjoying himself, for 24 hours a day, day in and day out, over a span of six years. Nor can he make sure of enjoying himself even for the briefest spells; and, if luck does favour him that far, his foreknowledge that one day he is going to die will be lurking all the time at the back of his mind. The skeleton was simply being brought out of the cupboard in the Egyptian custom, also recorded by Herodotus,[4] of exhibiting a miniature wooden model of a mummy at a feast in order to remind the revellers of the grim fact of death, which they were trying to put out of their minds for the moment. Eating, drinking, and being merry is, like war and revolution, an intrinsically transient activity. It is, in fact, another name for "sowing one's wild oats", and it is only in fairy tales that this conventional escapade is followed by "marrying and living happily after". In prosaic real life, it is followed by the anxieties and fatigues and maladies of adult life—congenital evils of our human condition, which, if they are severe and long drawn out, may make a human being actually look forward to death as an eventual relief on which he can count for certain.

   (b) *Pessimism.* The most obvious alternative to the illusory solace of hedonism is to conclude that life is so wretched that death is the lesser evil. In the 5th century B.C., when the Greeks were at the height of

[1] Horace, *Odes*, Book I, Ode xi, line 8. Cp. Book I, Ode iv, passim.
[2] Isaiah, xxii, 13. Cp. Eccles., iii, 22.
[3] Herodotus, Book II, chap. 133.
[4] In Book II, chap. 78.

their achievement in all fields, the Greek poet Sophocles declared[1] that "it is best of all never to have been born, and second-best—second by far—if one has made his appearance in this world, to go back again, as quickly as may be, thither whence he has come." The Greek historian Herodotus attributed the same view to the 6th-century-B.C. Greek sage Solon.[2] According to Herodotus's story of Solon's conversation with King Croesus, the human beings cited by Solon as having been the happiest, save for one, within his knowledge, were, not Croesus, as Croesus had hoped, but two young men—a pair of brothers—who had died in their sleep at the height of their strength, achievement, and fame, when their mother had prayed to the goddess Hera to bestow on them the best lot that a human being can hope for. The comment that Herodotus puts into Solon's mouth is that the brothers "met with the best possible end that human life can have, and that God took this opportunity for making it manifest that, for a human being, it is better to be dead than to be alive".

"Those whom the gods love, die young."[3] In many military-minded societies, there have been young men who have looked forward, with pride and exaltation, to the prospect of dying prematurely in battle; and it is significant that when, in the 7th and 6th centuries B.C., some Greeks began to transfer their treasure from their community to their own individual lives, the elegiac and lyric poets who gave expression to this psychological revolution harped plaintively on the brevity of the springtime of an individual human being's life, and on the weariness of the long-drawn-out sequel of old age, with its burden of increasing ill-health and debility.[4]

However, in this age and in all subsequent ages of ancient Greek history, the Greeks continued to be enthralled by the Homeric epics. These were probably composed, or given their final form, in the 8th century B.C., and the hero of the *Iliad*, Achilles, is not at all reconciled to his foreknowledge that he is doomed to die young, nor does his mother the goddess Thetis take satisfaction, as some Spartan human mothers did in later times, in the prospect of her son's dying young on the field of honour. Young though he still is at the siege of Troy, Achilles has already had time to win matchless glory by his outstanding prowess. But the fame that Achilles has already achieved in a short life does not console him for death's imminence; and his experience after death, in the realm of the shades of the dead, justifies posthumously his reluctance, while alive, to lose his life prematurely. In the eleventh book of the *Odyssey*, his shade is represented as saying to Odysseus that the lot of an agricultural labourer who is the serf of a pauper in the land of the living is preferable to being king of all the dead;[5] and, after making this bitter

[1] In *Oedipus Coloneus*, lines 1224-6.
[2] Herodotus, Book I, chap. 31.
[3] Byron, *Don Juan*, IV, xii.
[4] E.g. Mimnermus, *Nanno*, Elegies I and II.
[5] *Odyssey*, Book XI, lines 489-491.

observation, he strides away, unresigned and indignant, though elated at the same time by the news, given him by Odysseus, of the military prowess of his son.[1]

The repining at the prospect of an early death which is attributed to Achilles in the *Iliad* may have corresponded to the average Greek young man's attitude in real life—even a young man who happened to have been born a Spartan and to have been conditioned by being brought up under the "Lycurgan" regimen. If his mother took the stand of the legendary Spartan mother, his private reaction may have been a wry one. At Sparta, and, *a fortiori*, in other Greek city-states, there is much evidence that the Greeks, even those who paid lip-service to pessimism, got much enjoyment out of life; were not eager to exchange it for death; and did not let the edge be taken off their enjoyment by brooding on a death for which they were in no hurry. The Greeks enjoyed passing the time of day in each other's company, discussing anything and everything; they enjoyed beauty; and they had a genius for bringing these two sources of enjoyment together in choral singing and dancing, theatrical performances, religious processions, and talkative political assemblies.

Compared with Greek pessimism, Indian pessimism has been radical, and it has also been sincere, as is demonstrated by the single-mindedness and the austerity with which it has been put into action. Hinduism regards man's universe as being an illusion; the Buddha, anticipating some of the schools of modern Western psychologists by about twenty-four centuries, held that the soul is an illusion too. He saw in the human psyche only a fleeting series of discontinuous psychological states, which are held together only by desire, and which can be dissipated if and when desire is extinguished. In the Buddha's view, the extinction of desire is the proper goal of human endeavour, because the achievement of this brings with it the extinction of suffering, and, for the Buddha, life and suffering were synonymous. Not death, but re-birth, is the arch-ordeal for a human being. The Buddha took it for granted that the effect of desire, precipitated in the form of karma (the cumulative spiritual effects of action taken in a succession of lives up to the present), is to keep a series of rebirths going *ad infinitum*, unless and until, in one of the lives in this chain, the sufferer, by successfully performing the strenuous spiritual exercises that the Buddha has prescribed, manages to bring the series to an end by attaining the state of extinguishedness (nirvana) in which all passion is spent and rebirth ceases because it is no longer brought on by the momentum of karma, now that karma has been worked off. In this spiritual struggle to attain nirvana, death (i.e. the death of the current life in the series) is an unimportant incident. Nirvana may be attained at death, but it may also be attained while the former sufferer is still living what will now have been the last of his successive lives.

[1] *Ibid.*, lines 538-540.

One index of pessimism is suicide. In a society in which life is rated at so low a value that death is held to be the lesser evil, suicide will be held to be one of the basic human rights, and the practice of it will be considered respectable and in some cases meritorious or even morally obligatory.

In the Graeco-Roman world, no stigma was attached to suicide, though the practice of it was not so common as it has been in South and East Asian countries in which the prevailing religions and philosophies have been of Indian or Chinese origin. There were cases of Greek statesmen who committed suicide in a political impasse. Demosthenes and King Cleomenes III of Sparta are examples. Under the Principate, Roman nobles were in some cases allowed to commit suicide as an alternative to execution. The Greek philosopher Democritus is said by Lucretius to have exposed himself to death voluntarily (perhaps by starvation) when he found that his mental powers were failing.[1] But the Greek spectators were surprised and impressed when Peregrinus Proteus burned himself to death ostentatiously at Olympia.[2] (A modern Western psychologist might have convicted him, as Lucian does, of exhibitionism.) It is possible that Peregrinus may have been influenced by an Indian precedent that could have been within his knowledge. According to the geographer Artemidorus of Ephesus, an Indian who had accompanied an Indian embassy to the Emperor Augustus had burnt himself to death at Athens. Strabo[3] cites Artemidorus as saying that "some Indians do this because they are finding life a burden, while others—of whom this one is an example—do it because they are finding life so good. The idea is that, when everything has gone as one likes, it is time to be off, for fear that, if one lingers, one may be overtaken by something that one does not like."

According to Artemidorus, this particular Indian "leaped on to the pyre, laughing, with nothing on but a loin-cloth and with his body well-oiled; and his tomb bears the inscription: 'Zarmanochegas, an Indian from Bargosa [Broach], who made himself immortal by following traditional Indian custom' ".

In Hindu society the commonest form of suicide has been *sati*. It used to be deemed a meritorious act for a widow to burn herself to death when her husband died; and, though *sati* was nominally voluntary, it seems often to have been committed under pressure. A widower was under no reciprocal obligation; but male devotees used to throw themselves under the wheels of Juggernaut's car to be crushed to death. In present-day Vietnam, Buddhist monks and nuns have committed suicide by burning themselves to death as a political protest. In China under the imperial regime, a censor who had felt it to be his official

[1] Lucretius, *De Rerum Natura*, Book III, lines 139-141.
[2] Lucian, *De Morte Peregrini*.
[3] *Geographica*, Book XV, chap. 1, §. 73 (C.720).

duty to present a memorial to the Emperor, cr
conduct, might follow up this act by committing
tion of sincerity with loyalty that would increa
Emperor while releasing the censor himself fro
Japan, it has been a point of honour to commit
political protest, but as a sign of respect for a
atonement for some failure in duty, or for som
which, in a Westerner's eye, would be a quite i
making such drastic and such irrevocable amend
observer had no objection to suicide in principle.

There have been cases in which Jews, Phoenicians, and Lycians have committed suicide *en masse* rather than allow themselves to be taken prisoner by a victorious enemy. On the other hand, Christians, whose religion is of Jewish origin, have always felt an inhibition against committing suicide, and have branded a suicide as a *felo de se*, who has debarred himself, by his crime, from being given burial in consecrated ground. The Christian's view of this world as being "a vale of tears" is much the same as the Buddhist's view; but the Christian, unlike the Buddhist, does not consider that he has the right to decide for himself to put an end to his life. For the Christian, this is not man's prerogative; it is God's; and it is impious wilfully to anticipate God's action. If this is a Christian superstition—and it is a superstition in Greek, Roman, Hindu, Buddhist, Confucian Chinese, and Japanese eyes—it is a Christian tradition that dies hard. At the present day, many ex-Christians, who have abandoned almost all the rest of the Christian tradition, still retain the Christian feeling that suicide is shocking.

In a community of Australian natives who live by food-gathering and migrate, in search of food, in an annual orbit, the aged will voluntarily drop out and stay behind to die, in order to relieve the community of the burden of continuing to maintain them. In the present-day Western world the average expectation of life has been increased, without any accompanying increase in zest or relief from pressure, while the loosening of family ties has left many old people out in the cold, socially and spiritually. If they had been Australian natives, they would have allowed themselves to die; if they had been Chinese peasants, there would have been a place for them in the home, with their children and grandchildren, as long as they remained alive. Being Christians or ex-Christians, and therefore feeling the traditional Christian inhibition against committing suicide, many old people in the Western world today linger on, lonely and unhappy, until medical ingenuity ceases to be able to keep them physically alive.

The Christian inhibition against suicide applies, *a fortiori*, to giving to incurably and painfully ailing human beings the merciful release that humane Christians give, as a matter of course, to animals when these are in the same plight. Hitler was not prevented by the conscience of the German Christian public from murdering millions of Jews; yet

man Christian conscience that did not prove effective for
ing Hitler from committing the crime of genocide did make it
ossible for Hitler to carry out his plan of killing off aged, infirm,
d feeble-minded Germans in order to relieve physically and mentally
fit Germans of the burden of continuing to look after the unfit when
German energies were being mobilised by Hitler for the waging of the
Second World War.

(c) *Attempts to circumvent death by physical countermeasures.* One of the
commonest primitive assumptions regarding death is that a dead
person's life can be prolonged after death by providing the corpse with
the food, drink, paraphernalia, and services that were formerly at the
disposal of the person whose living body this corpse once was. The
burial with the dead of objects that are useful to the living has been a
world-wide practice. Archaeologists have been able to reconstruct a
culture from the contents of graves in sites in which there has been little
or no trace left of the apparatus used by the living. Ancient tombs have
been preserved in far greater numbers than ancient dwellings once
inhabited by the living. Besides yielding up tools, weapons, ornaments,
and clothes, some tombs have been found to contain the remains of
slaughtered domestic animals and of human servitors, whose services
the dead owner of the tomb was expected still to be able to command.

This naïve strategy for circumventing death was carried to extremes
in Ancient Egypt. If the tomb representing a dead pharaoh's house was
magnified to the dimensions of a gigantic pyramid, if the furniture
deposited in his tomb was as lavish in both quantity and quality as the
gear that was buried with Tut-ankh-amen; and if the tomb was
endowed with lands whose revenues would pay, in perpetuity, for the
provision of victuals and for the performance of ritual by priests, it was
felt that death could be counteracted and overcome by this massive
application of physical countermeasures—in fact, by sheer physical
force. Still more naïve was the assumption that preserving a dead body
by arresting its natural decay was tantamount to keeping the life in it.
Mummification was practised not only in Egypt but in Peru. The
dryness of the climate in both coastal Peru and Upper Egypt was an
assistance to the embalmer's work, yet this fine art was manifestly just
as incapable of keeping life in a corpse as the Zoroastrian practice of
exposing corpses to putrefy until they have been consumed by scavenging birds and beasts.

Another strategy for the circumvention of death by physical countermeasures has been to seek for the tree of life or for the elixir of
immortality. But the fruitlessness of this quest has been recognised in
mythology. When Adam and Eve had eaten of the fruit of the Tree of
Knowledge, they were expelled from the Garden of Eden by the angel
with the flaming sword before they had had time to baffle Yahweh by
eating the fruit of the Tree of Life as well. Translated into present-day

prosaic terms, this myth signifies that man's acquisition of science and technology has not enabled him to acquire immortality as well. The outcome of the Sumerian hero Gilgamesh's quest for immortality was likewise ironical. After performing a series of Herculean labours, Gilgamesh was on the last stage of his journey home with a branch of the Tree of Life in his hand when he accidentally dropped this into the water, where it was immediately snapped up by a snake. So Gilgamesh arrived home still mortal. His labours had, after all, been in vain.

The futility of trying to circumvent death by taking physical counter-measures was demonstrated dramatically in Ancient Egypt at the fall of the Old Kingdom. The fall of this regime was accompanied by a social revolution in the course of which the tombs of the pharaohs and of their courtiers were rifled and the funerary wealth accumulated in the course of three-quarters of a millennium was impudently plundered. The irony of this ignominious end of such careful and elaborate physical provision for the circumvention of death is one of the themes of surviving Egyptian works of literature written in the age of the Middle Kingdom. Yet this recognition of the futility of the practice did not deter succeeding generations from persisting with it, and the principal beneficiaries of the costly furnishing of Egyptian pharaohs and nobles came to be, not the dead themselves, but living tomb-robbers. Tomb-robbing became as fine an art as mummification. The robbers penetrated the most massive and most cunningly contrived defences and eluded the watchful eye of the public authorities. They battened on the Egyptian people's invin-cible naïveté. Yet it is conceivable that the robbers themselves were not altogether immune from the prevailing superstition. We can imagine them going about their professional business with mixed feelings of cynicism and guilt.

(d) *Attempts to circumvent death by winning fame.* Though a dead body cannot be kept alive by physical measures, the memory of the dead, as they were when they were truly alive, can be transmitted to succeeding generations. In an illiterate society the main media of commemoration are the memorisation of genealogies and the composition and recital of oral poetry. When a society has become literate, poetry can be reduced to writing and can be supplemented by inscriptions engraved on stone or impressed on clay tablets or written on papyrus or parchment or paper or palm-leaves or slivers of bamboo, to record the foundation of temples and the annals of reigns. These official records, in turn, can be raised to the level of biographies and historical works of literature which can take their place side by side with poetry.

This attempt to circumvent death by commemoration is more sophisticated than the attempt to circumvent it by physical measures; but the outcome of this attempt is ironical too in ways of its own. For instance, the recorder eventually wins greater fame than the men of action whose fame has been preserved by the recorder's pen. Most of what we know about the Athenian statesman Pericles and the Spartan soldier Brasidas today is due to the fact that a minor naval commander, Thucydides, was given the leisure for becoming a major historian thanks to his having been cashiered and exiled, perhaps unfairly, for having failed to prevent Brasidas from capturing Amphipolis. When Horace wrote "non omnis moriar",[1] he underestimated the length of the time after his death during which his poetry would preserve the memory of the poet himself. He reckoned that his poetry would continue to be read as long as the ritual of Rome's official religion continued to be performed. This ritual was suppressed by the intolerant Christian Roman Emperor Theodosius I in the last decade of the 4th century of the Christian Era, only four centuries after the date of Horace's death. Yet Horace's poetry is still being read in the 20th century by readers whose mother tongue is not Latin, and, in the earlier decades of the 19th century, it was still being quoted in speeches made in English by members of the parliament at Westminster.

Horace himself, however, has pointed out the precariousness of this circumvention of death by commemoration—sophisticated and ethereal though this method is by comparison with the naïve circumvention of death by physical measures.

> Vixere fortes ante Agamemnona
> multi; sed omnes illacrimabiles
> urgentur ignotique longâ
> nocte, carent quia vate sacro![2]

The relics of Agamemnon's predecessors who are not commemorated in the Homeric epic have now been disinterred by modern archaeologists. These have proved to have been mightier monarchs than Agamemnon himself, and, whether or not they employed court poets whose works have not yet come to light, we have now retrieved some of their records—not romantic minstrels' lays but prosaic official inventories, corresponding to what present-day governments call "forms". These pre-Agamemnonian Mycenaean official documents are at least four or five centuries older than the *Iliad* and the *Odyssey*, and we have specimens of rudiments of the Sumerian cuneiform script that date from before the close of the fourth millennium B.C., but mankind's first five millennia of literacy are dwarfed by the dark night of the preceding million years during which our ancestors were already human yet have not left any surviving memorial except their tools and their cave-paintings—and even these Late Palaeolithic paintings are estimated to be not more than about thirty thousand years old. Our thousand past millennia of oblivion are a long span of time, compared

[1] Horace, *Odes*, Book III, Ode xxx, line 6.
[2] Horace, *Odes*, Book IV, Ode ix, lines 25-28. "There were mighty men before Agamemnon—there were any number of them; yet, one and all, these are buried in a long, long night, unknown and unmournable—and this just because they had no inspired bard" [to commemorate them, as Agamemnon has been commemorated by Homer].

to our subsequent 30,000 years of pictorial commemoration and 5000 years of literacy. But mankind's first million years, as well as his latest 5000 years, are dwarfed by the span of 2000 million years which is reckoned to be the expectation of life on the surface of this planet. It is difficult to imagine that any existing works of man, either monumental or literary, will have survived until the day when this planet becomes no longer habitable. Will any of the now current languages then still be intelligible? Will any works written in these still survive? Will not the pyramids, and the still more durable tumuli and railway-embankments, have been worn down flatter than the most archaic of the rocks that now crop out on the earth's surface?

(e) *Self-liberation from self-centredness by putting one's treasure in future generations of one's fellow human beings.* Another way in which human beings have sought to reconcile themselves to the fact of death has been so ubiquitous and so constant that one might almost venture to infer that it is innate in human nature. Down to this day, since the earliest date to which our surviving records reach back, most human beings have reconciled themselves, to some extent, to their mortality as individuals by putting their treasure in their descendants, while some human beings have expanded their concern to embrace all the other representatives of future generations who, though not their physical descendants, will be their successors and will perhaps be their spiritual heirs.

In the genealogy in the 11th chapter of the Book of Genesis, the high point in the life of Shem and each of his successive descendants is his age when his first child is born. The remainder of his life, from that red-letter day onwards till his death, is represented implicitly as being an anticlimax.

In Yahweh's successive promises to Abraham, the god never promises his human client personal immortality. What he promises him is progeny. "I will make of thee a great nation";[1] "I will make thy seed as the dust of the earth, so that, if a man can number the dust of the earth, then shall thy seed also be numbered";[2] "look now toward heaven and tell the stars, if thou be able to number them: and he said unto him, so shall thy seed be";[3] "thou shalt be a father of many nations";[4] "Abraham shall surely become a great and mighty nation";[5] "in multiplying I will multiply thy seed as the stars of the heaven, and as the sand which is upon the sea shore".[6] Whether or not this prospect of becoming the ancestor of the Hebrew peoples reconciled Abraham to the prospect of his own death, it is evident that the promises that were held to have been made to Abraham by Yahweh were felt, by the authors and editors of the Book of Genesis, to be more valuable and more satisfying than any promise of personal immortality would have

[1] Gen., xii, 2.
[2] Gen., xiii, 16.
[3] Gen., xv, 5.
[4] Gen., xvii, 4.
[5] Gen., xviii, 18.
[6] Gen., xxii, 17.

been. If the Israelite writers of these passages believed that, after death, the shades of the dead retained a shadowy existence in Sheol, they will have shared the feelings of the author of the 11th book of the *Odyssey*, who, as has been remarked earlier,[1] describes the shade of Achilles as exulting, in Hades, at the news of his son's prowess on earth, unreconciled though Achilles himself was to his own state after death.[2]

It is significant that the belief in the resurrection of the dead did not gain a foothold in the Jewish community until the 2nd century B.C. This belief seems to have been introduced to the Jews through their becoming acquainted with a foreign religion, Zoroastrianism. One of the considerations that led some Jews to believe, from the 2nd century B.C. onwards, in the eventual resurrection of some individuals is thought to have been their confidence in Yahweh's sense of justice. They will have felt that this was bound to move Yahweh to reward those Jews who had suffered martyrdom in resisting the Seleucid Emperor Antiochus IV's attempt to coerce the Palestinian Jewish community into adopting the Greek way of life; and these martyrs would not be adequately rewarded if they were not eventually raised from the dead to become living participants in the messianic kingdom when this was eventually established. The belief that, not only the Jewish martyrs, but all the dead, were destined to rise again seems, in the development of Judaism, to have come later.

It is also significant that this addition of a new article to the traditional corpus of Jewish beliefs was not accepted immediately by the Jewish people as a whole. It was adopted, at first, by the Pharisees only. It was rejected by the Sadducees on the ground that there was no warrant for it in the written Mosaic Law, and that the written Law alone was valid. The Pharisees were originally dissenters; the Sadducees represented the "establishment". The Sadducees were in control of the Temple at Jerusalem, and held at least the key posts in the officiating priesthood. The Sadducees maintained their dominant position in the Palestinian Jewish community, and persisted in their rejection of the belief in the the resurrection of the dead, until the destruction of the Temple in A.D. 70. It was only after this that the Pharisees' hitherto controversial belief became part of the orthodox faith of the Jewish people as a whole; and, among the Jews, this general adoption of the belief in the resurrection of the dead has not weakened the desire for the continuous survival of the Jewish people as a community that perpetuates itself from generation to generation of the mortal men and women who are its successive ephemeral representatives.

The pre-Pharisaic Israelites and Jews were not peculiar in reconciling themselves to the prospect of death by taking comfort in the prospect that their race would be perpetuated in their descendants. A prospect that has caused greater anxiety and distress than the prospect of death

[1] See pp. 70-71.
[2] *Odyssey*, Book XI, lines 538-540.

has been the prospect of dying without being survived by any descendants. According to the Book of Genesis,[1] Abraham felt that Yahweh's announcement that he was going to be Abraham's "exceeding great reward" was meaningless so long as Yahweh suffered Abraham to go childless; and this passionate desire to have descendants, that is attributed to Abraham in this passage, has been widespread. It has been particularly strong in societies, such as the Hindu and the Chinese, in which it has been held to be important for a human being that, after his death, he should be commemorated and be venerated in a cult performed by a surviving son and by this son's descendants in their turn.

Where the cult of ancestors is practised, this is evidence of a concern about what is going to happen after one's own death, but this concern may not be solely a concern for the perpetuation of the race; it may be partly self-centred. The ancestor who has demanded the cult has presumably sought commemoration for himself in the belief that this will have some posthumous value for him; the descendant who performs the cult may be moved to undertake this burden not only by love of a parent or by a feeling of piety towards a more remote ancestor, but also by a belief that dead ancestors have it in their power to benefit or injure their descendants, and that it is therefore advisable for their descendants to give them satisfaction by carrying on the cult. Abraham's longing to have a child is not un-self-regarding either. He points out to Yahweh that, if he dies childless, the heir who will inherit his estate will be, not one of his own kinsfolk, but "one born in my house", i.e. a child of one of Abraham's slaves.[2]

This self-regarding aspect of the desire to be survived by a legitimate successor is likely to be prominent in cases in which the estate that the present holder of it will leave behind him at death does not consist just of private property, such as Abraham's flocks and herds, but is the succession to the throne of a kingdom. In this case, no doubt, the self-regarding desire to be succeeded by a descendant may be accompanied by a concern for the public welfare. The reigning sovereign may forebode that, if no near kinsman of his survives to succeed him, his own death may be followed by a dispute over the succession that might give rise to disorder. If the reigning sovereign has imposed on his subjects reforms that are radical and controversial, and if he is conscious that his own ability and will-power have been the principal agencies by which his reforms have been instituted and have been maintained, his desire that his life-work shall outlast his own lifetime may be stronger than his desire that his successor shall be one of his descendants.

The classic case is Peter the Great's treatment of his son and heir Alexei. After disinheriting Alexei, Peter had him flogged to death. One of Peter's motives for committing this dreadful and unnatural crime was a personal antipathy that was mutual; but Peter was also moved by

[1] Gen., xv, 2-3.   [2] *Ibid.*

concern for the future public welfare of the Russian state and people, and this concern of Peter's was justified by facts. Alexei was not, by nature, a man of action; he hated being involved in public affairs and was incompetent in them, and he was under the influence of people who were opposed to Peter's reforms and who would have pressed Alexei to undo these if Alexei had survived Peter and had succeeded him. Posterity will agree with Peter that, for Russia, this would have been a calamity.

The extreme step taken by Peter to ensure that the reforms which he had carried out in Russia should not be undone after his death brings out the truth that it is difficult to feel concern for the future welfare of posterity without also trying to give practical effect to this concern by taking steps to influence or even determine what shall happen after one's death in so far as this lies in one's power. If one feels concern for posterity, one will have one's own ideas about what is going to be beneficial for or detrimental to posterity, and one will then be moved to try to ensure the welfare of these future generations as one sees it, and to secure them against suffering harm as one sees that too. Heads of states who have a life-long tenure of office are, of course, not the only people whose concern for posterity may incline them to try to make their power last longer than their own lifetime by fixing, while they are still alive, what shall happen after they are dead. This possibility also arises whenever any private person makes his or her will, especially if the testator is making bequests, not only to kinsmen and friends of his, but to religious, educational, or charitable institutions. The exercise, by the dead, of this posthumous power has been found so burdensome for posterity that, in some countries, legislation has been enacted that limits a testator's freedom to dispose of his property altogether as he chooses.

However, neither private testators nor rulers with a life-long tenure have been so successful in governing the life of posterity as the founders of the historic philosophies and higher religions. Hundreds of millions of human beings who are alive at this moment are being swayed, on many issues, great and small, by the commandments and precepts of Marx, Muhammad, Saint Paul, Jesus, the Buddha, Confucius, and the redactors of the Pentateuch. The posthumous power of these spiritual authorities has been, and continues to be, incomparably great. Yet the exercise of this posthumous spiritual power has its ironical aspect.

Some of the authentic commandments and precepts of these religious leaders were drafted and promulgated by them on the spur of the moment for dealing with some urgent but local and temporary situation. Cases in point are Saint Paul's epistles and the chapters of the Qur'an that were issued by the Prophet Muhammad when he was the head of the government of the city-state of Medina. Both Muhammad and Paul would probably have been disconcerted if they could have foreseen how literally and earnestly even the most casual of their pronouncements were going to be taken by millions of devout posthumous adherents of theirs, and this for hundreds of years to come. There are other zealously obeyed commandments and precepts and statements that have been attributed falsely to the religious leader whose name has lent them their authority, and some of these might have shocked their alleged authors. What would Jesus, for instance, have felt if he could have foreseen that, after his death, his followers were going to worship him, in company with Yahweh and with the Holy Spirit, as one of the members of a divine trinity? On the evidence of the Gospels themselves, Jesus was an orthodox Jew. He is reported to have said to an enquirer: "Why callest thou me good? There is none good save one; that is God."[1] This saying is likely not only to be authentic but to have been notoriously authentic at the time when the Gospel according to Saint Mark was composed. If it had not been, it would surely have been expurgated; for it is a contradiction, out of Jesus's own mouth, of his posthumous Christian followers' thesis that he was God himself.

Peter's murder of Alexei also brings out, through being an extreme case, the truth that the future generations in whom a living human being can put his treasure may comprise a far wider circle than his own physical descendants. The choice that confronted Peter was not, in itself, a unique one. The reigning occupant of an hereditary office— whether he is the sovereign of a state or the director-in-chief of a family business—may feel obliged to disinherit his son, or some less close kinsman, because he judges him to be unfit to take over the duties of the office and because his conscience tells him that the interests of the realm or the business—i.e. the interests of people who are not his relatives but for whose welfare he is responsible—ought to take pre-cedence over his family obligations to his "kith and kin". The disin-heriting of an heir who is his heir by virtue of kinship does not normally require that he should put his disinherited kinsman to death. The Roman emperors Nerva, Trajan, Hadrian, and Antoninus Pius each in turn handed on the imperial office to a successor who was his son only by the legal fiction of adoption, and in doing this they were making the future welfare of the Empire and its inhabitants their paramount concern; but none of them murdered any disinherited kinsman of his, as Peter murdered Alexei. On the other hand, Marcus Aurelius did a bad service to the Empire when he departed from the consistent practice of his four immediate predecessors by bequeathing the imperial office to his actual son Commodus. For Commodus was not only incompetent in public affairs and uninterested in them, as Alexei was. Unlike Alexei, Commodus was a vicious character.

Peter the Great's concern for the welfare of future generations embraced a nation that was already a large one, but that was, at the same time, only one among a number, with some of which it was at enmity. Marcus Aurelius's four predecessors' concern embraced the

[1] Mark, x, 18.

F

whole population of an empire that was a world-state in the eyes of its rulers and their subjects, in the sense that the Roman Empire contained within its frontiers as much of the contemporary civilised world as was within its inhabitants' ken. Today, anyone who is concerned with the welfare of future generations has to expand his concern not only from his family to his nation, but from his nation to the whole human race. For, in our day, "the annihilation of distance" by the progress of technology has linked together, for good or for evil, the fortunes of all sections of mankind, while the invention of the atomic weapon has put the human species in danger of extinction once again for the first time since, in the Later Palaeolithic Age, Man definitively got the upper hand over all other living creatures on the face of this planet except bacteria. No doubt, Lord Russell was thinking in these ecumenical terms if he said, as he is reported to have said, that, when one has reached old age, it is important to care immensely about what is going to happen after one is dead.

In the present state of military potency, political tension, and scientific knowledge, this means putting one's treasure in seventy million future generations of mankind which will have come and gone, after the present generation has died off, before the surface of this planet will have ceased to be habitable for living creatures. Can a human being reconcile himself to the fact of death by putting his treasure in future generations of all mankind in these almost un-imaginably large numbers? Can the transfer of one's concern from one's own puny self to so vast a posterity give meaning, value, and zest to life and deprive death of its sting?

It may seem audacious to say that posterity on this scale is not something great enough to draw a human being completely out of himself, and so to reconcile him entirely to his foreknowledge that he himself is going to die. Yet to sink one's self-centredness in a concern for all future generations of one's fellow human beings would be wholly satisfying only if one knew that mankind was the be-all and end-all of the universe. We do not know this; we have no means of discovering whether or not it is the truth; and it seems unlikely to be the truth, considering that our own planet, solar system, and galaxy are only minute fragments of a physical universe whose bounds, if it has any bounds, are beyond the reach of our powers of observation. Moreover, there is, within the psyche of any single human being, a psychic universe that is apparently proving to be at least as vast, in its own medium, as the physical universe is. Furthermore, the psychic universe, the physical universe, and the relation between the two are not self-explanatory; they are mysterious; they can hardly be the ultimate reality. Can a human being get into touch with this ultimate reality? And, if he can, can he reconcile himself to death by entering into eternal communion with the ultimate reality or by merging himself in it?

(f) *Self-liberation from self-centredness by merging oneself in ultimate reality.*
To get into touch with Ultimate Reality and to merge oneself in it has
been an Indian quest. In India, this has been the principal quest of
philosophers of all schools for the last 3,000 years at least. Round about
the turn of the 6th and 5th centuries B.C., the quest produced a sharp
cleavage between two schools which gave different reports of the
findings of introspection and consequently worked out different prescriptions for reaching spiritual goals that were perhaps identical.

The adherents of one school reported that, when a human being
succeeds in bringing into the light of consciousness the very centre of
his psyche, he finds there a "dweller in the innermost"—a soul—that is
identical with Ultimate Reality itself. This finding has been expressed
in the three words "That art thou"—"that" meaning Ultimate Reality,
and "thou" meaning a human soul. Was the recognition of the identity
of "thou" with "that" held to be tantamount to the merging of "thou"
in "that"? Possibly it was; for the recognition of the identity is not just
an intellectual discovery; it is the consummation of long and hard
spiritual travail.

The opposing school was the school founded by the Buddha. The
Buddha's findings were quite different from those of his contemporaries,
and, so far from being the final consummation of long and hard spiritual
travail, they were a fresh starting-point for this.[1] The Buddha reported
that in the psyche there was no soul; he found there only a series of
discontinuous psychic states, held together and kept moving only by
the momentum of the karma engendered by desire. His prescription for
merging the self in Ultimate Reality was not to penetrate to the self's
core and recognise the identity of Ultimate Reality with this; it was to
stop the flow of psychic states by extinguishing desire—i.e. self-
centredness—and thus attaining to the state of "extinguishedness".
(nirvana).

A present-day Western observer is likely to be more conscious of the
common ground of these two opposing Indian schools of thought than
of the differences that loomed so large in the minds of their respective
Indian initiators. Both schools take it for granted that all sentient
beings are doomed to go through a round of rebirths which will
continue unless and until, in one of the successive lives, the sufferer
succeeds in bringing the series of lives to an end. Both schools hold that
rebirth is a far greater evil than death, and that to circumvent rebirth,
not to circumvent death, ought therefore to be the supreme goal of
human endeavours. Both schools also hold that the spiritual exertions
required for attaining this goal are long and hard, though their prescriptions for striving to attain it differ. A human being who adheres
to either of these schools of Indian philosophy will have little difficulty
in reconciling himself to the fact of death. The fact (taken by him for
granted) that death is going to be followed by another rebirth will be

[1] See below, Ninian Smart, "Attitudes Towards Death in Eastern Religions", p. 95 ff..

this man's nightmare. I have never forgotten the radiant smile that came over the face of a Japanese scholar, Professor Anesaki, when, at a conference held in Kyoto in 1929, he announced: "I am from Tokyo, but also from Kyoto, because I am coming here after I am dead." My guess is that Professor Anesaki's smile was evoked by two thoughts: the thought of the natural beauty of the city that was to cherish his mortal remains, and the thought of the ineffable beauty of nirvana.[1]

(g) *The belief in the personal immortality of human souls.* Hindus believe in a supra-personal immortality (i.e. in the identity of the essence of a human being's psyche with Ultimate Reality). Buddhists believe in a depersonalised immortality (i.e. in the possibility of extinguishing the self through self-release from self-centredness). I have suggested that these two beliefs of Indian origin prove, on analysis, to be more closely akin to each other than they might appear to be at first sight and than they have been held to be in Indian philosophical controversies. A further feature that they have in common is that both alike are more credible than the belief in personal immortality.

It is credible that a human being, in his psychic dimension, may be part and parcel of Ultimate Reality in its spiritual aspect, and it is demonstrable that, in his physical dimension, the same human being is part and parcel of the universe in the material aspect in which we apprehend the universe with our senses and interpret our sense-data in scientific terms. On the other hand, no living human being has ever been able to demonstrate conclusively that he has been in psychic communication with a disembodied human psyche (i.e. with the psyche of a human being whose body was, at the time, not alive, but was either a corpse or had decomposed into the chemical elements of which the corpse had consisted at the moment at which it had ceased to be a living body).[2] *A fortiori*, no one has ever been able to demonstrate that he has been in psychic communion with an unembodied human psyche that has never yet been embodied or that has, at the time, been temporarily unembodied in an interval between two successive incarnations (a conception that requires the undemonstrated assumption that a psyche can be, and is, repeatedly re-embodied in successive living bodies, human or non-human, without losing its identity).

Every living human being whom any other living human being has ever encountered has been a psychosomatic entity; and the life of every one of these human psychosomatic entities, like the life of every other sexual living organism inhabiting this planet, has moved, or is in the course of moving, in the time-dimension, on a trajectory which describes a course up from birth through infancy to its prime and from its prime through old age down to death, supposing that the human being in

[1] For a fuller discussion of the quest for Ultimate Reality, see below, Ninian Smart, "Attitudes Towards Death in Eastern Religions", pp. 101-102.

[2] But see below, Rosalind Heywood, "Death and Psychical Research", p. 219 ff.

question lives out his or her life to the end of its full natural span, and that this particular life is not cut short prematurely by disease, accident, or violent death inflicted by other human beings in war, by law, or by private enterprise.

Death, whatever its cause and its circumstances may be, is an event in which the former living body becomes a corpse which decays (unless its physical decomposition is artificially arrested), while, at the same moment, the psyche passes out of human ken (i.e. ceases to be in communication with the psyche of any human being who is alive at that moment). It is impossible to conceive of a human body being alive without being associated with a human psyche. It has been found possible to imagine a psyche being alive without being associated with a living body. However, this feat of imagination is so difficult that attempts to work out its implications in detail have run into incongruities, inconsistencies, incompatibilities, and self-contradictions.

When believers in personal immortality have sought to describe the state of disembodied souls, they have found no way of describing this hypothetical state that does not involve the drawing of some analogy with the psychosomatic life on earth of which we have actual experience. The shade that has been consigned to Sheol or to Hades or to the underworld as conceived by the Sumerians and their Akkadian and Babylonian cultural heirs is an enfeebled replica of the now dead person who was once alive in psychosomatic form. In fact, the author of the 11th book of the *Odyssey* takes it for granted that the only condition on which the living visitor, Odysseus, can put himself into communication with the shades of the dead in their shadowy world is by partially and temporarily re-endowing them with a modicum of physical life. In order to enable them to talk to him, Odysseus has first to administer to them a physical stimulant. He gives each of them, in turn, a drink of the blood of non-human psychosomatic animals—sheep—which Odysseus has slaughtered for this purpose.[1] As for the privileged minority of the departed who are imagined to be enjoying a blissful existence in the Kingdom of the West or as a star in heaven (if the departed grandee has been an Egyptian pharaoh), or in Elysium (if he has been a pre-Christian Greek hero), or in Valhalla (if he has been a pre-Christian Scandinavian warrior), these favoured few are credited with a vitality that is of a superhuman or even godlike exuberance.

This inability to conceive of disembodied spirits in non-psychosomatic terms also besets those believers in personal immortality who hold that the destiny of the departed is determined, not by their former rank, but by their former conduct. The torments of the damned in hell are depicted on the walls of Etruscan tombs and of Eastern Orthodox Christian refectories in monasteries on Mount Athos, and are described in Dante's *Divina Commedia*, in crassly physical terms—and some of these imaginary torments are so extreme that no living human being

[1] *Odyssey*, Book XI, lines 23-50, 82, 88-89, 98, 153, 232, 390.

could be subjected to them for more than a few seconds without dying of them, though, incongruously, the disembodied spirits that are believed to be suffering these lethal torments are held to have been made immortal in order that their suffering may be everlasting. There have been a number of different conceptions of the nature of the personal immortality of a disembodied or unembodied soul, but they all have one significant feature in common. In some degree, they all involve some incongruities, inconsistencies, incompatibilities, and self-contradictions.

One conception of the immortality of the soul has been that souls are not only immortal but eternal: i.e. that every soul has been in existence eternally before it ever came to be embodied, and that it will remain in existence eternally after having become disembodied once for all. Of all the divers conceptions of the personal immortality of the soul, this is the one that comes nearest to the Indian conception of a supra-personal or a depersonalised immortality. This belief was held by some pre-Christian Greeks, but never, so far as we can judge, by more than a small sophisticated minority. Another small minority believed that, at death, the soul was annihilated. The majority probably believed, from the beginning to the end of the pre-Christian age of Greek history, that each human soul comes into existence together with the body with which it is associated in life, and that, after death, it continues, as a shade, to lead, in Hades, a shadowy life of the kind depicted in the 11th book of the *Odyssey*.

The most prominent of the Greek believers in the eternity of souls were the Pythagoreans (an esoteric semi-philosophical semi-religious organised fraternity) and the Orphics (an unorganised and unsophisticated sect). Both these Greek sets of believers in the eternity of souls were also believers in the transmigration of souls from one incarnation to another, and this latter belief is so arbitrary and so peculiar that its simultaneous appearance, in the 6th century B.C., in the Greek world and in India can hardly have been fortuitous. One possible common source is the Eurasian nomad society, which, in the 8th and 7th centuries B.C., had descended upon India, South-Western Asia, the steppe country along the north shore of the Black Sea, and the Balkan and Anatolian peninsulas in one of its occasional explosive *völkerwanderungen*.

A belief in the personal immortality of souls which does not involve a belief in their being eternal as well as immortal is bound up with the attempts, noted already, to circumvent death by physical countermeasures. The pre-Christian and pre-Muslim Egyptians, for instance, believed in the conditional immortality of the souls of the dead—or, strictly speaking, in the conditional immortality of one of the several souls that were believed to appertain to a human being. The particular soul known as the "ka" was believed to remain in existence, haunting the dead person's tomb, so long as posterity continued to keep the tomb in proper spiritual condition by performing the requisite ritual there and by providing the requisite supplies of food, drink, clothes, and furniture which were conceived of as being necessities of life after death, as they had been before death. This belief was held simultaneously with the incompatible beliefs that the dead person's soul might have migrated to the Kingdom of the West or might have ascended to heaven to shine there as a star or might have descended into the underworld presided over by the god Osiris.

This Egyptian belief in the conditional immortality of souls after death has also been held, though it has not, in all cases, been worked out so systematically, by all the numerous other peoples that have practised ancestor-worship, e.g. the Chinese.

Three other varieties of a belief in the immortality of souls after death that does not involve a belief in their pre-existence before birth or in their eternity have been mentioned already. There has been a belief in a dismal habitation of the souls of the dead, which retain a shadowy existence there. This is the Hebrew Sheol, the Greek Hades, and the Sumerian counterpart of these. There has been a belief in a blissful abode for the souls of dead persons who had been in privileged positions in their lifetime. This is the Egyptian Kingdom of the West and Kingdom of Heaven, the Greek Elysium, the Scandinavian Valhalla. There has also been a belief in the existence of two alternative destinations for the souls of the dead—destinations that are determined, according to this more ethical belief, not by previous rank, but by previous behaviour. The souls of the wicked are consigned, as a punishment, to hell—an everlasting abode which is not merely dismal, as Sheol or Hades is, but is excruciating. On the other hand the souls of the righteous are admitted, as a reward, to Paradise or heaven—an everlasting abode which is as blissful as Elysium or Valhalla, but which, unlike them, is attained in virtue of previous merits, not of previous rank.

For believers in Hades and Elysium, the consignment of a dead person's soul to the one or the other of these two alternative abodes is automatic. It is decided by the dead person's former social rank in his lifetime. For believers in hell and heaven, the decision depends on the dead person's conduct during his lifetime; his conduct cannot be assessed without being examined and appraised; and this requires the passing of a judgment by some authority. The belief in a judgment of souls after death is a necessary corollary of the belief in heaven and hell.

This belief in a judgment of souls after death made its appearance at two widely different dates at two far apart places (far apart, that is to say, before the very recent "annihilation of distance"). The belief appeared in Egypt perhaps as early as the age of the Old Kingdom in the third millennium B.C., and it also appeared in North-Eastern Iran or in the Oxus-Jaxartes basin round about the turn of the 7th and 6th centuries B.C., i.e. in the lifetime of the Prophet Zarathustra, who was the promulgator of the belief in this region. We have no evidence as to whether the Egyptian and the Iranian belief in a judgment by which the soul, after death, is consigned either to hell or to heaven had a common historical origin. It is noteworthy, however, that the Egyptian and Iranian beliefs have a further feature in common. The judge of the souls of the dead—Osiris in the one case and Ahura Mazdah in the other—is a good god who has triumphed, or who is going to triumph, in a hard struggle with a wicked god or wicked semi-divine being. Osiris, after an initial defeat, has been given an eventual victory over his wicked brother and adversary Seth by the prowess of Osiris's son Horus and by the devotion of his sister and wife Isis. Ahura Mazdah is going to be victorious, eventually, over his wicked adversary Ahriman.

The Egyptian belief in a judgment of souls after death, to determine whether they shall be sent to hell or to heaven, was presumably the source of the same belief in the Greek world in the Hellenic Age. Here it was probably a legacy of Egyptian influence in Crete in the Minoan Age. Osiris, in his capacity of serving as the judge of the souls of the dead, has a Cretan counterpart in Rhadamanthus. In Egypt the pyramid texts, inscribed for the benefit of pharaohs in the age of the Old Kingdom, and the later "Book of the Dead", circulated for popular use, are collections of formulae, spells, and instructions designed to help the dead person's soul to find its way successfully to a blissful terminus without falling into any of the pitfalls, traps, and obstacles that will beset the soul in the course of its difficult and dangerous passage. The contents of the Orphic tablets are similar and are designed to serve the same purpose.

In both cases the purpose is practical guidance, not edification, and, in so far as purification enters into it, this is purification in the ritual, not in the ethical, sense. In the pre-Christian Greek picture of hell, Tityus, Sisyphus, Tantalus, and Ixion are four classical representatives of the damned who are suffering everlasting torments. The wall-paintings in Etruscan tombs show that the Greek picture of hell made a strong impression on the Etruscans; and it may not be fanciful to guess that there may have been an Etruscan component (preserved in subsequent Tuscan folklore), as well as a Christian component, in the mediaeval Christian Tuscan poet Dante's lurid description of the torments of the damned in the Christian hell.

The Christian and Muslim conceptions of the judgment of souls after death and of the heaven and the hell to which the souls are consigned respectively, in accordance with the verdict, are evidently derived, in the main, not from the pre-Christian religion of Egypt, but from Zoroastrianism—presumably via Pharisaic Judaism, which—unlike the Sadducean Judaism of the post-exilic Jewish "establishment" in Judea —laid itself open to Zoroastrian influences that played upon Judaism after the incorporation of Babylonia, Syria, Palestine, and Egypt in the Persian Empire in the 6th century B.C.

In Christian belief the individual judgment of souls immediately after death, and their consignment, immediately after judgment, to hell, limbo, or heaven, coexists with the incompatible belief in the universal judgment of all souls—both the souls of the resurrected dead and the souls of the human beings alive at the moment—when the Last Trump sounds to give the signal for the resurrection of the dead and for "the Last Judgment" of living and of resurrected dead human beings alike.

When the belief in personal immortality is associated with a belief in a judgment after death—a judgment that will consign the dead to either eternal bliss or eternal torment—the price of a human being's belief in the survival of his personality after his death is anxiety during his lifetime.

"For we know Him that hath said, 'Vengeance belongeth unto me; I will recompense', saith the Lord. And again, 'The Lord shall judge his people.'

"It is a fearful thing to fall into the hands of the living God."[1]

(h) *The belief in the resurrection of human bodies.* A disembodied or unembodied soul is more difficult to imagine than a soul that is associated with a living body in the psychosomatic unity with which we are familiar through our acquaintance with ourselves and with our fellow living human beings. This union of soul with body in a life after death is easier to imagine if it is represented as being a reunion, in which the body with which the soul is now associated is the body—reconstituted, reanimated, and resurrected—with which this soul was associated before soul and body were parted by death and the body consequently became a corpse. On the other hand the reconstitution, reanimation, and resurrection of a corpse is virtually impossible to imagine, considering that, after death, a human body immediately begins to decay and eventually decomposes completely, unless the entrails are removed and the rest of the corpse is preserved artificially by being mummified.

The audience that Saint Paul had attracted at Athens listened to him patiently till he made the statement that God had raised a man from the dead; but this assertion brought the meeting to an end. Some of Paul's listeners laughed, while others, more courteously, told him that they would wait to hear more from him till they found another opportunity.[2] If Paul had stated that Jesus had an immortal soul which had pre-existed and would continue to exist eternally, his Greek audience might have been willing to hear him out. Personal immortality of souls was a familiar and not incredible hypothesis for Greeks of Saint Paul's generation, but to be asked to believe in the resurrection of the dead was, for them, tantamount to being given notice by the speaker himself that he was wasting their time by talking nonsense.

Paul might have obtained a better hearing for his declaration of

[1] Hebrews, x, 30-31.
[2] Acts, xvii, 32.

belief in bodily resurrection if he had been preaching in contemporary Egypt; for in Egypt, since at least as far back in time as the third millennium B.C., it had been believed that one corpse had come to life again—and this after it had been cut up into fourteen pieces that had been scattered and had had to be reassembled. In Egypt this story was told of a god—the god Osiris who, since his own bodily resurrection, had become the judge of souls after death. When Paul told the Athenians that Jesus had been raised from the dead, he referred to Jesus as being a man and said that it was God who had raised him; but at the same time Paul cited this act of God's as evidence that God had appointed Jesus to judge all mankind at a future date that was already fixed;[1] and Paul believed that Jesus was in some sense God, though he did not divulge this belief of his on this occasion. It will be recognised that the role of being a god who is put to death and is resurrected in order to become mankind's judge is attributed to both Osiris and Jesus.

The belief that Jesus has risen from the dead, the belief that he is to judge mankind, and the linking of these two beliefs with each other thus have an Egyptian precedent; but there is also another tenet of Christianity in which a belief in resurrection is linked with a belief in judgment, and this tenet appears to be of Zoroastrian, not Egyptian, origin. According to Christian doctrine, Christ's judgment of mankind is not an *ad hoc* judgment of the souls of the dead individually, immediately after the death of each of us; it is a future judgment of all mankind simultaneously, including the people who will be alive at the time, as well as all those who will have lived and died by then; and the dead will be brought to judgment by a resurrection of their bodies, which will be brought back to life for the occasion and will be reunited with their souls. This belief in the bodily resurrection of all dead human beings is common to Christianity and Islam, and, like the belief in judgment, noted earlier,[2] it seems to have been derived by both religions from Zoroastrianism via Pharisaic Judaism. According to Zoroastrian doctrine, the discrimination between the righteous and the wicked at the last and general judgment is to be made by means of a physical ordeal by fire and molten metal; and this indicates that, according to Zoroastrianism, in accordance with Pharisaic Judaism, Christianity, and Islam, the dead are expected to rise again physically.

Zoroastrianism anticipated Christianity in believing in two judgments: a judgment of each soul individually, immediately after death, and a final judgment of all human beings simultaneously, the dead as well as those alive at the time. This belief is so peculiar and involves such incongruities that there surely must be an historical connection between its appearances in these two different religions: i.e. Christianity must have adopted the belief from Zoroastrianism. Zoroastrianism's

[1] Acts, xvii, 31.
[2] See p. 88.

priority is indicated, not only by the chronological fact that Zoroastrianism is about six centuries older than Christianity, but also by the connection, in Zoroastrianism, between the belief in a future last and general judgment and the belief in a final and conclusive victory of the good god Ahura Mazdah over the evil spirit Ahriman in the current war between these two spiritual powers. Ahura Mazdah's coming victory over Ahriman is to have the general judgment of mankind as its sequel.

This belief that mankind is to be judged twice over, besides being incongruous—it seems superfluous to recall souls from heaven or hell, as the case may be, to earth in order to have the same verdict passed on them for the second time—also raises the question whether heaven and hell are to be thought of as existing in the psychic dimension or in the physical dimension. The locus of disembodied souls is presumably not physical. Yet the agony and the bliss of the souls of the dead before the general resurrection are depicted in physical imagery; and if, for the last and general judgment, the temporarily disembodied souls of the dead will have been reunited with their resurrected bodies, the heaven and the hell to which they will then be consigned must be physical localities, if the human beings who are sent there after this second judgment have been restored to the psychosomatic state in which they lived on earth before their deaths—not to speak of those who are overtaken, still alive, by the sounding of the Last Trump.

In Christianity and Islam, as in Zoroastrianism, the resurrection of human bodies is associated with a last and general judgment, which will consign—or re-consign—the resurrected dead, and will also consign the living, to either heaven or hell. Their common mother-religion, Pharisaic Judaism, however, seems—at any rate, to begin with—to have adopted the Zoroastrian belief in bodily resurrection in a version that was less close to the original than the Christian-Muslim version is.[1] In this original Pharisaic Jewish version the resurrection is apparently to be a privilege, not an ordeal. The Jewish martyrs who have given their lives for the Jewish faith and for the Jewish people are to rise again from the dead, not to attend a divine judgment which will consign them either to heaven or to hell, but to participate in the re-establishment on earth of the Kingdom of Judah by "the Lord's Anointed" (the Messiah): a scion of the House of David who will not only reinstate his ancestral kingdom up to its Davidic frontiers, but will transform it into a world-empire that will be the millennial Jewish successor of the successive world-empires of the Assyrians, the Persians, and the Macedonians.

This mundane Jewish adoption of a transcendental Zoroastrian belief brings out the truth that the resurrection of the body does not necessarily imply that the reconstituted psychosomatic human being is going to be immortal. The Messiah himself seems to have been thought

[1] See p. 78.

of originally as being a mortal man who would be distinguished from his fellow mortals only in being the legitimate Davidic heir to the Kingdom of Judah and in bearing rule over a world-empire that would be still more extensive and more mighty than the realm of the Messiah's ancestor David himself. In the course of nature the Messiah would die, like David and like every one of David's successors and the Messiah's predecessors who, from the 10th to the 6th century B.C. had, each in turn, reigned over the Kingdom of Judah as "the Lord's Anointed", i.e. as the legitimate living representative of the Davidic dynasty. If the Davidic restorer of the Davidic kingdom was destined to be mortal, like his ancestor, the resurrected martyrs would presumably prove to be mortal too. They would be resurrected only to die again eventually—dying, in their exceptional case, for the second time.

It will be seen that, in this first phase, the adoption by the Pharisaic Jews of the Zoroastrian belief in bodily resurrection was subordinated to the traditional Jewish view—expressed in the legend of Yahweh's successive promises to Abraham—that the supreme blessing for a mortal man was to be assured, not of securing personal immortality for himself, but of leaving behind him descendants who would per-petuate his race. It was taken as a matter of course that the Jewish martyrs would be raised from the dead expressly for the purpose of witnessing the eventual military and political triumph of Judah to which they would have contributed by having sacrificed their lives. It was assumed that they would be well content to "depart in peace", together with the Messiah himself, when their eyes had seen God's salvation which He had prepared before the face of all peoples[1]—a salvation that would be the corporate salvation of the Jewish people, and a glory that would be the political glory of a re-established Jewish state which, this time, would be, not a petty local principality, but a veritable world-empire.

(i) *The hope of heaven and the fear of hell.* A Hindu who, as a result of intense introverted contemplation, has attained, as a personal experi-ence, the intuition that the essence of his soul is identical with Ultimate Reality, has presumably been liberated by this experience from all hopes and fears about either life or death. He has become aware of a truth that assures him of the unimportance of life and of death alike. A Buddhist who has learnt that it is possible to make a definitive exit into nirvana from the sorrowful series of rebirths, and who has also been instructed in the strenuous spiritual exercises by means of which this goal may be attained, will be too absorbingly preoccupied with the pursuit of his practical spiritual endeavours to concern himself with either life or death or to entertain either hopes of fears. On the other hand, lively hopes and fears about a human being's destiny after death will be aroused by a belief in personal immortality, whether the believer

[1] Luke ii, 29-32.

in this expects to survive everlastingly as a disembodied soul or expects his soul to be reunited, at the sounding of the Last Trump, with his resurrected body, to live on everlastingly thereafter as a reconstituted psychosomatic unity: i.e. as a human being constituted like his own present living self and like the living selves of his contemporaries who, like him, have not yet suffered death.

What is the effect of the belief in personal immortality after death on the feelings, attitude, and conduct of the believer? To what degree, if any, does it influence his behaviour while he is alive in the psychosomatic form of life which is the only form of it that is known to us in our experience?

The believer in a conditional personal immortality—an immortality that is dependent on the perpetual performance of rites by the believer's descendants—is likely to suffer anxiety. He will be anxious to make sure both that he is going to leave descendants behind him and that these will have both the will and the means to perform, punctiliously, all that is requisite in order to maintain the immortality of this ancestor of theirs. The believer in a personal immortality in the shadowy realm of Sheol or Hades will repine at the brevity of a human being's full-blooded zestful psychosomatic life on earth—unless, of course, he undergoes so much suffering before death that he comes to contemplate even the bleak prospect of Sheol or Hades with resignation. The grandee who is confident that his own destination is not Sheol or Hades but is Elysium or Valhalla may be nerved by his aristocratic self-assurance to face the prospect of personal immortality after death with equanimity, or even with the pleasurable anticipation with which a Buddhist —the polar opposite of the pagan barbarian warrior—looks forward to his exit into a nirvana in which his personality will have been extinguished.

The believer in a personal immortality which he may be going to spend either in heaven or in hell, according to the verdict that will be passed, after his death, on his conduct while he was alive, ought, if he holds this belief *bona fide*, to be the most anxious of all; and his version of the belief in personal immortality ought to have the greatest effect of all on his present behaviour. He is committed to the belief that the credit or debit balance of the account of his good and evil deeds during his brief life on earth is going to decide, once for all, whether his destiny is to be weal or woe in the everlasting future of sentient personal life that awaits him after death.

In practice, there is in some cases a considerable discrepancy between the belief on the one hand—even when the believer believes himself to be sincere—and the believer's state of mind and behaviour on the other hand. I have, for instance, known one believer who was intensely afraid of the prospect of death, though he was conscious of having lived righteously in the main and though he was also utterly confident that he was one hundred per cent correct in his theological tenets. Logically, he

ought to have felt assured that, after death, he could not only go to
heaven but would be received there as a V.I.P. All the same, he was
unable to face the prospect of death with equanimity. Conversely, there
have been people who have believed that the infallible penalty for the
commission of serious sins in this life is condemnation, after death, to
everlasting torments in hell, yet who have not been deterred by this
belief from committing sins that have been so heinous that, according
to the sinner's own belief, his condemnation to suffer everlasting torment
in hell will be inescapable.

Such discrepancies between belief and behaviour indicate that belief
has to be supported by experience if its influence on behaviour is to be
effective. All beliefs, whatever they may be, that relate to what is going
to happen or is not going to happen to a human being after death are,
intrinsically, beyond the range of experience, and they are perhaps even
beyond the range of realistic imagination.

In so far as the belief in personal immortality after death does
captivate a living person's imagination, the believer's mental picture
of hell seems generally to be livelier than his mental picture of heaven.
The torments of the damned in hell have, on the whole, been depicted
and described more vividly than the bliss of the salvaged in heaven.
Lucretius, in the third book of his *De Rerum Natura*,[1] in which he is
arguing that death spells complete and permanent annihilation,
presents this as a consoling thought for the living, because the prospect
liberates them from the fear that, after death, they may be condemned
to suffer the legendary everlasting torments that are believed, by the
credulous, to be being inflicted on the mythical arch-sinners Tantalus,
Tityus, Sisyphus, and Ixion.[2] As Lucretius drives his point home at the
close of this passage, it is in this world only that life ever becomes hell,
and this only for people who are such fools as to believe in the reality
of a life in hell after death.

This fear of hell, which Lucretius is seeking to dispel, is offset, of
course, by the hope of reunion, after death, with beloved fellow human
beings from whom one has been parted either by dying before them or
by surviving them. Bereavement through death is harder to face and to
bear than death itself; and the pain of bereavement is mitigated if the
separation that death brings with it is believed to be not everlasting but
only temporary. The coming reunion is usually pictured as a blissful
one in heaven; yet even the torments of hell are eased if they are shared.
The most moving passage in Dante's *Inferno* is his depiction of Paolo
and Francesca[3] locked in each other's arms in everlasting love as they
are swept round together in an everlasting wind of anguish.

[1] Lines 978-1023.
[2] Cp. *Odyssey*, Book XI, lines 582-600.
[3] *Inferno*, Canto Quinto, lines 73-142.

2. Attitudes towards Death in Eastern Religions

by NINIAN SMART

THE MOST important centre of religious influence in Asia has been India. This is not merely because India itself has given birth to a number of faiths—Hinduism, Buddhism, Jainism, Sikhism, etc.—but because one of these, Buddhism, came to influence profoundly the culture of virtually the whole of East Asia. It is therefore convenient to approach the problem of death first through Buddhist eyes. Thereafter we can treat of the attitudes to mortality in other Indian religions and in the traditional religions of China (Confucianism and Taoism) and Japan (Shintoism).

Buddhism

A controlling factor in the Buddhist view of death is the doctrine of rebirth. In a number of respects, this doctrine differs profoundly from traditional Western and Semitic concepts of the after-life. First, the individual is regarded as virtually everlasting, unless and until he attains liberation (nirvana), when there will be no more rebirth. The individual has come through a vast succession of previous existences, and will continue thus so long as he remains in the grip of craving and spiritual ignorance. This cycle of existence can be seen against a wider cosmological background, in which there is a continuous recurrence, over vast ages, of cosmic collapse and expansion. One finds a similar cosmology in Hinduism and Jainism. Something of its flavour can be gathered from the Hindu calculation that each *kalpa* or eon is 4,320,000,000 years long and constitutes a day in the life of the god Brahma; he lives 100 years, and each day is complemented by a night. So each great age (*mahākalpa*) constituted by the life of a Brahma, is 311,040,000,000,000 years long. Then the whole process starts again with a new Brahma.

Second, belief in rebirth gives a somewhat ironic twist to conceptions of heaven, purgatory and so on. For in Buddhism there is no denial of higher and lower realms of existence beyond the plane of this world, nor is there a denial of the gods, even if the doctrine of a Creator is repudiated. Good deeds may lead to an individual's being reborn in heaven; but this does not constitute final liberation. Heaven is impermanent like everything else. So, fortunately, is hell. So indeed is the great god Brahma, and the other deities. Ironically they have to learn from the Buddha, and it is through human existence that one can hope to gain nirvana. Gaining nirvana is achieving something higher, then, than heaven and higher than divine status. A not dissimilar conception is to be found in some Hindu systems of doctrine. This leads to a paradox encountered by, but for the most part quite unrecognised by, Christian missionaries. In so far as Christian salvation is conceived as the attain-ment of heaven, it will be looked on as only a second-rate form of salvation by those who are brought up in the ambience of the doctrine of rebirth as described above.

Third, the Buddhist doctrine of rebirth (as distinguished from the major Hindu conception) does not involve belief in a soul. There is no permanent self underlying physical and mental states. So liberation is not the attainment of the release of the soul. It does not mean the individual's becoming somehow blissfully eternal. Rather it is the replacement of the impermanent states which constitute the individual by a permanent state, nirvana. In nirvana, there is no person, for the person is simply a succession of impermanent states bundled together. For this reason, the Buddha (at least in Theravada Buddhism, i.e. the Buddhism of Ceylon, Burma and parts of South-East Asia) can no longer properly be said to exist. There is no possibility of transactions with him, and hence no prayer or worship of him. Temple ceremonies are rather a mode of expressing reverence for the departed Teacher. So, then, true liberation leaves the individual behind. The true saint is one who neither wishes to cease existing nor to go on existing. By a paradox:

Only suffering exists: there is no sufferer.
There is action: but no doer of the action.
There is nirvana: but no person who enters it.
The Path exists: but one can see no traveller on it.

So at the highest level, one should not hope for individual immortality. The desire for it is a sign that one has not gained the serenity and insight of the saint. This was one reason for the Buddha's rejection of belief in an eternal soul or self. Another was that there was no need or room for such a conception in a world characterised by impermanence: if everything is impermanent so am I. Moreover, one event is brought about by another, and something unchanging, such as an eternal soul, can have no effect: it contains no events or changes, and thus cannot bring about changes. It is a useless and misleading idea, then, to ascribe a soul to man.

Fourth, just as the individual can gain heavenly or hellish states of existence, so too he can become an animal or other living creature. Some of the most charming popular tales in Buddhism are concerned with the previous lives, often in animal form, of the Buddha. The whole of the world of living things is seen as a continuum: there is not the sharp break between men and animals found in the Western tradition.

Fifth, and very significantly, rebirth is sometimes described in early texts as redeath. The prospect facing the individual is seen negatively as a succession of deaths. But death itself is brought about by birth. The problem is not so much that one is going to die and so strives for a salvation which will after all confer immortality. It is rather that one is condemned to life, to a life which displays (most importantly through its leading to death) its essential unsatisfactoriness. This is what lies behind the Buddha's doctrine of *dukkha*, literally "ill-fare" but commonly translated "suffering". Everything is a mass of ill-fare. Life is characterised by birth, which is painful, old age, sickness, death.

Many Westerners have taken this as a highly depressing account of the world; it is puzzling that the adherents of what seems so gloomy a faith are so often cheerful. The depressing impression is to some extent misleading, however. It is necessary to remember that the dark side is complemented by a light side. The serenity of nirvana, the calm of the saint—these positive goals remain. Further, the Buddha was not denying the reality of human joys, but pointing to their underlying unsatisfactoriness (this is where the translation "suffering" is too strong): true happiness is to be found in treading the Path. This is the way to overcome the redeath which makes a mockery of human achievements and satisfactions.

It can be seen then that the Buddhist doctrine of rebirth places death in a special perspective, different indeed from that of which the West is chiefly accustomed. The problem is not to gain immortality, but to transcend it.

This is why nirvana is described as the "deathless place"; but it is not deathless because life goes on indefinitely. Nirvana is, as we have seen, beyond the realm of change and therefore of individual existence. It has sometimes puzzled commentators that one of the "undetermined" questions which the Buddha refused to answer, not because they were just ill-advised or irrelevant, but because they were wrongly framed, was the question of whether the Buddha or saint on the attainment of final nirvana at his decease does or does not survive. The Buddha declared that it was neither right to say he does, nor that he does not, nor that he both does and does not, nor that he neither does nor does not. He compared the case to asking where a fire goes when it goes out. Does the flame go north? The question, being intrinsically absurd, cannot be properly answered. Likewise, if individual life is constituted by changes —a flow of mental and physical events—there is no individual existence in nirvana, and yet nirvana exists.

Since also the Buddha rejected belief in a supreme personal Creator, there could be no possibility of describing release as a kind of union or communion with Him. In reaching the deathless place one by-passes the gods. They are tolerated by the Buddha as mythological entities dwelling in the heavens and elsewhere within the cosmos. But, as the Buddha remarks in one passage in the scriptures, one does not get to the end of the world by travelling. The ascent to the heavenly realms is in that respect quite unnecessary. The end of the world lies within one's own grasp, at the end of the Path. The knowledge of what it is like can be gleaned from the life of those who have attained it, above all the Buddha himself.

As we shall see, Buddhism in its Mahayana form (the form which became dominant in China and Japan) in effect modified the above doctrines. Meanwhile, let us look at the way in which Buddhist attitudes have been symbolised and realised existentially by those treading the Eightfold Path. Buddhism, unlike Hinduism, has a centralised mythology of evil, as expressed in the figure of Māra, roughly equivalent to Satan. Māra is literally the "one who causes death". At one level he is the leader of the animistic forces besetting the ordinary man in the cultures which Buddhism has permeated, so that through the legend of the Buddha's complete victory over Māra the ordinary man may feel that hostile powers have been finally overcome. At another level, Māra symbolises the temptations and allurements which constitute an obstacle to the attainment of true welfare, nirvana. Through the symbol, men are led beyond popular religion to a higher conception, and are given a vivid symbol of the enemy that has to be fought. Yet we also find that in the last resort Māra is only a symbol. The Buddhist scriptures give a doctrinal and psychological account of the obstacles to liberation, and from this perspective one can dispense with the mythology. Nevertheless, Māra plays an important role historically in the life of the Buddhist Order of monks (and nuns), as a symbol to encourage the continuous striving for deeper serenity and insight.[1]

It might be thought that much of this emphasis on the higher life would pass the laity by. As we shall see, the laity's desires for a more immediate salvation than that held out by the possibility of rebirth as one who would become a monk was given expression in the Mahayana. But even from earliest times we can detect a strong solidarity between laity and monks, which still makes Buddhism a cohesive social force. The layman has the monk before him as also a symbol of the conquest of redeath. In early Buddhism, the truths were not only conveyed to the laity by symbols such as Māra, but also by parables. The most famous perhaps is the parable of the mustard seed, where the Buddha tells a bereaved mother, who sobbingly cannot get over the tragic loss of her dear little son, to search the city for grains of mustard seed from a house in which no one has died. This will be the medicine to cure her condition. But of course she cannot find such a house, and comes to see existentially the universality of death. She goes to the burning-ground and cremates her son.

Since death is the most fearsome sign of the impermanence and ill-fare of the world, there is a great deal of exhortation in the Buddhist tradition to meditate upon death. One should be mindful of death:

[1] I am indebted here to Trevor Ling's excellent *Buddhism and the Mythology of Evil* (George Allen & Unwin, 1962).

"But if you should make any plans that do not reckon with the inevitability of death, you must make an effort to lay them down again, as if they were an illness which attacks your own self. Not even for a moment should you rely on life going on, for Time, like a hidden tiger, lays in wait to slay the unsuspecting."[1]

The most spectacular and gruesome method of meditating on death is for the monk to seat himself at the burning ground, amid the skulls and charred remains. This keeps him vividly aware of what otherwise might be tucked discreetly out of sight and out of mind. Thus death itself is treated not only as an event, but as a symbol of the underlying dissatisfactions of human life, when the latter is lived unrealistically as though joys can be lasting.

For various historical and religious reasons the Mahayana developed doctrine and cults which went beyond those described above. One important belief was in celestial Bodhisattvas or Buddhas-to-be. According to the story of the Buddha's Enlightenment, Māra tempted him to keep his saving truth to himself and achieve immediate release. The Buddha, however, rejected this allurement and spent many arduous, though serene, years travelling around preaching, forming the Order and so on. He put off his final decease for the good of living beings. This theme is taken up in a more dramatic and mythological way in the belief in Bodhisattvas. They put off their nirvana, their Buddhahood, for countless lives, during which they heroically serve others and help them to liberation. Religiously, this belief functioned as a focus for worship or loving adoration (*bhakti*). The Buddha-to-be acquires such a vast treasury of merit through his countless lives (an enormous credit-balance) that he can transfer some of it to the otherwise unworthy faithful, enabling them to approach liberation through faith in the Buddha-to-be. This modification of the doctrine of karma was supplemented by another, in the Pure Land School (ultimately influential in both China and Japan, though with its roots in Indian developments).

The great Buddha Amitabha (better known under his Japanese name of Amida) has created a paradise, the Pure Land to the West. Those who call with faith on the name of the Buddha will be translated thither on death. There the conditions for attaining final liberation are peculiarly propitious. Not unnaturally, the splendours of paradise, vividly described in some of the Mahayana scriptures, came to replace nirvana in the popular imagination as the supreme goal. In this way Buddhism developed a strand of belief in a celestial after-life with analogies to what is found in Islamic and traditional Christian theism. The Pure Land School was perhaps well adapted to Chinese conditions, where there had been no belief in rebirth, so that at a popular level at any rate the promise of immediate paradise made more sense than the long quest for nirvana.

[1] Translation by E. Conze, *Buddhist Scriptures* (1959), p. 112.

Also of increasing importance in the Buddhist tradition, whether Mahayana or Theravada, is the concept of the future Buddha, Maitreya, who will restore the glories of the faith at the end of the present period (one of decline—hence the need to rely on faith in paradise rather than on the works of meditation and deep self-discipline). Rebirth in the time of the future Buddha thus becomes a hope, and to this extent Buddhism contains an eschatological element analogous to the myths of the "last things" in Christianity, Zoroastrianism and elsewhere.

Despite the changes which occurred to Buddhism in its migrations, even the most luxuriantly developed form of Buddhism, that of Tibet, incorporated indigenous elements in a characteristically Buddhist way. Thus the *Tibetan Book of the Dead* makes use of pre-Buddhist mythology, but within a general framework of Buddhist doctrine. The book describes the fate of the individual after death, when he passes into an intermediate state before being reborn. The brilliant light of Ultimate Reality shines so whitely that most individuals are unable to bear it: they do not gain liberation, but are destined for rebirth. All kinds of terrifying and sensuous images beset the individual, and the book gives advice on how to avoid the worst fates, such as rebirth in hell. The work puts in symbolic language the message that our desires and dispositions make us cling to life, and prevent us from serenely accepting the loss of individual existence in the bright emptiness of nirvana.

To sum up the general Buddhist teaching about death: the main message is not "You can accept death, because it is the prelude to immortality: in your essence, death will not destroy you"; nor is it the agnostic "You can accept death, for you then need no more fear the heat of the sun." Rather it is: "Accept death as the chief sign of the impermanence of all hopes that you could possibly have: when you neither long for it nor fear it, you are on the way to transcending both life and death, and gaining the Permanent."

Jainism

Jainism, which may date back to the 8th century B.C. or even much earlier, has some affinities with Buddhism—notably the doctrine of rebirth and the absence of belief in a supreme God. Something of the same structure of beliefs about the afterlife is found there, but Jainism is less concerned with the psychology of liberation than Buddhism. The Buddha emphasised more strongly the mental attitudes leading to serenity, and so nirvana. Jainism has been more typically ascetic in its conception of how to manage the law of karma. So extreme indeed has Jain self-mortification been that the most heroic way to pass out of the cycle of rebirth is by giving up food altogether and so committing slow suicide. Such suicide however is only right and efficacious if the saint is genuinely a saint; this heroic course is not recommended for those ill-prepared. A powerful symbol of the Jain attitude are the great statues, such as that at Sravana Belgola in Mysore State, of Jain heroes, nude, rapt, so indifferent to the world that the creepers are growing up and twining themselves round their legs. This sublime indifference to worldly values and proprieties depicts one road to the conquest of death, by conquering life itself.

Hinduism

We have already noted something of the wide range of Buddhist beliefs. The multiplicity of schools and cults is even more evident in Hinduism. Some forms of Hindu doctrine are atheistic; others stress the unity of the world, the soul and Ultimate Reality; others again are theistic. Some groups worship Shiva, others Vishnu, and there is a fabulous richness of different mythological traditions. These variations make considerable differences to concepts of liberation and salvation. Still, the doctrine of rebirth has become virtually universal in Hindu belief and this gives some common structure to attitudes to death. What was said earlier about the immensity of the cosmos and the cycle of existence applies to both Buddhism and to Hinduism (and indeed to Jainism). Yet, curiously, the doctrine of reincarnation is absent from the earliest hymns, and makes its first unambiguous entry into the sacred tradition in the Upanishads (roughly contemporaneously with the Buddha). Earlier beliefs about death contemplated the possibilities of the soul's ascending to the world of the gods, to the world of the Fathers, or more gloomily to the House of Clay. Some of these conceptions are retained in modern funeral customs, even though not altogether consistent with the doctrine of rebirth. Thus the ceremonies are designed to release the dead person from the state of being a ghost, and to send him on his way to the Fathers or on to a new incarnation.

Undoubtedly the most influential system of teaching within Hinduism in recent times has been Advaita Vedanta (the Non-Dualistic interpretation of the scriptural tradition), given its form mainly through the writings of Sankara (8th century A.D.), who was in some degree influenced by Mahayana Buddhism. The ultimate goal is realisation of one's identity with Brahman, the Holy Power or Absolute lying behind the world of appearance. This realisation is indeed liberation, but it does not change one's essential status, for all the time unknowingly one's inner essence is the one true Self. Since there is but one Self, Sankara's doctrine excludes belief in innumerable eternal souls, which elsewhere characterises Hindu doctrines. Thus there is an analogy between Sankara's system and that of the Buddha: both deny individual immortality (save in the sense of rebirth), but for Sankara there is an underlying Self at the bottom of consciousness, while for the Buddha there is no more than the capacity to attain nirvana. The latter capacity, in his teachings, replaces the belief in a Self or soul. Since, according to

Sankara, there is only one Reality, the Brahman-Atman (Absolute-Self), the world as we ordinarily conceive it is illusory. In thinking of it as other than the One Reality, we are implicated in illusion. Consequently the ordinary person's perspective on the divine Absolute, which is to see It as a Creator, is in the last resort misguided. Yet the belief in a personal God is not harmful, and eventually leads to its being transcended in the mystical realisation of one's identity with the Absolute. Thus the conquest of death and rebirth is a radical going beyond the categories of the empirical world, and even beyond religion as conventionally understood.

But though Sankara's teachings, modified in various ways, for example by ex-President Radhakrishnan, by Swami Vivekananda and others of the excellent Ramakrishna mission, by Aldous Huxley in his *The Perennial Philosophy* and by many other reinterpreters of the Hindu heritage, have been influential, there have been other important, and rival, conceptions of release from the cycle of existence. Prominent among these have been the expositions of Ramanuja (12th century A.D.) and Madhva (13th century A.D.). The former taught the doctrines known as Qualified Non-Dualism, another version of Vedanta. He was heavily influenced by the religion of worship and loving adoration of God which flourished in South India in his time, and which not only supplied a counter-balance to traditional Vedic ritualism as mediated by the Brahmins, but also expressed the fervent piety of many who could not aspire to the rules of a religion essentially reserved for the upper castes. Ramanuja, a follower of Vishnu, represents God as personal, the world as real and the individual as capable of salvation from the cycle of existence by loving faith of the Lord. He can thereby gain a life of bliss, close to God, in heaven, Vaikuntha, the abode of the great Vishnu. Ramanuja rejected the monism of Sankara, and stressed faith rather than the spiritual knowledge which overcomes the ignorance holding men in bondage to the illusory world and the round of rebirth.

Madhva even more strongly rejected Non-Dualism (his system being known as Dvaita or Dualism). He was unique among the major theologians of the Hindu tradition in affirming the possibility of eternal damnation: he has various grades both of salvation and punishment, among them the consignment of some souls to hopeless perdition; elsewhere, as we have noted, the Indian "hells" are really purgatories—one works off one's evil karma eventually. This is one reason why some scholars have held that Madhva was influenced by Christianity (established from quite ancient times in South-West India), though there are reasons within Madhva's system for this doctrine, and the influence may not be genuine.

Thus within the Vedanta there are varying ideas of release. Those who stress the personhood and otherness of God contemplate the possibility of heaven. Sankara, more in line with Buddhism, yet at the same time characteristically Hindu, looks to the transcendence of individuality in the identification of the Self with the Absolute.

Among other accounts of salvation in Hinduism, the most notable is that of Yoga. The Yoga system (a separate school of thought, though yogic methods are used in varying ways throughout Hinduism, Buddhism and Jainism—one can speak thus of Yoga as a group of methods of self-control and contemplation, but of Yoga as the system practised by the school in question) lays down a path of liberation. But here the conquest of the suffering which is intrinsic to empirical existence does not mean union with the Absolute or communion with God. On the contrary, the eternal soul, once disencumbered of the psychological and physical states which manifest when it is implicated in the round of reincarnation, exists in splendid isolation. This isolation is free of pain, but otherwise inert. The original form of Yoga was probably atheistic (that is, denying a personal Creator), though later developments indicate belief in a Lord, the one soul never implicated in the round of rebirth: meditation upon Him can aid the Yogin in his quest for liberation. It will be seen that the general doctrines of Yoga approximate to those of Jainism and early Buddhism, despite the latter's denial of an eternal soul. Thus after-life liberated states are not, in any of these teachings, associated with a mythology of heaven, nor with union with the Divine Being. Death and redeath are not conquered essentially by reliance on God or the Other, but by one's own efforts, in accordance with various prescriptions of meditation, austerity, and so on. For Yoga, then, there is no realisation of one's unity with the Absolute or the presence of God, but the isolation of the soul, so that it is no longer implicated in matter. In this state of splendid isolation the soul does nothing, but is at least released from the pain which material existence inevitably brings.

Hindu mythology

These various doctrines of liberation, though important, have to be understood in the general context of the mythological and symbolic imagery which feeds the imagination of the Hindu in approaching a higher reality. Thus Sankara's teaching is presented in the milieu of the worship of Shiva, that destructive, creative, fierce, merciful, sensuous, austere, dancing, reposeful deity, who dynamically and kaleidoscopically mingles opposites in his own person. He is both creator and destroyer, for the world is perpetually in the flux of creation and destruction. As Time, Shiva symbolises the forces of decay, even though as the King of Dance he expresses the exuberance of life. This ambiguity in Shiva is in accord with the principle that both good and evil trace back to a single source: the wise man transcends both good and evil. This indeed is the way to the overcoming of death. This is brought out by Shiva's being not only Time but Lord of Yoga, the patron of those who tread the contemplative path to liberation. For as Time, Shiva brings death, but as Great Yogin he incorporates the principle for overcoming death. And he too, if one is to take Sankara's doctrines seriously, vanishes in the last resort: for when I realise my oneness with the Absolute, I am beyond the dualisms of worship and of religious imagery. I am beyond the Creator, who is implicated in the illusoriness of the world he creates.

This illusoriness connects up with the Buddhist doctrine of impermanence. The major sign that the world is illusory, according to Non-Dualist teaching, is that it is impermanent. Still, there are overtones of the Hindu concept which need to be brought out. God is, as it were, the great illusionist; through his magical power he creates the insubstantial world. We who look on it as real are taken in, like the man who sees a rope and thinks it is a snake. If the illusion is dispelled, we see Reality. So the mythology of Shiva connects with the doctrines: we must transcend both life and death in order to conquer death.

There is less of this sense in the cult of Vishnu, a kindlier representation of the ultimate. The Bhagavad Gita, for instance, which is the greatest testament to the religion of Vishnu in the Indian tradition, is more concerned with reliance on God than going beyond Him to a transcendental state in which all distinctions are lost. Those who do their daily duties in reliance on the Lord will not go unrewarded. Death is conquered, then, through faith, and the power of karma released through the gracious action of God. This graciousness is also seen in His desire to make himself known to men through avatars, such as Krishna: like the Buddha, he restores true faith when it is in decline, though unlike the Buddha he attracts worship and adoration, rather than reverence. There is, however, another motif in the Gita which is in a way at variance with the loving nature of God there depicted, and certainly at variance with the principles of Gandhi who yet found in the book so much inspiration. Gandhi preached non-violence, in accordance with the ancient traditions of Buddhism and Jainism and parts of Hinduism. Yet the Gita can comfort the hero, Arjuna, who is trembling and anxious at the slaughter which is bound to ensue in the battle which he awaits (against his kith and kin, moreover), by remarking that the killer who thinks he kills is wrong. The eternal soul is not killed by the sword. Arjuna needs to go on with his duty, however unpleasant. He will be saved if only he renounces the fruits of his action, and relies upon the Lord. In this way the effects of karma will be short-circuited by the gracious action of God, complementing the faith of Arjuna.

This emphasis on the essential deathlessness of the soul (and so of the inmost person) seems, as I have said, at variance with the teachings of non-violence, for it reverses the usual direction of argument about the soul: one principle affirms "Do not destroy him, for he has an immortal soul"; but another asseverates "Why not kill him? He cannot die".

Nevertheless, the main message of the Gita is reliance on God, and it is roughly true to say that where such a fervid personal theism is well-developed in the Indian tradition the whole doctrine of rebirth becomes less important. As in the Buddhist case, there is the possibility of immediate salvation through faith, where the Lord takes men to himself in love, without waiting for the long effects of karma to work themselves out through countless lives. On this "kindlier" doctrine of death and salvation, there is a ready means to the conquest of impermanence and dissatisfaction, through calling on the name of one's chosen God.

Woven into the mythology of Shiva and Vishnu are many other motifs and figures. There is Yama, the lord of the dead, a figure drawn from the Vedic period of early Brahmanical religion: Yama, the first man to die and now the one who presides over the dead as judge, ably assisted by his book-keeper Chitragupta ("Manifold-Secret") who reads out the account of the dead man's deeds. Shiva is called Yamāntaka, or "Ender of Yama", in as much as at the end of every world-period he dissolves the universe and gives living beings a rest from the recurrance of death and judgment. Yama has an aspect reminiscent of one feature of the *Tibetan Book of the Dead*. According to the latter the transcendental mysteries appear luminously lovely to those who have conquered selfishness; but those still in the grip of craving find them horrifying, like a bad dream. Likewise, Yama appears gracious to those who have been virtuous, terrifying to those of evil character.

But even those of good character are likely to find the representation of Kali, Shiva's consort, terrible. She wears a garland of skulls and a skirt composed of severed arms; she drinks blood; she presides ferociously over destruction and death. Yet as female she is also the source of life, and the mainspring of Shiva's creative powers. This is symbolised by the figure of the recumbent Shiva, a corpse beneath her feet. When the universe has collapsed into quiescence, all that remains is the power of Time (Kali herself), awaiting the moment when the cosmos will begin again to unfold.

These variegated images and many others bear on the attitudes to death, destruction and life in the Hindu tradition: this mythic, symbolic foreground against the background of doctrines of rebirth and liberation. The paradoxicalness of the images in part springs from the sense that both good and evil have a single source. Not surprisingly, as with the doctrine of the eternal soul, different conclusions can be drawn. The main teaching of the images and doctrines is that the ultimate conquest of death is either by the Yogi's stilling of life or by reliance on the graciousness of God to break the bonds of karma. Yet also the destructive Kali could be inspiration and justification of murdering highwaymen (the Thugs). The ambiguous attitudes to death and destruction also have something to do with the shape of Indian society.

The quest for holiness

It has long been a vital religious tradition that the man who seeks the highest spiritual insight withdraws from society. The Buddha left his wife and young child: likewise the Jain teacher Mahavira. In the Hindu context, there evolved the doctrines of the ashramas or stages of life. This was a somewhat artificial schematisation, but reflects the course followed by at least some. First one is a child and student, living celibately with one's teacher. Then one marries and becomes a householder. With sons grown up, one begins to shed worldly responsibilities. Finally one becomes a wandering ascetic or *sannyāsin* in old age. In this last stage one is beyond society and beyond, therefore, the requirements of following the complex rules governing Hindu society. In general, the holy man has gone beyond good and evil, and is "dead" to the world. He may have attained *jivanmukti* "liberation while still alive", only waiting for the body to run down, like a potter's wheel when the potter has ceased to work with it. Thus the idea of attaining a transcendental state beyond rebirth and redeath is mirrored in society, where the holy man has transcended his social obligations and ordinary desires and ends of life.

But of course most men remain in society. For them there is always the distant ideal of true holiness and liberation. But for them the actual operations of karma are more important than the method of conquering it. At the popular level, good and evil deeds are conceived as conducive to higher and lower status in the next life. The time and mode of one's death is likewise so determined, so that from the ordinary man's point of view there was a kind of logic in the disasters and misfortunes of life —surely they could ultimately be traced back to some prior misdeeds.

Rites of passage

Yet death retains its fearfulness, expressed not only in popular demonology, where the spirits of evil and uncared for men can haunt the community, but also in the uncleanness surrounding the corpse. As elsewhere in Hindu society, there tends to be elaborate ceremonial controlling rites of passage, especially for the upper classes. The corpse must be cremated; preferably by a river, into which the ashes are consigned. On the third day the bones are gathered up and likewise consigned to the river. In succeeding days offerings are made to the dead person, who now has a ghostly status, and needs nourishment to acquire a subtle body enabling him to travel onwards to his next existence. Only after ten days are the relatives who have performed these ceremonies ritually clean, so that they can resume their ordinary avocations. These orthodox rites represent a fusion of an early Aryan conception of the after-life and the later pervasive view of rebirth. But though cremation has been widely practised in India, it has not been universal. In South India and elsewhere there are instances of burial, and in older texts there are instances of exposure of corpses to animals and birds, such as vultures (the latter playing a prominent part in the funeral customs of Parsees to this day). But ideally one's ashes are scattered in a river, and above all the Ganges. In floating downwards to the Ocean they symbolise the way in which ultimately all return to the one divine Reality.

The conquest of death

The conquest of death, then, in the Indian tradition is generally conceived as a long business, and often therefore a strenuous one, since one must transcend the whole series of lives constituted by rebirth. Virtue can, it is true, give one a limited blessedness in heaven, but only in some branches of the tradition can there be a blessed immortality in such a state, through the action of God. Here it is one's faith in God, rather than one's virtues which are relevant, and the karmic process is short-circuited, either by Vishnu, in the case of Ramanuja's teachings, for instance, or by the Buddha Amitabha, for instance, in the Mahayana. But in the absence of a strongly developed pietism, the picture is of a hard struggle to achieve serenity and insight. In Jainism, the struggle is severely ascetic, and it requires powerful self-mortification to destroy the effects of previous karma. In Buddhism and Advaita there is more stress on psychological attitudes and understanding. The practice of a moderate Yoga geared to the stilling of the senses and to the knowledge of impermanence can, for the Buddhist, culminate in a special flavour of detachment, in which neither life nor death disturbs tranquillity. This is not world-negating as such, for any wish to negate the world is as much to be suspected as any wish to affirm it. For Sankara, the path to the conquest of death is more complex, for Sankara accepts, but only at a lower level of reality, the religion of worship, together with the sacrificial and other rites of the ancient past. One may be helped by such piety; and indeed the ambiguous and striking mythological representations of God as Shiva can give an insight into the transcendence of life and death, good and evil. But finally, one disappears beyond these images, and they are seen essentially to be only a conventional and lower way of pointing to what lies Beyond. The world itself, with all its joys and vicissitudes, takes on the atmosphere of a great conjuring-trick. Liberation is like waking from a dream; and death itself is only part of that dream.

Yet if the way is often strenuous, one can be relaxed about it, since one will be reborn many times. The doctrine of rebirth functions as a softening of the rigours of the higher life. But it is not intended as a kind of fatalism (though there have been some fatalistic teachers in the Indian tradition). There is always an explanation of death, but there is always too the possibility of changing the direction of one's destiny. One can do this in one's ordinary life: for the vast majority the time has not yet arrived to leave that. Hence the quest for a higher conquest of death is juxtaposed in the Indian tradition to a great exuberance of this-worldly culture and the pursuit of men's usual mundane ends. In these respects, the common Western myth of Oriental fatalism, austerity and world-negation is profoundly misleading.

One final point about the Indian tradition, before we pass further East: until the mediaeval period, there was a not insignificant materialist school in India, which denied rebirth and the possibility of nirvana, release, heaven, etc. Its strictures on Brahmanical orthodoxy were often severe, religion being seen as a fraud. One explanation of consciousness given, to combat arguments for rebirth drawn from the existence of a soul, was that it is a new property occurring when certain elements are put together—just as drink mixed in a certain way may become alcoholic, though none of its original constituents were. Some materialists, somewhat paradoxically, are described as ascetics, but the most frequent inference drawn from the mortality of the self is that one can gain satisfactions in this world, even if they be impermanent ones. Not everyone, thus was convinced by the common religious claim that only the Eternal can be fully satisfying.

China

It is common to speak of the "three religions" of China, but it was largely as a response to Buddhism, already well institutionalised, that Taoism and Confucianism began to take on the form of religions in the full sense. In the centuries before Buddhism penetrated China, from the 1st century A.D. onwards, there were a number of movements or traditions of teaching, the most significant being those going back to Confucius and to the most probably legendary Lao-Tse. There were, as it happened, aspects of Taoist teaching and practice with affinities to Buddhism—its quietism, the emphasis on contemplative techniques, etc., so that ultimately there emerged from the interplay between the two that characteristically Chinese contribution to Buddhist religion, Ch'an (or, to use its better-known Japanese transliteration, Zen). However, it is chiefly with Taoism that we are here concerned.

The *Tao-te-ching*, the main source of early Taoist thought, though associated with the name of Lao-Tse, reputedly of the 6th century B.C., was a later anthology of teachings, yet one which has a fair amount of cohesion. However, there are very widely differing interpretations put upon it by modern scholars. Suffice it here to outline some important traditional interpretations, which bring out the Taoist attitude to death. The key concept in the work is that of the Way (*Tao*) or principle governing the universe. The sage is one who by living in accord with the Way thereby actually participates in it.

This identification with the eternal Tao is reminiscent of some other forms of mysticism, e.g. those of Sankara and the Mahayana. There is another analogy too. Though the *Tao-te-ching* does not teach rebirth and karma, it comes to a conclusion not unlike that reached in some phases of Indian religion: the way to escape the affects of action, according to the latter, is by a kind of inaction—the repose of the Yogin. So in early Taoism, identification with the Tao is achieved by *wu-wei*, no-action. Nature itself acts effortlessly, spontaneously: it acts by not acting. A sublime passivity is the true way to power; the sage seeks the Emptiness, and in so doing conquers all. In emptying himself (like Nature) of desires, he achieves the highest contentment—for what is the cause of discontent but the having of unfulfilled desires, and being covetous? This passivity of early Taoism expressed itself in pacifism and a kind of gentle anarchism, opposed to the Confucian school, emphasising etiquette, correct behaviour and the concerns of government and administration. It is not hard to see that early Taoism belongs to the contemplative, mystical side of religion, and though it was false for Taoists, after Buddhism arrived in China, to suppose that Lao-Tse had gone westwards to teach the truth, so that Buddhism was an offshoot of Taoism, the speculative claim had at least a basis in the resemblance between the two contemplative paths.

It followed from the above general outlook, that the sage attains a kind of immortality. In being identified with the Tao he becomes eternal. In being beyond desires, and so beyond concern either for life or death, he cannot be assailed by misfortune. As the *Tao-te-ching* says, the true sage is impervious to the stings of insects, and the attacks of wild beasts and birds of prey. No doubt this is not meant literally, but symbolises the self-sufficient calm of the man who finds strength in weakness, and the eternal in emptiness. There is perhaps too an analogy with certain trends in modern existentialism: the acceptance of death as limiting and indeed mocking our hopes itself gives the key to authentic existence (Heidegger is reported to have said that if he understood D. T. Suzuki, the famous exponent of Zen Buddhism, aright, Suzuki was saying everything that he, Heidegger, had been trying to express). But the quietism and mysticism of early Taoism was not to remain the only important contributor to the later, more elaborate religion known as Taoism. Not everyone can achieve the heights of inner experience, and eternal life can be interpreted materialistically as a kind of immortality.

In later Taoism, the quest for eternity is increasingly replaced by a more mundane desire for longevity and post-mortem security. At the same time a rather elaborate mythology, partly drawn from Chinese tradition and partly from elsewhere, attached itself to the teachings, as did a hierarchical priestly organisation. As in one or two other phases of the history of religion, mysticism became implicated with alchemy and other magical or quasi-magical practices. The desire for immortality led to the quest for the famous elixir of life, and at least the ordinary man could settle for means of prolonging his own life. The inner core of adepts could, through breathing exercises, alchemical and other means, gain immortality of the body, mysteriously transplanted on death to the sacred island of Paradise, where dwell the holy Immortals. The laity could hope for lesser boons. On death they would go to the world of the dead, in a favourable position if they had been pious: maybe their descendants might cause them too to be translated to the Paradise of the Immortals, through appropriate "masses" for the dead. The preoccupation with long life naturally tied in with concerns about sickness, sometimes itself regarded as a defilement or sin. Taoism thus attracted to itself a prominent place in the practice of traditional and quasi-magical medicine. Though the educated Confucians might despise much of this form of religiosity, together with Buddhist piety, much of Taoism could co-exist in popular life with the two other of the "three religions". If later Confucianism catered for official needs and gave sanction to ancestral cults, Buddhism and Taoism in differing ways catered for private aspirations and anxieties.

The "materialisation" of the Taoist concept of eternal life was itself partly a reaction to the presence of Buddhism, which, despite its alien teaching of rebirth, effectively catered for men's hopes of Paradise, especially in the Pure Land School, and of a mythological focus of worship and adoration, in the shape of the Bodhisattvas and celestial Buddhas. But Taoism was less successful in welding doctrine and myth and practice together, so that there remained a split between the organised religion, which was essentially popular, and Taoist philosophy, as expressed in the *Tao-te-ching* and elsewhere. This was a cause of the great decline of organised Taoism in modern times.

Both Buddhism and Taoism gave shape and substance to beliefs about an after-life which were rather sketchy in ancient Chinese ancestor-worship (better called the cult of ancestors, "worship" being much too strong a word). The cult had a widespread ritual and social significance, in reaffirming and promoting the solidarity of the family and of wider groups, but there was no promise here of a highly personalised immortality or religious release. Though it is an exaggeration to say that Confucius was agnostic in religion, there was great restraint in his answers about such topics as the after-life. His attempt to restore and reorganise ancient values led him to take a favourable view of the cult of ancestors, but he rather stressed its social and moral use: thus one should address the ancestors as though they were personally present—in this way respect for persons is enhanced. On his death-bed, when asked to pray, he replied that he had already been praying a long time: the implication being that it is the whole of life that leads to a good death, not special invocations at the last. On death, he remarked that to know about it one must know about life. Neither from the point of view of Confucian propriety, nor from the point of view of the popular cult, was there a well-developed eschatology such as Buddhism and Taoism were later to provide.

Thus the departed spirits stayed around as individual entities for some generations, then gradually disappeared. It is true that men with powerful charisma might persist longer in the ghostly state, and in later times great men could thus virtually attain the status of gods, notably Confucius himself, who was incorporated into the State cult, partly to give ideological sanction to his teachings, especially important as a codification of upper-class behaviour, partly as a counter to Buddhist influence.

Later Confucianist philosophers attempted to co-ordinate these somewhat exiguous beliefs to the conception of the Yin and the Yang, the former being the dark, female principle, associated with the earth, the latter the light, masculine principle, associated with heaven. Through the interplay of these two principles the universe is governed. There are elements within the human being corresponding to them— the "higher" soul which is of the nature of Yang, and the "lower" soul which is of the nature of Yin. The latter is simply the animating force- which sustains the vital functions of the body, and on death ceases, being reabsorbed in the earth. The former is more detached, and maintains activity for some time, enabling the person, in this somewhat attenuated form, to receive the offerings made to him in the cultus.

A not altogether different approach was displayed in the Neo-Confucian revival (11th and 12th centuries A.D.), only here there was greater influence from Buddhism (especially Ch'an) and from Taoism. The most important thinker, in point of historical influence, in systematising Neo-Confucianist doctrines, Chu Hsi (12th century A.D.), likewise saw the universe as governed by two main principles, the realm of transcendent essences (*li*) and a vaporous material factor (*ch'i*). Things and persons represent a kind of combination of the two, some- what like the form-matter doctrine in Greek philosophy. The *li* of man is good, but muddied over by its material accompaniment. The aim of the sage is to realise his true self, the *li*, in all its purity. In so doing he will participate in the Supreme Ultimate, the Form of the Good, which unites the transcendent essences of all things.

The way to achieve realisation of one's *li* bears a close resemblance to the contemplative methods of Buddhism and philosophical Taoism. But though such contemplation could bring participation in the highest Reality, and so a kind of omniscience and a sense of unity with all things, through their essences, there was a vital difference between Neo-Confucian attitudes and those of Buddhism and Taoism, especially organised Taoism. The Neo-Confucian sage remained highly critical of the monastic ideal. He achieves his enlightenment by staying in the world and performing his social and moral duties, and he typically repudiates the desire for nirvana, which he sees as a flight from attachment to the world symptomatic of an underlying attachment. The Confucian way can bring full knowledge and full love, and life having been lived thus is terminated by a peaceful death. One can gain harmony with the universe as it actually is: one does not seek release beyond it. Thus Neo-Confucianism represents in sophisticated form two recurring themes of the ancient Chinese tradition—the need to live in harmony with the whole process in which men find themselves, and the importance of social ties and correct action. If the ancestor-cult is incorporated in the latter, it gives Confucianism a certain projection beyond death; but the educated man is not taken in by the popular fantasies of the Pure Land or the Paradise of the Immortals. To this extent, despite the remarkable symbiosis between the "three religions", often overlapping in the lives of the people, there has been some split between the educated class, in so far as it continued to maintain the Confucian tradition, and the masses. This has sometimes led Westerners to an imperfect appreciation of the force of religion in Chinese history, through being in main contact with officials and scholars imbued with Confucianist humanism.

Japan

Naturally enough, some of the values of Chinese religion, especially Buddhism and Confucianism, were carried over into Japanese culture, which owed so much to the mainland in the development of its civilisation. Certain trends already present in China were intensified and remoulded in Japan—for instance, the Pure Land pietism reached intenser levels in the teachings of Honen and Shinran (13th century A.D.), promising salvation through the act of faith. Nichiren, of the same period, adapted such pietism to nationalism. It is common to such schools that celibacy and other works supposed to bring advance along the Buddhist Path are useless, and there is a strong analogy to the Reformation doctrines of Luther. Thus in Japan, the Pure Land more strikingly manifested the revolution in Buddhism which offered immediate salvation to all, if they but repeated the name of the Buddha Amida in faith. The older, more strenuous way, towards the transcendence of death and life itself was no longer applicable.

However, such pietism was complemented in Japan by other Buddhist movements, such as that of Zen, which brought new techniques to bear on the ancient Buddhist Yoga. By so doing it went beyond monasticism, in offering a discipline, during the mediaeval period, whereby laymen could through their ordinary pursuits gain illumination—hence the various Zen methods of enlightenment through sword-play, archery, flower-arrangement and so on. In part this was a reflection of the curious combination of meditative practice and mediaeval feudalism. The *samurai*, chiefly lower knights serving feudal princes as warriors, could paradoxically combine Buddhist values with the pursuit of a self-sufficient martial ethic. This helped to inform the spirit of *bushido*, with its ideals of stoicism and of honourable suicide. The flavour of this contempt for death was later to pervade State

Shinto, in its attempt to provide an ideology for militarism. A very rough differentiation between Zen and Pure Land attitudes to death is this: that for the former, the achievement of *satori* or illumination in this life (even as a layman) puts one beyond the vicissitudes of life, and thus one can face death with equanimity, while for the latter there is a Paradise in the after-life awaiting those who can have faith, and so one can face death in pious hope.

Shintoism in earliest times was not much concerned with problems of an after-life, the dead usually being thought to go to an inferior region below the earth: only a few exalted persons could ascend to the heavenly sphere. But over a very long period, Shinto co-existed with Buddhism and Confucianism: as in China, it was largely Buddhism that supplied an eschatology. With the Meiji restoration, Shinto was given a special position as the State cult—it having always supplied a framework for reverence for the Emperor. The State cult, though essentially antipathetic to Buddhism, came to incorporate a popular doctrine of Paradise, as, however, a reward for valour and commitment to the Emperor rather than as a consequence of faith in the Buddha. Blending this with the tradition of aristocratic contempt to death, it provided a viable ideology for militarism. This was a main reason for the dissociation of Shinto from the State in 1945, after the surrender. But shrine Shinto, carrying on the ancient traditions of naturistic worship, continues as a vital force.

It is probable, but not certain, that Shinto from the earliest period incorporated the cult of ancestors; in any event these features have long been significantly important in Japanese life, reinforced by the incorporation of similar practices in the Confucianist tradition.

General patterns

It is now possible for us to draw out some general patterns from the varieties of cults and faiths of South and East Asia. At one level, in the cult of ancestors, etc., there is not a highly developed concern with personal survival, though a desire to affirm the solidarity of the family and of society, and to reverence the dead. This reverence of the dead often goes, in popular religious practice, with a fear of them, and a sense of the uncleanness of corpses and the uncanny possibilities of the return of the deceased, unless properly cared for. This fear merges into the general fear of spirits and other inferior spiritual entities infesting the life of the cultivator. Buddhism, we noted, provides a symbol, in the figure of Māra, for unifying these threatening forces and for displaying them as ultimately robbed of power by the victory of the Buddha over them.

In Hinduism and Buddhism there are more developed ideas of personal salvation, survival and release. Because of the belief in rebirth, salvation ultimately means transcending death in a very

radical way, by being taken out of the stream of existence to a transcendental realm. Where the contemplative life is stressed, the way to
this is seen through the treading of a Yogic path; where there is faith
in a personal God, piety and commitment supply the conditions of
salvation.

The contemplative path sometimes takes the form of a withdrawal
from ordinary social pursuits, as in Buddhist monasticism, in Taoism,
in the life of the Hindu *sannyasin*. This tends to emphasise the minority
character of the higher life. But with the growth of concern over death
and release, there is a quest for a pattern of salvation more readily
available to men in their normal pursuits. Though the doctrine of
rebirth itself supplies an answer to this problem, by projecting the
individual's higher spiritual quest to a future life, the pressure for more
immediate salvation persists, especially in cultures such as those of
Japan and China where belief in rebirth did not antedate the arrival
of Buddhism. The "democratisation" of the path beyond death takes
two principle forms: one by the evolution of a Yoga adapted to ordinary
life, as in some phases of Zen, where even the warrior could attain
illumination through disciplining his avocation in a spiritual direction,
the other by the gradual substitution of heaven for the hope of transcendental release. The latter course depended in large measure on the
growth of personalistic ideas of God or of celestial Buddhas, etc.,
capable of granting heavenly existence to the faithful.

The former course tends to be associated with a metaphysics in which
one can be in touch here and now with an Ultimate Reality which
pervades the whole of life. Thus in the Mahayana, we have the
paradox that nirvana and *samsara* (the cyclical flux of existence) are
identical: the Suchness or Void is not only an Absolute transcending
the world, it is the very fabric of phenomena. So we swim, so to say,
in a sea of liberation, if we could but see it. In Taoism, similarly, the
sage is able to participate in the Eternal Tao by conforming himself to
it through non-action. In Neo-Confucianism, one can gain knowledge
of the Supreme Ultimate embracing the essences of which the world
about us and ourselves are formed. Such patterns of thought tend to go
with a difference of emphasis in regard to the conquest of death.
Having participated, so to say, in Ultimate Reality I already have the
secret of eternal life, and so can face death with equanimity: there is no
need to postulate some eternal state of the soul (as in Jainism and Yoga,
for instance) beyond my final death.

Though here and there, ideas of a post mortem judgment appear in
Eastern religions, the framework of rebirth on the one hand, and the
comparative scepticism of Confucianism on the other, give them little
importance. Through karma, the serious "judging" is done through
my own past and present deeds. Looked at from another perspective,
as in the *Tibetan Book of the Dead*, the terrifying nature of the Beyond,
as symbolised by hellish punishments, is the consequence of the indi-

vidual's failure to find peace and illumination in it. There is something of this in the mythic dimension of Hinduism, where God is both the source of good and of evil: the purified soul rises beyond these terrors.

The pietism of the Pure Land school, the *bhakti* religion of Ramanuja —these and other manifestations of reliance on a loving Lord have some strong resemblances to Christian piety, however different the mythological framework may be. The presence of such hopes of heavenly communion with the Lord must be noted, for often there is an oversimplified view of the essence of Eastern religion. At the same time, it is not this aspect of Eastern faiths which presents a contrast to the Jewish, Christian and Islamic hopes; the combination of belief in rebirth and the stress on Yoga give a different perspective—in which death is conquered by going beyond heaven, and by attaining a purified peace here and now.

3. Death in the Judaeo-Christian Tradition

by NINIAN SMART

THE ATTITUDES to death in the Judaeo-Christian tradition can roughly be seen under two aspects. First, there is the evolution of various beliefs about the after-life. Second, there is the valuation of experiences and ways of living as manifesting true or eternal life, as contrasted with alienation from God, of which natural death is the most powerful symbol. Beliefs about the after-life themselves should be seen in relation to the latter symbolism of death.

Death in the Old Testament

The Old Testament expresses the first stage of beliefs about death in the tradition which bifurcated with the rise of Christianity and yet which shared so much in common with it. In the Old Testament, death is mainly regarded in a naturalistic way, as the dissolution of the individual. Yet there were intimations of a life after death. The deceased person retained a certain power after his passing. This power enabled him to drag on his existence in Sheol, the "underworld". There the individual joined his ancestors: he was "gathered to his fathers". Yet such an existence was a mere shadow of the life of those still in this world. This underplaying of the theme of immortality in part was the consequence of the Old Testament stress (echoed less strongly elsewhere in the cultures of the Ancient Near East) on the divide between mortal man and immortal God. This was a major theme of the *Epic of Gilgamesh*; but it has special prominence in the Bible, because of the strong monotheism expressed in it, with its implication of the gulf between the Lord and men—only God had the power to save, and so any holiness and salvation which he could bestow was his prerogative. Men are not naturally immortal: immortality belongs to God. A further reason for the relatively exiguous treatment of immortality in the Old Testament was that the transactions between God and man (in particular Israel) were seen as involving the Lord on the one hand and the community on the other. Individual survival, from this perspective, paled in comparison with the survival of the community.

These attitudes to survival are reflected in the principal idea of man in the Old Testament—namely as being a psychophysical entity, not a being divided into two parts, as it were, viz. a soul and a body. Admittedly, the essence of life tended to be identified with breath or spirit; but this notion of the spiritual aspect of the individual was not developed in such a way as to imply any doctrine of an intrinsically immortal element in man.

The concept of resurrection

However, towards the end of the Old Testament period, and more importantly in the interval between the composition of the bulk of the Old Testament documents and the time of Christ, there was increased interest in belief in the resurrection of the dead (an idea deriving partly from Zoroastrian influences). This belief became a major feature of the piety of the Pharisees, with whom early Christianity had closer links than the Gospels might seem to imply. The idea of resurrection combined three features of earlier attitudes.

First, resurrection implied that a saved or higher existence would still be essentially like existence at the present time: salvation would involve a renewal of psycho-physical existence, not the immortality of a disembodied soul. Second, resurrection was typically conceived, in the period up to and beyond the life of Christ, as a communal event, linked with a judgment by God. Admittedly, distinctions between individuals would be made in such a universal judgment. Still, it was important to the conception that there would be a simultaneous treatment of men at the "end of history" rather than the piecemeal decision on individuals as they passed out of individual existence. Third, the belief in resurrection reinforced a characteristic view of history developed in the Bible. If God works through temporal events and through the ongoing history of a particular people, it was not unnatural to think of a kind of symmetry between the past and the future, bridged by the history of Israel. The creation of the world led into the creation of the chosen people through the Covenant; the consummation of the historical process there begun would occur at the "end" of time, with a final resurrection and judgment. Thus ideas of resurrection latched onto the notion of a "materialistic" or psychophysical account of the individual, a sense of the inherence of the individual in the community and a feeling for the significance of the future in symmetry with the significance of the past.

Resurrection beliefs were given a new dimension in early Christianity by faith in the resurrection of Jesus. This was a pivotal part of the preaching of the early Church. On the whole, current ideas of resurrection were communal: but here there was the resurrection of a particular person here and now, and not in the consummated future. This belief expressed, for early Christians, the sense that the things of the future were already present in the present. Christ was seen as the "first-fruits", the anticipation of the salvation which was available to those who could share in his resurrection. This sharing in the kingdom, in the anticipated salvation, brought very closely together the ideas of eternal life here and now, through participation in the grace and mystery of the living God, and of the working out of God's purpose in history, culminating in resurrection and judgment.

However, many in the early Church looked on resurrection as essentially in the near future. But what was to be said when such a near future did not materialise? What of those who "fell asleep" in the interim? Faith in Christ promised salvation, and there was a sense that such salvation culminated somehow in the after-life. The problem of the interim condition of the faithful between death and resurrection came to be seen from the perspective of current beliefs in the Hellenistic and Roman world into which the new religion so successfully penetrated. It became natural to adopt belief in an immortal soul, current in various forms in Greek (and so Roman) philosophy.

Immortality of the soul

Apart from the fact of cultural osmosis, there was another reason for the increasing emphasis on belief in immortality among Christians. The faith itself contained strongly the idea of a community, but this community, the new Israel, was not constituted traditionally and as it were "naturally". It could not like the old Israel be identified with a national tradition. It was constituted by those who individually acknowledged the Lordship of Christ. The Church was thus open to more individualistic conceptions of salvation, and these were more easily expressed through the doctrine of the soul residing in the individual than through the belief in a communal resurrection. One should not of course see early Christianity in over-individualistic terms, for there was always the counter-balance that the substance of the faith had to do with a sharing of life with Christ and so with the risen Christ. The members of the Church saw themselves as organically related together through the person of Jesus.

Still, there was seen, in the early centuries of the Church, the evolution of a doctrine of soul-immortality, and thus we reach the third stage of Judaeo-Christian beliefs about the after-life (in Judaism likewise there emerged faith in immortality of the soul). The first stage involved a rather shadowy idea of persistence of men after death in Sheol. The second stage is represented by the increasing influence of an eschatology of resurrection and judgment. The third stage brings in the wedding of immortality to the ideas of resurrection.

This wedding was not always clearly worked out, and there has remained a tension between the two partners. This has been partially reconciled in later Christianity through such doctrines as that of the general and particular judgment. The general judgment lies at the end of history, with the consummation of God's plan. In this, God judges the whole of mankind, consequentially upon the resurrection of the dead. The particular judgment, on the other hand, concerns the individual and has been typically taken in Catholic theology to occur at the time of death. It reveals to the soul its relationship to God: and the concept of such a judgment is a natural adjunct to the doctrine of immortality of the soul.

Heaven, hell and purgatory

Although Christianity came to adopt belief in soul-immortality, it nevertheless emphasised that the soul is created by God: immortality is something which remains essentially the gift of God, and does not arise from the intrinsic nature of man. Further, the doctrine was closely linked, as we have seen, to the idea of judgment by God. Of greater importance than survival is the question of the *quality* of survival. Already in the New Testament the after-life, symbolising the consequences of faith and unfaith, is seen as divided into paradise (later identified with heaven) and Gehenna, the place of punishment and destruction. There are hints of a possible intermediate state—these later to be worked up into the Catholic doctrine of purgatory. However, in the New Testament there is little if anything of a metaphysics of the after-life. The future is described symbolically and through parables. It was only under the slow pressure of cultural synthesis and the elaboration of a code of conduct and teaching in the Church that there evolved the classical picture of heaven, hell and purgatory. A principal plank of the Reformers, however, was the denial of this last state, since it was linked in practice to the cult of saints and the granting of indulgences and in theory tended to run contrary to the doctrine of justification by faith alone.

In one respect, the essential division is between heaven and purgatory on the one hand and hell on the other. For, in the Catholic doctrine, those who enter purgatory are saved, but they require to expiate their venial sins and the consequences of forgiven mortal sins. Nevertheless, belief in purgatory represented a mitigation of the doctrine of eternal damnation, since a person in this life who had not shown great saintliness or goodness might nevertheless be regarded as destined for salvation, if penitent. The idea of purgatory also provided a partial explanation of the state of many souls between the particular judgment and the final resurrection. In their final state of beatitude and salvation souls would have had their sins and defects purged away and could then be united to bodily existence through the creation by God of resurrection bodies.

This latter notion played a role also in the mediaeval picture of heaven. St. Thomas Aquinas, following Aristotle, regarded the soul as the "form" of the body, and a division between the soul and its body as unnatural. Thus for full existence after death the soul must be reunited to a body. Hence, those saints who pass to heaven on death still await the full consummation of blessedness at the "end" of history with the general resurrection—here interpreted as involving the creation in the next life of renewed bodies.

The bliss of heaven has been thought of centrally in the Catholic tradition as focused on the beatific vision of God. This direct perception of God is not possible in this world (though Aquinas claimed that it was granted exceptionally to Moses and to St. Paul); all that is given is a foretaste (e.g. to contemplative mystics) of the beatific vision. In heaven, however, the blessed souls enjoy this bliss-making and glorious experience eternally.

The situation of those in hell is a stark contrast. The damned souls are excluded from God's presence and so cut off from happiness, and they suffer torments. These have been depicted vividly, not to say sadistically, in popular imagery. One problem for theologians contemplating the problem was that there were obstacles against a psychological interpretation of hell. It has been argued that hell simply involves the remorse and misery occasioned by the soul's recognition of being alienated from God. But *ex hypothesi* the person who is damned is impenitent: he does not want to turn back to God. How then should he regret the alienation? This is one reason for the traditional picture of an external agency (symbolised by fire) tormenting souls in hell.

The Protestant Reformers attacked the doctrine of purgatory, as we have seen. But belief in eternal damnation remained important to them, however inscrutable God's will might be in choosing those who were to be saved. But already there was a revival of interest in views propounded by some of the big figures in the first centuries of the Church. For instance, Origen had held that hell was more in the nature of a purgatory, and that the next life would give everyone ultimately the realisation of salvation. Origen's works had become available again in the 16th century. A number of the more radical Protestant movements, such as the Anabaptists and the Moravians, considerably modified the traditional teaching about hell. The former, for instance, treated hell as purgatory: thus eventually all would attain salvation (though admittedly there was much suffering to go through for most folk). The Socinians argued for the annihilation of the wicked, as indeed do some modern sects: that is, the wicked would simply die at death—only the saved would be raised to joy.

Demythologising death

In Protestantism there has been a decline in the imagery of punishment and hell, and one of the most important figures in the history of Protestant thought, Friedrich Schleiermacher, could argue for universalism—the universal salvation of everybody. A variety of causes has brought about a diminution of interest in the after-life. One was that mainstream Protestantism tended to preach a this-worldly ethic and a new form of this-worldly piety. Another factor was the work of scholars on the Bible and the rediscovery of the symbolic, mythic and parabolic aspects of New Testament language, not lending itself so easily to the codifications implied by traditional doctrines of the after-life. Another has been the change in secular theories of punishment. Eternal damnation is not so easy to square with a reformatory rather than a retributive theory of punishment. Another has been the virtual abolition, within Protestantism, of the practices which vivified the traditional Catholic theology of death—prayers of intercession to the saints and above all to the Blessed Virgin Mary, indulgences, masses for the departed, etc. (Anglicanism, of course, retains an intermediate position in these matters.)

The emphasis on a "this-worldly" piety naturally encourages a renewed emphasis on eternal life as to be enjoyed and experienced here and now. Correspondingly it tends towards a demythologising of death. The Church has seen physical death as somehow the consequence of the Fall: this has expressed the connection between death as the limiting of men's life with men's alienation from God. But as men have attracted death through their solidarity with the first Adam, so they can gain life and overcome death through solidarity with the second Adam, the risen Christ. This mythic representation of the interplay between death and eternal life has to be reinterpreted once the belief in a real primeval Adam fades (as it has done, taken literally, through the modern discovery of the prehistoric and evolutionary past). This is one reason for the concern with existential interpretations of eternal life and of the conquest of death—a concern which I have discussed elsewhere in this book.

4. Changing Attitudes towards Death in the Modern Western World

by Arnold Toynbee

In the modern western world, attitudes towards death have been changing progressively in the course of the last 300 years. These changes have been one of the consequences of the contemporary progressive recession, in the West, of the belief in the tenets of Christianity. A whole-hearted genuine belief in Christian doctrine is something more than an intellectual assent to a set of theological propositions. It is an act of faith which commits the believer to action on the moral and spiritual, as well as on the intellectual, plane. It commits him, among other things, to the Christian attitude towards death.

The Christian view

Christianity is one of the religions that include, among their tenets, a belief in the personal immortality of human souls. This belief is common to Christianity and modern (i.e. Pharisaic) Judaism—the only non-Christian religion that (at the price of severe penalisation) was tolerated in Western Christendom until towards the close of the 17th century. The belief in personal immortality is also one of the tenets of Christianity's sister-religion Islam; and Islam was the only non-Christian religion, besides Judaism, with which the peoples of Western Christendom were in contact until 1498, when the Portuguese made contact with Hinduism at their landfall in India. Down to that date, the belief in personal immortality was the only living belief about the sequel to the death of a human being that had come within the range of Western Christian experience.

It is true that Western Christians had always had access to the surviving remains of pre-Christian Latin literature, in which other beliefs that are incompatible with the Christian belief are recorded and, in some cases, are commended. For instance, in Lucretius's poem *De Rerum Natura*, the belief in the annihilation of the personality at death is powerfully and passionately advocated as a liberating and consoling release from an excruciating anxiety that is groundless. At the Renaissance the Western world's acquaintance with pre-Christian Latin literature had been reinforced by the recovery, in the West, of an acquaintance with pre-Christian Greek literature, and both these classical literatures had been studied enthusiastically from then on. However, in the early modern age, Western Christians had managed to respect and admire the Greek and Latin classics without allowing these to shake their Christian faith on points on which the Greek and Roman attitude to life and death conflicted with the Christian attitude. Western Christians had also managed, from the close of the 15th century onwards, to make acquaintance with a number of living non-Judaic religions and philosophies besides Hinduism—e.g. Buddhism and Confucianism—without allowing their Christian faith to be shaken by this experience either.

Nor had the schism in Western Christendom at the Reformation shaken, in the West, the traditional orthodox Christian belief about the sequel to death; for this had not been one of the points on which the Protestants had dissented from the Roman Church. The Calvinist Protestant doctrine of predestination had accentuated the hopes and fears about a soul's destiny after death that were inherent in the Zoroastrian-Jewish-Christian-Muslim belief in immortality. But this belief itself, and the attendant beliefs in the two polar alternatives, after death, of bliss in heaven and torment in hell, had continued to be held by all Western Christians, as well as by all non-Western Christians, all Jews, and all Muslims. On the test of fundamental Christian doctrine, as formulated in the Christian creeds, Westerners in general had still been orthodox Christians at the opening of the 17th century. If, at this date, there had been any unbelievers, they had still been rare, and the open avowal of unbelief had been almost unheard of, since the penalty for it, under Catholic and Protestant regimes alike, had still been capital punishment in the particularly painful form of being burnt at the stake. On the other hand, before the close of the 17th century, unbelief was already not only rife among a small sophisticated minority of Western ex-Christians, ex-Catholics as well as ex-Protestants; this unbelief was also now being avowed implicitly or, at any rate, hinted at discreetly with impunity. This 17th-century change of attitude towards the Christian religion is one of the greatest revolutions that there have been in Western history so far, and it is a revolution that has been making increasing headway from the later decades of the 17th century down to the present day. It has spread more and more widely and at the same time it has been avowed more and more openly.

The 17th-century revulsion from a religion that had been accepted unquestioningly in the West throughout the preceding thirteen centuries had been aroused, in the first instance, by the scandal of the 16th-century and 17th-century Western wars of religion. These wars had been a shocking exhibition of malice, uncharitableness, fanaticism, and also hypocrisy. The theological controversialists on both sides had been fanatical in so far as they had been sincere; the politicians had been hypocritical in exploiting sincere religious fanaticism for furthering the interests of their respective states; the combatants, whatever their motives and aims, had been guilty of committing appalling atrocities. This spectacle had been excruciating for sensitive spirits; and, in the course of the 17th century, there had been a deliberate move— illustrated by the history of the foundation of the Royal Society in England—to turn away from acrimonious and inconclusive theological controversies to scientific investigations, in which the truth could be established indisputably by observation and experiment and in which the incontrovertible findings could be turned to practical account for the improvement of technology with a view to the betterment of the material conditions of human life.

The growth of the scientific attitude

This transfer of Western man's intellectual interest and psychological libido from theology to science has had consequences that were not foreseen by the pioneers who initiated it 300 years ago. Christian theology confidently assumes that the universe in which a human being awakes to consciousness has been created, as man finds it, by an omnipotent God who is a person in the sense in which a human being is one. It assumes that the universe is under its creator's control, and that it is governed by a scheme that the creator himself has conceived and is putting into execution. In this scheme, man's position, first in life in this world and then in life after death, is both central and certain, whether for weal or for woe. The progress of scientific knowledge in the West, since Western man began to give science the topmost place in the hierarchy of his intellectual interests, has reduced man's position to apparent insignificance in both the space-dimension and the time-dimension.

In the space-dimension the progress of astronomy has shown that the planet earth, so far from being the centre of the stellar universe, is a satellite of a sun which is only one of a vast number of suns constituting one galaxy out of a host of galaxies whose number is unknown and is perhaps unknowable because it may conceivably be infinite. Already, within Pascal's lifetime (1623-1662), the astronomers had arrived at an estimate of the physical scale of the material universe that daunted a Westerner whose intellectual, as well as his spiritual, stature was outstanding. Pascal has put it on record that he was frightened by "the silences"—the inhuman unsolved enigmas—of the vast spaces of the stellar cosmos. These spaces, as estimated in the 17th century, were vast indeed on the standard of the traditional geocentric picture of the physical universe, as depicted, for example, by Dante in the *Divina Commedia*. Yet they were, of course, trifling compared to the scale of the physical universe as this is estimated by the astronomers of our day.

In the time-dimension, the traditional estimate—or, rather, dogmatic reckoning—of the age of the earth and of the whole physical universe was revolutionised by the advent of the modern science of geology at the turn of the 18th and 19th centuries. In Western Christendom since the 6th century, events had been dated by years before and after the supposed date of the birth of Jesus. In Eastern Christendom and in the Jewish community, events had continued to be dated by "years of the world" (i.e. the number of years that were believed to have elapsed since the creation of the world by God). The Eastern Orthodox Christians' starting-date for the "years of the world" was 5509 B.C.; the Jews' starting-date was 3761 B.C. In a book published as recently as A.D. 1650, Archbishop J. Ussher, an immensely industrious, learned, and naïve scholar, computed that the world had been created at 6 p.m. on the evening before October 23rd (Old Style), 4004 B.C. Today we know that there was already a city at Jericho by that date. The geological evidence has revealed that life made its appearance on this planet about 2,000 million years ago. The astronomers, in their work in the time-dimension, have estimated that the planet itself may have been in existence for at least twice as long as that, and they forecast that it will remain habitable for living creatures for another 2,000 million years (unless, of course, its human inhabitants, in the present generation, choose to risk making it uninhabitable by waging an atomic world war). Thus, in the time-dimension, a human being's life-span turns out to be as infinitesimally short as, in the space-dimension, a body turns out to be infinitesimally minute. This has given a shock to Jews and Christians. For Indians, on the other hand, it is, of course, no surprise. It is merely a belated and laborious verification, by Western scientists, of time-magnitudes on the multi-aeon scale that had already been apprehended by Indian philosophers intuitively at least 2,500 years ago.

The conclusions suggested by our modern Western scientific discoveries are ironical. The discoveries are, in themselves, astounding products and proofs of man's intellectual genius; yet, at the same time, these self-same intellectual feats of his have revealed to him that the universe in which he finds himself is so vast, both in its space-scale and in its time-scale, that its human denizens' role as natural phenomena is utterly insignificant. A recognition of these recently established scientific facts is impossible to reconcile with the traditional Zoroastrian-Jewish-Christian-Muslim belief in the physical resurrection of human bodies, and is difficult to reconcile with the traditional belief of the same group of religions in a God who is conceived of as being a person in the human sense of the word. It is still more difficult to believe that the physical universe, as we now know it, was created by a God of this kind. It is most difficult of all to believe that this God—or one person of a divine trinity—chose to become incarnate in human form on this particular planet out of concern for the salvation of this planet's human inhabitants. "After all, this is a small star", as Einstein once comforted himself by reflecting at a moment when he was feeling depressed at the spectacle of mankind's folly and wickedness.

The truth is that all God's—or Nature's—eggs are not in this one little basket. The astronomers tell us that, considering the scale of the stellar universe, there are probably innumerable other planets that are habitable and, for all that we know, are actually inhabited, by human-like beings—even though the nearest of these other habitable planets to our own planet may be millions of light-years distant from it in some other galaxy that is barely discernible by us, even with the aid of our most ingenious astronomical instruments and techniques. If we believe that Christ was moved by love and compassion to be crucified for man's sake on this planet, are we not also bound to believe that He has undergone the same voluntary torment for the same reason on countless other stars? This would seem to be, for Christians, an inescapable corollary of the belief in a plurality of worlds. The Roman Catholic ecclesiastical authorities who put Giordano Bruno to death in the year 1600 for having avowed this belief were aware of its implications for the traditional Christian picture of the universe. But their act was, of course, one of those blunders that are worse than crimes—as they themselves might have realised, if they had reflected that their pre-Christian predecessors had made Christianity's fortune by allowing themselves to be trapped into making Christian martyrs. The martyrdom of the neo-Democritean philosopher Bruno played its part in speeding modern astronomy on the way to its triumph. In 1686, Fontenelle published, with impunity, a book with the title *Conversations on the Plurality of Worlds*.

A physical universe of a kind that seems to rule out the possibility of the existence of a personal God who is its creator must also seem to rule out the possibility of personal immortality after death for the human inhabitants of a planet that is one of any number of habitable specks of dust scattered almost infinitely far apart from each other in the perhaps endless spaces whose sinister silences daunted Pascal. What, then, has been the effect on modern Western man's attitude towards death of the accelerating advance of science and recession of Christianity in our Western world in the course of the last three centuries?

The spread of unbelief

The effect is difficult to gauge, because a human being's attitude has at least three facets. What he publicly professes to believe may be different from what he admits privately to himself, and this again may be different from his true belief—or disbelief—that would come to light if he were to elicit it by analysing himself or by allowing himself to be analysed by a professional practitioner. There is usually a time-lag between a person's arrival at an actual state of belief or unbelief and his admission of this to himself, and a further time-lag between his admission of it to himself and his avowal (if he ever does make this) in public. If he has, in truth, ceased to believe the tenets of his ancestral religion, he may be upset psychologically if and when he becomes aware of his loss of faith, even if he does not divulge this disquieting discovery. If, in the meantime, someone else, who has had the same inner experience, has the courage or brazenness or tactlessness to proclaim his loss of faith from the housetops, his disingenuous fellow-apostate may turn and rend him—and this all the more savagely because he is aware—or, at any rate, is semi-conscious—that this candid avowal of unbelief by one of his contemporaries is threatening to tear from off his own face a mask that conceals a rather ignoble hypocrisy.

This was Gibbon's experience in 1776, the year in which he published the first volume of *The History of the Decline and Fall of the Roman Empire*. Gibbon was surprised both by the acclaim with which his public greeted the volume as a whole and by the fire that was drawn by this volume's last two chapters. These chapters deal with the rise of Christianity and with its eventual conversion of the Empire, and they suggest a number of non-supernatural causes that might account, at least in large part, for the Christian Church's remarkable achievement. In viewing Christianity's triumph in these matter-of-fact terms, Gibbon was seeing this historic event with the eyes of a cultivated Westerner of his generation, and it seems probable that some, at least, of his critics did not differ from him appreciably in their heart of hearts. The offence for which Gibbon was vigorously, and, by some critics, viciously, attacked was that he had said in public what many of his contemporaries thought in private.

The outward profession of an ancestral religion dies hard; and it dies the harder if and when the adherence to a church, whether sincere or not, is found to be an economic or social asset.

For instance, towards the close of the 19th century, a section of the French bourgeoisie that had been anti-clerical or agnostic or atheist since at least as far back as the time of the French Revolution reverted to a profession of Roman Catholic orthodoxy in a more or less cynical mood, because they had come to think that the Roman Catholic Church's deeply ingrained conservatism was now making the Church a bulwark of private property in an age in which socialism was on the march. Many of these re-converts of the first generation had their tongues in their cheeks, For them, property was worth a mass, as Paris had been for Henri IV.

Religion as a social convention

At the present day, a section of the middle class in the United States cherishes its church-membership—whatever may be the church to which a particular family happens to adhere—for a reason that, like the French re-converts' reason, is not religious, though, in the American case, the reason is social, not economic. Of course, the American middle class is as eager as the French middle class is to retain its affluence.

Probably it is even more eager, considering that it has a good deal more to lose; and, in the political field, its action in defence of its own material interests is at least as vigorous as the action of the corresponding class in France. In the religious field, however, the American middle class's motive for adhering to a church—and for supporting its church financially with characteristically American generosity—is that, since the United States changed from a largely agricultural to an overwhelmingly urban society, its population has become increasingly mobile and is therefore feeling a growing need to strike even temporary roots of some kind in the chillingly impersonal environment of some mammoth city in which an American family may have been constrained to take up its abode by the exigencies of the urban employment from which it earns its living. In these circumstances, a church may serve as a welcome social centre through which social waifs and strays can establish personal relations with other members of a micro-community that is on a humanly small scale.

If you walk through the streets of Houston, Texas—a modern Western commercial city which is growing rapidly in size and in which the non-negro and non-Mexican section of the population is affluent—you will find numerous churches, of many different denominations, that have been recently built or are in process of being built at the moment. "Find", not "see", is the right word; because, in many cases, the church itself—i.e. the "house of God" dedicated for worship—is dwarfed and smothered by a surrounding complex of buildings used for non-religious social purposes. These secular buildings that throttle the church itself are nominally auxiliary but are actually dominant. Their uses are innocent, and, indeed, are for the most part valuable. These other buildings are libraries, club-houses, lecture-rooms, theatres. The feature that is common to them all is that their social functions are non-religious.

Now take a plane from Houston, Texas, to Mexico City (it is a quick flight) and make a tour round the villages of the Puebla district on the Mexican plateau. The contrast will strike you. In a Mexican village in this region, the church is the largest and most conspicuous building in the place. It is also likely to be a handsome building in the renaissance or baroque style. It will have been a legacy to the villagers from the early post-conquest generations of one or other of the Roman Catholic religious orders, and you will find that the villagers—unsophisticated and even illiterate though many of them are—appreciate their church for both its aesthetic and its religious value. The act of common worship in church is the main form in which these peasants express their sense of community. Unlike their neighbours in the United States, they need no subsidiary buildings to supplement the church for secular social purposes, and, unlike their bourgeois French Roman Catholic co-religionists, they do not rally to the Roman Church as a bulwark of private property. A Mexican villager's private property is exiguous by

French, not to speak of United States, standards; and he finds satisfaction in spending part of the tiny surplus that remains to him after he has met his family's elementary needs for subsistence on tending his village church—replacing damaged tiles on the roof or regilding the pate of the statue of some saint or the figure of some cherub in the interior.

Of course, Mexico, in contrast to both the United States and France, is a semi-Westernised country that, in the current vocabulary of international cant, is still only "developing" and is not yet fully "developed". In other words, the outlook and spirit of a present-day Mexican village-community are survivals of those that were prevalent in the Western world as a whole before the great spiritual and intellectual revolution that started in the West in the 17th century and that has been gathering momentum there ever since.

Western man and the fear of death

Human beings who are imbued with the spirit of pre-17th century Western Christendom find it easier than their descendants find it to face the fact of death frankly and robustly.

In any community, whatever its particular religion and culture may happen to be, the celebration of a marriage is a joyous occasion. This joyful note is to be found in "the Form of Solemnisation of Matrimony", in the Book of Common Prayer of the Episcopalian Church of England the earliest version of which was compiled in the 16th century; yet the crucial declaration, made by each of the two human beings that are being wedded, contains the phrase "to love and to cherish till death do us part". These words are outspoken not only about the painful fact that both parties to the marriage are going, one day, to die. They are also outspoken about the still more painful fact that, save for the exceptional possibility that husband and wife may die simultaneously by some physical accident or by murder, one or other of them is going to suffer the pain of bereavement—a pain that is far more grievous than the ordeal of one's own death for a wife or a husband who does truly cherish his or her partner in marriage.

Among Westerners of the present generation, some of the few who speak unselfconsciously and unfalteringly about death are to be found among the monks of the divers Roman Catholic orders. Monks are not callous; far from it; they have a deep affection for their brethren and an abiding love for their mothers (whose sons, if monks, have no wives to claim a share in their sons' love for a woman). Monks can speak serenely and even cheerfully about death—not excluding the deaths of those people who are the most dear to them—because they have an unshakable belief in personal immortality. In their belief the parting inflicted by death is temporary and is therefore tolerable; and, though their own and their fellow human beings' destiny after death hangs in the balance as long as life in this world lasts, their destiny is going to be decided by

I

their conduct during this life, and conduct is something that, with God's help, lies in a human being's own hands. A present-day Christian monk's stalwart Christian faith makes death, for him, a comparatively unimportant incident, as it is for a Buddhist who believes in the possibility of obtaining nirvana, or for a Hindu who believes that "the Dweller in the Innermost" of a human being's spirit is identical with the Ultimate Spiritual Reality that lies behind a universe that is illusory.

However, since the great 17th-century revolution in Western man's outlook, the inability to face with equanimity the fact of death—an inability that is the nemesis of a loss of belief in personal immortality or in nirvana or in the intuition that "Thou art That"—has overtaken, not only many of those Westerners who have lost their belief in the tenets of their ancestral religion, but also some of those who have retained their belief unquestioningly. In the 18th century, Dr. Johnson (1709-1784), who was a believing Christian, was notoriously terrified of death. His terror of it comes out, again and again, in his conversation as recorded by Boswell. It would hardly be an exaggeration to say that this was one of Johnson's major themes. I myself have been a first-hand witness of this Johnsonian terror of death in a 19th-century believing Christian whose great-nephew I am. Captain Henry Toynbee (1819-1909) was born and brought up on a farm near Boston, England, became the master of an East-Indiaman and was noted for the scientific precision of his nautical observations. He was not only an unquestioning believer in the tenets of Christianity; he was also convinced that he was one of very few Christians who had ever got his Christian belief exactly right. (My great-uncle was an ultra-low-church Anglican.) Yet the thought of his own coming death appalled him. It looks as if, by a kind of spiritual osmosis, even some of the surviving Western believers in Christianity in the age of progressive unbelief in the Western world have become infected insidiously with an inability to face death by the *Zeitgeist*—a *Zeitgeist* which they themselves have repudiated energetically in so far as they have been aware of it.

This more and more prevalent post-17th-century fear of death in the West reveals itself in various ways. The typical modern Western man or woman has allowed one of the most characteristic and most noble faculties of human nature to atrophy; or, if it is has not atrophied, he or she tries deliberately to suppress it. This is the faculty—cultivated so earnestly and so effectively in India—of communing with oneself and, through oneself, not with oneself alone but with the Ultimate Spiritual Reality behind the universe. This faculty of spiritual contemplation is one of the features of human nature that makes us human. We turn sub-human if we lose this faculty or destroy it. Yet the average modern Westerner becomes uneasy if he is by himself. Science, applied with sensational success to technology, has substituted the physical conquest of non-human nature for the spiritual conquest of himself as Western man's ideal paramount objective. Modern Western man is therefore inclined to spend the maximum possible amount of his time and energy on work, except in so far as he curbs this inclination by restrictive practices for protecting his work from being exploited unduly for other people's profit; and the time and energy that is not consumed in working, feeding, and sleeping is occupied by some form of "entertainment". If gregarious entertainment is not obtainable, he turns on the television set or the radio or the gramophone. Anything and everything is acceptable that will preclude "the flight of the alone to the alone". Confronted by death without belief, modern man has deliberately been clipping his spiritual wings.

The word "death" itself has become almost unmentionable in the West—particularly in the United States, which, of all the "developed" countries, is today the most extremely "developed" in the sub-human connotation of this euphemistic word. Death is "un-American"; for, if the fact of death were once admitted to be a reality even in the United States, then it would also have to be admitted that the United States is not the earthly paradise that it is deemed to be (and this is one of the crucial articles of faith in "the American way of life"). Present-day Americans, and other present-day Westerners too in their degree, tend to say, instead of "die", "pass on" or "pass away". When the mourners at a Western funeral pose for the camera-man, they have to put on the photographer's conventional grin, as if they were attending, not a funeral, but a wedding or the races.

Worst of all, there is a reluctance in the present-day Western world to tell a dying person that he or she is dying.[1] Doctors, nurses, and relatives are reluctant to tell, not only when the patient is reluctant to hear, but also even when he or she suspects the truth and is being kept in spiritual suspense and pain by this suspicion that he or she is not being granted the human right of being treated as an adult human being—in other words, the right to be told the truth in time to prepare oneself for death spiritually.

The traditional Christian view is that a dying person ought, as far as possible, to be forewarned that he or she is dying, in order to be given all the spiritual help towards preparing himself or herself for death that the Church is able to give. On this view, to die unprepared is the worst spiritual misfortune that can befall a human being. This belief is expressed in the lapidary Italian curse "accidente"—a "portmanteau word", as Lewis Carroll's Humpty-Dumpty would have called it— which concentrates the *ne plus ultra* of malice in nine letters of the alphabet. When "accidente" is spelled out, it means: "I spell-bind you to die by a sudden violent accident, in order that you may 'fall into the hands of the living God' without having had the time to obtain the services of a priest to hear your confession and to give you absolution

[1] For a fuller discussion of this, see above, John Hinton, "The Dying and the Doctor", p. 36 ff.

and extreme unction. In that event, if you are a sinner—and I bet you are one—you will be condemned to spend the maximum time in Purgatory or—better still, from my point of view—you may find yourself permanently domiciled in hell."

Malice could hardly go farther than that; yet the ultra-malicious Italian curse-word "accidente" does imply, in its very perversity, a belief in human dignity, whereas a loss of this belief is implied in the Americanism "pass on" as an anodyne substitute for the word "die". Man's sense of his dignity may be outraged by his knowledge of his mortality; yet, so long as man retains this sense, it demands of him that he should meet death like the human being that he is, and not like one of "the beasts that perish". An uncle of mine, whose name I have the honour to bear, and who died suddenly at the age of 30, had written (prophetically of himself, as it turned out): "Man lifts his head for one moment above the waves, gives one wild glance around, and perishes. But that glance, was it for nothing?" Our Christian Western forebears knew that it was not for nothing. Their descendants have to recapture this knowledge if the Western civilisation is to survive.

5. Some Inadequacies of Recent Christian Thought about Death

by NINIAN SMART

A MAJOR trend in 20th century Christian theology has been towards a reaffirmation of biblical faith, but in the new context of historical criticism of the scriptures. There has been also, for various reasons, an increased scepticism about older attempts to wed Christianity to a scheme of metaphysics. Whereas a hundred years ago one could find frequent discussion of the problem of the immortality of the soul, today there is scarcely any; and this reflects both the fact that the New Testament does not have a systematic doctrine of survival and the fact that for philosophical and scientific reasons it is not so easy to hold to a belief in a mind-body dualism which would render immortality intelligible.

A recurrent theme in much modern biblical theology is that the thought-forms of the Bible differ markedly from those of the ancient Greek world; yet traditional theology, and in particular doctrines of the soul, leans rather heavily upon philosophical ideas ultimately taken over from the Greeks. In differing ways, Karl Barth and his successors in expounding the theology of the Word have tried to maintain a certain biblical purity accommodated to the critical approach to the scriptural material developed by historical criticism. The result is to emphasise biblical concepts, while riding often loosely to the historical and miraculous claims of the New Testament. Alternatively, as was pointed out in an earlier section,[1] the concepts themselves are treated rather radically, the attempt being to understand their function in the early Church and then to replace them by modern ideas (often existentialist): in this way, the Gospel is no longer encumbered by mythic elements at variance with present ways of looking at the world.

At the same time, there is an increasing trend in Christian thinking to emphasise the "materialistic", this-worldly side of Christianity. This was one of the motives in John Robinson's *Honest to God*—to get away from an apparent split between this world of human concerns and a God "out there". It is more strongly seen in theologians such as Paul van Buren (in his *The Secular Meaning of the Gospel*) and Harvey Cox (in his *The Secular City*). The fading of interest in an other-worldly God is naturally accompanied by a lack of concern about exploring the idea of an other-worldly consummation of human life. Paradoxically, a not dissimilar result can come from stressing the transcendence of God: his

[1] "Philosophical Concepts of Death", pp. 33-4.

being beyond thought and his absence from the world can mean that man has the freedom to operate autonomously in the secular world—this theme is found in some Catholic writers, such as Karl Rahner and Hans Urs von Balthasar.

New interpretations of biblical mythology

These trends bring about some characteristic ways of looking upon God's saving activity. If we remain within the ambit of biblical thought forms and do not attempt to demythologise them, stress tends to be placed upon God's action in history, through the Incarnation to a future consummation of history. The New Testament has much to say about the coming of the Kingdom and the resurrection of the dead. In one respect, the Kingdom is already here, being realised in the life of Christ. But in so far as Christians have hope, it must be in the second coming and resurrection of the body. But the reaffirmation of these mythic ideas is necessarily hampered by the difficulty of giving them precise content, and by their traditional connection with the idea of God's judgment, a concept which was bound to become eroded with changes in ways of looking at punishment and reward. (The retributive theory of punishment no longer commands the allegiance that it did.)

One way of trying to give a future consummation of history some content is by relating it to the evolutionary process, as in the work of Teilhard de Chardin; but this itself implies an extensive reinterpretation of biblical categories. It may be noted too that the stress on a future consummation is more directly relevant to the salvation of the community than of the individual: the latter's justification comes largely through his being a co-worker with God in moving towards the full realisation of the Kingdom of God.

At the other pole, it is possible to replace biblical mythology in such a way that the message of the Bible has essentially to do with the individual's relationship to God (or even his relationship to himself). Thus the myth of the Fall becomes symbolic of the state of alienation of man from God (or his alienation from his essential nature—a theme found in the writings of Paul Tillich). The picturesque imagery of the Apocalypse and similar eschatological motifs in early Christianity become symbolic of the finitude of the individual in the light of his inevitable death. This theme is developed in Rudolf Bultmann. The resurrection of Christ—the central sign and cause of the conquest of death—becomes the experience of new life in the disciples, derived from Jesus. Paul van Buren uses this idea in treating Jesus of Nazareth as being the source of a "contagious freedom" which has carried on down history.

This individualistic and existential approach to the "last things" must inevitably lay its stress upon an interpretation of eternal life as operative here and now. The implication of the approach is that it is not meaningful to speak of a continued existence beyond the grave (indeed, the very idea of immortality robs death of its significance and causes the New Testament mythology to lose its force in summoning us to immediate decision here and now). There is, though, as we shall see, a way of combining the existential approach with belief in the resurrection of the body. But in the meantime, it can be noted that the crumbling (from the point of view of radical theology at any rate) of the negative side of the idea of salvation has correspondingly put emphasis on the positive aspects of the Incarnation, just as the crumbling of the ideas of immortality, judgment, heaven and hell has led to conceiving of the conquest of death in terms of positive ideas of authentic existence (eternal life) in the face of death. Thus the Fall (from the radical point of view) cannot be treated historically: Christ is not the second Adam, (save symbolically) who came to remedy the situation brought about by the first Adam. Salvation is not so much treated as salvation *from* an historical predicament: rather it is easier to treat it as the positive creation of new life through Christ. All this emphasis on the positive side works in well with the renewal of positive attitudes towards the world, in contrast with "other-worldly" interpretations of the faith as expressed by the promise of heaven as a counter-balance to the sufferings of men in this life.

But as has been said, it is in principle possible to combine existential approaches to life and death with the traditional teachings about the resurrection of the dead. Paul, it may be recalled, spoke of a "spiritual body" as incarnating the saved individual. There are few who would today go back to earlier theological speculations about the necessity for the particles composing the physical body to be reassembled at the general resurrection. It is more common to look on the "spiritual body" as being some kind of (unimaginable) vehicle of personhood. Karl Rahner hints that the resurrection of the dead can be interpreted as the raising up of the individual, whose life nevertheless, as one moving through time, is already completed by his death. Rahner's central emphasis, however, is on the acceptance of death in this life, so that in a sense death is the supreme act of the Christian life, wherein one is united with Christ in *his* death. He therefore in essence rejects the idea of a continuing after-life beyond the grave, and lays his stress upon eternal life as realisable here and now.

Disbelief in immortality

There is a double tendency in modern theology to reject or ignore a belief in immortality which would be of universal comfort or relevance. One is the effect of the kind of scepticism about biblical mythology which we have touched on, and the feeling of a need to reinterpret the faith in contemporary terms. This involves a rather general scepticism about the possibility of life after death. The other motive for not taking the immortality of the soul very seriously derives from the biblical concepts themselves, and from certain fundamental elements of religious experience. The notion that men are in any case immortal does not so easily square with the biblical emphasis on eternal life as a gift of God; this emphasis in turn is connected with the experience of grace and the sense of the unique holiness of God. God alone can save; and so God alone can confer eternal blessing on men. The idea of the intrinsic immortality of the soul suggests that the after-life is of a natural rather than of a supernatural or divine origin. Admittedly, this sentiment can be taken care of by postulating that God's gift consists in one's place of destination rather than one's survival (heavenly life is a gift of God; otherwise there is purgatory or damnation); but as we have seen, the traditional conceptions of reward and punishment do not seem relevant today, to many people.

The gap between theology and popular religion

Although modern Christian radicalism has much to commend it, for it faces up with a certain realism to the problems confronting the presentation of the faith in the changed situation of the 20th century; and although a merely conservative reaction to these problems is likely to alienate those who have been affected by the intellectual difficulties of traditional belief; there nevertheless remain some important criticisms of the trends depicted above. First, the churches in fact are bound to rather conservative formulations of belief, and traditional attitudes are built heavily into the hymns and other liturgical expressions commonly in use. It is doubtful whether the implications of radical theology for beliefs about death are understood widely among those who actually participate in Christian practice. This is an aspect of the present confused state of Christianity. One is reminded of the situation in the late 17th century and early 18th century, when many theologians in Britain were critical of or sceptical about belief in hell, but in general forbore to make this attitude public, since it was commonly thought that the fear of damnation was essential for the maintenance of public morality.

Second, theology has been considerably preoccupied with the (admittedly important) problems of interpreting or replacing biblical myth. The recent "reforming" trends in Catholicism after Vatican II have caused Catholic theology to spend more of its energies on a rediscovery of the scriptural basis of faith. This preoccupation with the Bible among many of the most gifted of theologians in Europe and America has led to a relative neglect of the philosophical and scientific problems about the analysis of personhood and the possible implications of recent research. It could be that the latter in some measure favour the "materialism" of much of the biblical approach to the nature of man; but the reinterpretation of the Christian message may need to be much more empirically based. For example, the positive notions of authentic existence and acceptance of death need to be defined in some practical detail before they can escape the charge of spiritual rhetoric. There also needs to be some proper investigation of whether symbols (such as those of eschatology) in fact function for people in the way required by theologians.

Third, it is not possible to theologise in the abstract about death. There is perhaps a feeling that a denial of the after-life, as traditionally interpreted in a rather literal sense, might upset many of the faithful. But here we need to dig deeper into the concrete motives for people's desires for comfort and reassurance. Theology needs too to consider whether its own traditional doctrines are not in any case fearful, and themselves perhaps a cause of harmful attitudes to death; but this too is in substantial measure an empirical problem, not just a matter of speculation. Consider the following quotation:[1] "Epicurus, with more insight than some of his modern disciples, saw that what man fears is not that death is annihilation, but that it is not; that the horror of death is not extinction but 'the wrath to come'." Perhaps men should fear this, but surely this has to be gauged in part by the actual effects upon them of this kind of imagery.

Because of all these problems, it is not likely that there can emerge easily a Christian consensus on death and the after-life, at any rate for a long time. The boldness of Christian self-criticism at the present time is encouraging; but it does not conduce to comfort and agreement. But the least that can be expected is a straightforward willingness to discuss more openly and clearly the question of death. It has been approached, on the whole, obliquely in recent theology, as elsewhere.

[1] H. F. Lovell-Cocks, *By Faith Alone*, p. 57, quoted by Alan Richardson in *A Theological Word Book of the Bible*.

6. Death and the Decline of Religion in Western Society

by NINIAN SMART

IT IS a commonplace (though not everywhere justified by the facts) that religion in the West is declining, and has been doing so steadily since at least the turn of the century. With the main exception of the United States, where a remarkably high proportion of the population regularly attends church or synagogue, most industrially advanced Western countries have experienced a diminution in formal religious activities. The proportion of Easter Day communicants in the Church of England has gone down by about a third since 1900 (though as it happens, the absolute number has slightly increased—but the total population has, of course, gone up even more). In the 1950s, only a quarter or less of French and Belgian Catholics attended mass; in Lisbon and Vienna about 20 per cent. Figures are better for Italy and Spain, but in recent years some marked decline has occurred in Italy. Conversely, church membership has about trebled in the U.S. since the beginning of the century. On the whole, and neglecting the New World, the most marked secularisation has occurred in predominantly Protestant countries: but there is a real question as to whether this has something inherently to do with Protestantism or whether it has to do with these countries' earlier reaching a relatively high standard of economic development or for some other particular constellation of causes.

However, the above sample of statistics concerns formal acts of religion. In speaking of a "decline of religion", it is useful to be clear as to what constitutes religion. For it can be that those who abstain from church-going and the like, nevertheless believe in God, and pray in private. (There is, indeed, evidence on this point—the majority of Englishmen, for instance, believe in God or something like Him, even though the minority attend places of worship.) Religion can be viewed broadly under two aspects: first as a set of beliefs (including ethical beliefs), and second as a pattern of practices, including worship, prayer, alms-giving and so on. Typically, but not universally, the two sides are wedded closely together: God, for instance, is not seen just as creator, but as the supreme object of worship, the Person to whom one prays. But it is always possible to ask, about a decline of religion (or supposed decline) whether it represents a decline in belief, a decline in practice, or both. But a further point needs to be made about practice. For it too can have two aspects.

One aspect of religious practice in the Judaeo-Christian tradition is communal, collective or congregational practice—what we may call "public" practice, for short. In so far as the Christian faith, for instance, is institutionalised, it is largely through a Church which expresses itself centrally through acts of public worship. But acts of prayer and so on need not always be performed publicly and collectively, so that religious practice can also take a "private" form. Thus formal public religious practice may be performed only by a minority while private religious practice may be much more widespread.

It is also worth noting, to avoid confusion, that no judgment about values need be intended by saying that there is a decline in religion, whether in terms of belief or practice, public or private. Such a decline may or may not conduce to "Christian" behaviour in the sense of ethical behaviour in line with the spirit of Jesus' teachings. (This is what many people regard as the essence of Christianity, even if it means ignoring a major part of what the Christian faith has traditionally meant.)

Given these distinctions, it is possible to paint in broad outline some of the religious changes occurring over the last hundred years or less. (I shall here confine many of my remarks to the British scene, though they may also have wider significance—but there is a great variety of religious conditions even among the nations of the Western world, and generalisations are hazardous.) I shall relate the picture specifically to attitudes and customs relevant to death.

The crisis in religious belief

First, as to belief: there has been something of a crisis of religious belief in the West, which has hit different religious groups at different times and in different ways. The crisis has had three main roots. One has been the application of scientific historical methods to the scriptures, since the early part of the 19th century. The result has been less to undermine faith than to weaken a certain method of arguing for and formulating beliefs—namely, by taking texts from the scriptures and founding doctrines simply on the basis of scriptural testimony. The impact here has been particularly profound on Protestantism, less inclined to appeal to Church authority and so more reliant on scriptural authority. Its effect on Catholicism is being more widely felt in the new atmosphere issuing from Vatican II. The second root of the crisis of belief has been the effect of certain aspects of scientific thinking upon traditional ways of formulating Christian belief. The framework of biblical myth and cosmology had admittedly been considerably modified by mediaeval and post-Reformation thought; but it still retained a profound influence on the way people looked at the world. But the doctrine of the Fall, for instance, was difficult to maintain in anything like its original form after the publication of the theory of evolution. More widely, there seemed an incongruity between the miraculous and pre-scientific thinking of New Testament writers and the assumptions according to which we now try to understand the world about us. A third root of the crisis has been the more self-critical approach to ideas, religious or otherwise, brought about by the development of psychology and sociology in modern times. There is less inclination to accept beliefs before examining their possible particular origins, not in the Gospel and the Bible, but in our own psyches and societies.

This has left the churches in an uncertain intellectual state—one of excitement and ferment, perhaps; but one also where it is increasingly difficult to talk about *the* Christian position or about the teachings of Christianity. The crisis can provoke opposite reactions: one is to repudiate (in effect) the new thought-world, or at any rate to deny that it need modify seriously traditional scriptural formulations; the other is to attempt to evolve a new Christian radicalism. The former reaction is rather frequent among evangelicals, and has brought about rifts within denominations perhaps more significant than the divisions between denominations. The latter reaction has taken various forms—the attempt to harness existentialist motifs to a re-presentation of the Gospel without the old myths (Rudolf Bultmann, and to some extent Paul Tillich); an eclectic modernism (the Bishop of Woolwich); the so-called "death of God" theology in the U.S.; Catholic Marxism; and so on.

One of the effects of the crisis has been for new forms of radical theology to treat the eschatology of the New Testament (its picture of the "last things"—the resurrection, the judgment, the after-life) as essentially belonging to the mythic way of thinking of that age. The project of re-presenting the Gospel without out-dated myth has tended towards a scepticism about the next life, and a this-worldly or world-affirming view of eternal life as something to be tasted here and now through relationship to God and action in a suffering world. In any event, there are thought to be grounds for saying that the idea of an immortal soul is not characteristic of biblical thinking; and it is hard to know what the concepts of resurrection of the body or the coming of the Kingdom mean from the perspective of the 20th century. Some like to interpret these eschatological motifs in terms of evolution: hence the appeal of Teilhard de Chardin's picturesque promise of a consummation of evolutionary history in a future Christocentric harmony and unity.

Popular belief and public religious practice

But if these uncertainties afflict religious intellectuals, they do not to the same degree influence the man in the street. Something like half of British people appear to believe in an after-life. What is questionable, though, is whether many believe in it in the sense implied by traditional Christianity. Naturally, a substantial number of folk think of the after-life as a place, so to say, for rejoining their loved ones and friends: the doctrine of judgment might indeed preclude this.

The situation in regard to the public practices of religion in the last hundred years is less easy to diagnose briefly. But one important aspect of it has been the increasing divergence between meaningful church allegiance and the operation of religion's functions in administering rites of passage, such as baptism, marriages and funerals. In societies where religious rites are closely integrated into the fabric of social life, there is a small gap between religious belief and loyalty on the one hand and the solemnisation of key events in family and communal life. But the position of the churches in many countries now, and notably in Britain, is that they are in essence voluntary denominational associations. Although the Church of England in theory has a national purview, in fact its real membership consists of those who voluntarily sustain its activities, and in essence its status is no different from Congregationalism or Methodism. The mobility of modern society, starting from the massive geographical regroupings of the population brought on by the industrial revolution, has broken the parish principle: namely, that there is a correlation between a local community and a church community. Consequently, the expression of public worship depends upon private and variegated initiatives, and is less than ever it was an agreed community enterprise and obligation. This denominationalism in modern Christianity leaves over, however, certain ritual functions, in particular the solemnisation of rites of passage which attract widespread support. Thus in England, if 15 per cent of the population are to be found worshipping on an average Sunday, about 70 per cent of the population want to get married in church. Active church membership, of course, is greater than this 15 per cent; but even so there is a marked disparity between real membership and the number of those who make use of religious ceremonial at rites of passage. An even greater number of folk have the benefit of religious ceremoinal at death, partly because it is in any case rather hard to avoid.

Rites associated with death

One must not, of course, exaggerate the decline in religious practice of a public kind; only a minority were regular church-goers in England 50 years ago. But public religion operated more homogeneously and pervasively, partly because of its entrenchment in middle class be-haviour, and the middle class was the effective formulator of "public opinion". Further, there is an increased "isolation" of rites of passage, and in particular funerals. Traditionally, the funeral was followed by a period of mourning, somet mes quite extensive. This is well brought out in Geoffrey Gorer's reminiscences, in the introduction to his *Death*,

Grief and Mourning. Now the preparations for and sequels to death are skimpier and less formalised. This is perhaps in line with the trend of religion itself to be regarded as a private, personal matter. It is thus almost impolite to parade the ritual requirements of one's faith except in defined places and at defined times; likewise, it is almost impolite to display formalised mourning publicly and to all and sundry. In any case, the situation brought about by the denominationalisation of religion means that publicly agreed conventions connected with the solemnisation of death are largely eroded, and in the absence of an "etiquette" of mourning there is no assured way in which grief can be expressed acceptably.

It should be noted that what I have called here the "denomination-alisation" of religion does not constitute a full pluralism of religion in society, and this is one reason why even in the relatively pious United States mourning conventions have been whittled away. In a fully plural-istic society, as in India, it is expected that different religious groups will behave differently, in regard to their rites and public behaviour. But in Western societies which are at least pluralistic in the sense that there is a variety of religious affiliations, there is an expectation of roughly homogeneous public behaviour. A Jewish wedding or funeral will of course differ from a Christian wedding or funeral; but outside that immediate context, there is an expectation of general uniformity. Informality thus comes to replace an extended ritual of mourning.

One main connecting point between church beliefs and the administration of rites to the dying and the dead is, of course, the priest or minister. While Catholicism retains in good measure a confidence in the role of the priest, and a ceremonial and doctrine still rather unaffected by the changes mentioned earlier, the Anglican parson and the Nonconformist minister increasingly finds himself in difficulty as to his role and status in society. He is expected to administer rites to many who are not active members of the church; and he is expected to act pastorally towards the dying. This is often taken to mean the supplying of comfort to those who are dying and to the bereaved, and this in turn is often interpreted as meaning that he gives assurance about the after-life. He is thus, with the denomina-tionalisation of religion, in a doubly ambiguous position. He has to act within generally agreed social conventions and beliefs, but is expected to take a particular line. Yet about that "line" he is not very certain. The ferment in theology may leave him unhappy at simply repeating traditional assurances; nor is he certain that his duty to the dying and bereaved is specifically Christian. There is perhaps also the nagging thought that the psychiatrist is better qualified to deal with many of the problems brought to his pastoral attention by old age and death. To some extent these troubles are alleviated by the ecumenical movement and a strong contemporary interest in new modes of pastoral training for the clergy (making available to them some of the insights of "secular" workers in fields, such as geriatrics, which are of key pastoral interest). As to ecumenism, it seems to make easier a reaffirmation of a single Christian teaching on these matters, though so far this is but a promise. One of the difficulties here is that different denominations may not agree about doctrine, but at least the Bible is common—yet the biblical mythology (of the last things and of other matters) is precisely what is called in question by contemporary ways of looking at the world, and by historical criticism of the scriptural material. These points, it is true, do not apply to those who have reacted against contemporary radicalism; but a substantial number of clerics do not fall into this category.

A further factor in the decline of religious concern with death has been the development from within Christianity of a movement which tends to set the Gospel in Christ over against religion (regarded as a human creation). This contrast is found clearly in the writings of Karl Barth, but was developed further by Dietrich Bonhoeffer and by more recent exponents of "religionless Christianity". According to this doctrine, man, once he has "come of age" does not need religion, even though he may still need Christ. This form of radicalism is not conducive to taking Christianity's religious role in society very seriously. The conclusion of this line of thinking might well be that the social functions of religion might be turned over to some agency other than the church. The movement may well prove to be ephemeral; but it is symptomatic of the present crisis of belief and of a situation where belief in the Christian revelation is held only by a minority in societies which yet in theory remain Christian. Given the disparity between many ordinary men's degree of conviction and the teachings of the churches, it is a question as to whether the latter do not serve to obscure, rather than to illuminate, the message of Christ. The problem of death serves to underline heavily the dilemma of denominationalised Christianity; for however few or many people adhere to the faith, everyone sooner or later encounters death or mourning. In these circumstances it is hard to know how specifically Christian convictions can be incorporated into the expression of the rituals of death.

It is therefore perhaps surprising that little discussion has taken place of the desirability of a secular ritual of mourning, (as advocated for instance by Geoffrey Gorer) to correspond to the civil marriage, which caters for those who do not wish necessarily to be associated with specifically Christian (or any other religious) forms of ceremony. This would be one direction in which the thinking of "religionless Christianity" might tend.

Judgments on these issues in part turn on a wider view of the present trend in religious observance and belief. It is not obvious that the decline in religion, where it is occurring, need continue; and it is not self-evident that a decline in religion is a consequence of increasing industrialisation and of the growth of a technological society (we have already noted the comparative piety of the United States, and post-war Japan has witnessed a remarkable growth of new religious movements). There are sociologists who would argue, on the basis of a functionalist account of religion, that religion is a continuing necessity in human society—it only being that the forms of religion are liable to change with changes in society. If this estimate were correct, it would imply that the path of "religionless Christianity" was fundamentally mistaken, unless it adapted itself by treating religion itself as an area of human experience and practice to be served by Christians just as they serve other needs of mankind.

But whatever speculations may be relevant to the future, the present situation seems to be clear: that Christianity in the West is increasingly denominationalised and a matter of private decision; and for this and other reasons traditional beliefs and practices connected with death do not attract public agreement. The "solution" therefore is to treat death in a minimal and rather informal way. Since words themselves can be a kind of ritual, the less said about death the better. In a time of uncertain belief and behaviour, people are inclined to carry on with unclear hopes and exiguous rituals.

7. Death in War

by ARNOLD TOYNBEE

WAR IS not a spontaneous vent for human nature's innate pugnacity. This pugnacity is real, and war would be impossible without it. But the most pertinent facts about war are that it is an institution and that it cannot be a very old one. War is a recent institution measured by the time-scale of the age of the human race so far or, *a fortiori*, by the length of the race's present expectation of life on this planet.

The waging of wars is impracticable unless two conditions can be met. The first condition is that the war-making communities must have at their command a surplus of time, energy, and productivity over and above what they need to spend on just keeping themselves alive. War could not be waged by ruminant animals which have to spend on eating the whole of their time that they can spare from sleeping. Human beings, too, must have lacked the resources for waging war until the turn of the fourth and third millennia B.C., when, first in what is now Iraq and then in what is now Egypt, a considerable surplus was produced, for the first time in human history, by the draining and irrigation of soils, potentially rich for cultivation, that had previously been occupied by unutilisable jungle-swamp. These two immense feats of reclamation could not have been achieved except by an autocratic and also skilful organisation of the working-power of large numbers of docile human beings. The creation of the fertile fields of Sumer and Egypt required mass-discipline, and mass-discipline is also the second of the conditions that are required for the waging of war. If a human being is to be turned into a soldier, he has to be conditioned into risking his life, and perhaps losing it, in trying to kill fellow human beings of his with whom he has no personal quarrel. For committing this perilous public crime, docility and mass-discipline are as necessary as they are for carrying out large-scale productive public works.

Conventions of war

War, like other institutions, has its postulates and its conventions. The fundamental postulate of the institution of war is that, in war, "killing is no murder". Murder committed by private enterprise has been regarded, almost universally, as being a crime of the greatest magnitude, whether the motive has been hatred or covetousness. Murder committed under orders by public authorities in the collective interests (real or imaginary) of a community has been regarded as a virtuous and noble activity, except by a few small religious communities

K

(e.g. the Christians of the first few generations and, among modern Christians, only the Society of Friends, who hold that taking part in war is morally inadmissible in all circumstances). The moral sense of mankind in general has been obtuse enough to regard the killer in war as being righteous—at least, so long as he keeps, more or less faithfully, to the recognised rules. If he dies in battle, or if, whether dying or surviving, he shows prowess either as a combatant or as a commander, he is hailed as a hero. One of the conventions of war which was almost universal till recently, but is now being abandoned, was that women were exempt from having to serve as combatants (though not exempt, de facto, from being murdered or raped by male combatants). Another convention was, and still is, that a man on the war-path must dress the part. Even in the present age, when the technology of war has become sophisticated and when the soldier's equipment has become correspondingly "functional", the equivalent of the warrior's traditional war-paint and plumes survives in unobtrusive forms (stars, chevrons, buttons).

This dressing-up for war looks childish, and so it is; yet it has two serious functions, one psychological and the other practical. Psychologically it symbolises the abrogation of the normal tabu on killing fellow human beings; it replaces this tabu by a duty to kill them. Practically, the wearing of a uniform distinguishes soldiers visibly from civilians. This practical distinction has been more or less faithfully observed during two short periods of Western history: in 15th-century Italy before the French invasion of Italy in 1494 and in 18th-century and 19th-century Europe before the German invasion of Belgium in 1914 and the subsequent use in war of bomb-dropping aeroplanes. In the West between the end of the wars of religion and the outbreak of the First World War in 1914, war was, in theory at least, a killing-game played between men in uniform, in which civilians were not involved. Yet, even after the opening of the 19th century, it was still customary for a Western army that had taken by assault a fortified and defended town to loot, rape, and murder the civilian inhabitants—and this even when the defeated defending army had been a foreign one that had occupied and had been holding the fallen town by force, against the inhabitants' will, or at any rate without their having had any power to keep the foreign occupying army out. A notorious case was the British army's conduct in the Spanish city of Badajoz after they had captured it by assault from a French occupying garrison on April 6th 1812.

The religion of nationalism

War is not merely an institution; it is also one that is an act of religious worship. The god in whose honour this religious act is performed is the collective power of some fraction of the human race. The performance is a form of human sacrifice or ritual murder. The rulers of a state murder (by proxy) the soldiers of another state with whose rulers they are at war; and they do this at the cost of exposing their own young men, who have been turned into soldiers compulsorily if they have not volunteered, to be wounded, maimed, or killed by the soldiers of the opposing army, whom their own soldiers have been commanded to wound, maim, and kill to the utmost of their ability.

Communities consisting of fractions of the human race have been objects of worship, served by the performance of these criminal rites, ever since man got the upper hand definitively over non-human nature. Since then, the worship of non-human nature—man's main religion so long as he remained at non-human nature's mercy—has become virtually extinct, while man's worship of the collective power of fractions of the human race has continued to gain currency *pari passu* with the continuing increase in this power of his as a result of the progress of his technology. This idolatrous worship of collective human power, with its hideous ritual in the shape of war, has never been successfully suppressed by the relatively recent epiphany of the higher religions whose object of worship has been neither non-human nature nor collective human power, but has been the Ultimate Spiritual Reality behind the universe. Adherents of the higher religions have always continued actually, though not avowedly, to give a share of their allegiance to the sinister older gods.

In the modern Western world the 17th-century reaction against Christianity, out of revulsion from the fanatical vein in this higher religion, was followed in the 18th century by a spiritual lull during which "enthusiasm" (the 18th-century name for what we now call "fanaticism") was at a low ebb. Even then, the institution of war did not fall into abeyance. The motives of 18th-century Western war-makers were, indeed, more cynical than those of either their predecessors or their successors, because the 18th-century war-makers' motives were non-religious. The stakes for which they fought were moderate, but these 18th-century moderate stakes were naked economic and political interests. However, spiritual nature, like physical nature, abhors a vacuum; and, since the eruption of the American and French Revolutions, the spiritual vacuum left in Western souls by the recession of Christianity has been filled by the resurgence of the older, and always latent, worship of the collective power of human communities.

This post-Christian resurgent worship of collective human power in the West (and also in those non-Western societies that have latterly been adopting the Western civilisation, for evil as well as for good) has proved more virulent than the pre-Christian form of it as this was practised by, for instance, the Romans, the Greeks, the Sumerians, and the Chinese in the period of "the Contending States". In our post-Christian age, the worship of collective human power has been keyed up to a higher pitch by the infusion of ex-Christian fanaticism into it.

This post-Christian worship of collective human power is the evil religion whose name is "nationalism". It is un-Christian, except in the point of being Christianly fanatical. Unhappily, fanatical nationalism is today about 90 per cent of the real religion of about 90 per cent of the human race.

The increasing fanaticism of nationalism has exacted an increasing oblation of military human sacrifice. The increase can be measured by the increasing prevalence of military conscription since the *levée en masse* in France in 1792. In the modern Western world, conscription has been the twin sister of egalitarianism. The Prussian state introduced universal military service—an institution that is egalitarian, though not democratic—as its riposte to its humiliating temporary defeat by Napoleon. In the United States, whose citizens believe themselves to be the most democratic nation that there has ever been with the possible exception of the equally self-deceived Athenians, selective conscription has been imposed on two occasions: first, during the Civil War of 1861-5, on both sides, and then, in the reunited United States, from 1941 until the present moment.

Atrocities

Another index of the increasing fanaticism of nationalism, as measured in terms of the conduct of war, has been the accelerating recrudesence of atrocities. When, in the course of the 17th century, Westerners had desisted, at last, from fighting their Catholic-Protestant wars of religion, they had made a serious and partially successful effort —not, of course, to abolish the institution of war, but to reduce the inevitable accompanying atrocities to a minimum for the combatants themselves and, *a fortiori*, for civilians. Since August 1914 the relatively humanitarian standard that had been set by Westerners for their conduct of war since the close of the 17th century has been falling sharply—particularly as regards the exemption of civilians. When German troops shot batches of Belgian civilians in the course of their invasion of Belgium in August 1914, Western public opinion was deeply shocked. When the little Basque town of Guernica was destroyed by bombing from the air on April 26th 1937, with the inevitable indiscriminate slaughter of civilians of both sexes and all ages, a fresh wave of horror swept across the Western world. The bombing of Guernica was rightly felt to portend future bombings on a vaster scale. But, in the Second World War, atrocities that dwarfed those of the First World War in both scale and cruelty caused less perturbation. For producing a shock, atrociousness, by itself, is not enough; there must also be novelty. Human hearts become hardened to anything that has become familiar; and atrocities of the wars-of-religion degree had become familiar events again by 1939. In 1968 there must be Americans of my present age (79) who were horrified at the German atrocities in

1914 and at the bombing of Guernica in 1937, yet who, today, view with equanimity, on the television screen or in still photographs in a book, the spectacle of North Vietnamese villages being bombed more intensively than any European city was ever bombed in the Second World War, or the still more appalling spectacle of South Vietnamese soldiers torturing prisoners to elicit information, with American soldiers watching, acquiescing, and condoning.

In the United States today, scenes, from real life, of soldiers killing and wounding each other in battle in Vietnam have become regular features in television programmes. Little children are already familiar with them. The reaction to this first-hand view of the hideous realities of war ought, of course, to be a nation-wide insistence on the war in Vietnam being stopped immediately. I have been told, however, that, so far from bringing the realities of war home to people, the spectacle of them on the television screen makes them feel unreal, because the sub-conscious mental association of television-spectacles is with play-acting, not with real life. Battle-scenes, conveyed on the television screen, are transmuted, in the viewers' minds and hearts, from real life into "make-believe". Every child knows that, in "Westerns", the killings are not real; so real killings, presented as "Westerns", seem unreal too, and this makes the viewer of them, not sensitive, but callous.

The scale of the slaughter of European combatants in the First World War did appal all the belligerent peoples. It was a scale that they had not intended and not expected when they had gone to war with each other in 1914. All European peoples who had been belli-gerents in the First World War had to be whipped up into engaging in the Second. However, the degree of reluctance to go to war again differed markedly as between different peoples.

The French and the British were the most reluctant of all, and the Italians would, no doubt, have been equally reluctant if they had not then been living under a regime that would have inflicted extreme penalties on any outspokenly anti-belligerent individual Italian subject. The Germans were less reluctant than the French and the British, though, in the First World War, their casualties had been still heavier. Some Germans were stimulated by a thirst for revenge, but they were also willing to sacrifice their young men to a lust for conquest. Of the European peoples, the French and the Italians broke down; only the Russians, Germans, and British endured the Second World War to the end. Of the non-European belligerents in the Second World War, the Americans were stimulated, like the Germans, by a thirst for revenge— revenge, in the American case, for the Japanese attack on Pearl Harbour. In the First World War the American casualties had been relatively light, compared to those of the European belligerents. Japanese casualties had been lighter still in that war; but the Japanese spirit in the Russo-Japanese war of 1904 suggests that, even if the Japanese casualties in the First World War had been as heavy as the

German had been, the Japanese people would still have made war in 1941 unhesitatingly.

The Second World War ended with the dropping of two American atomic bombs on the Japanese cities of Hiroshima and Nagasaki. No weapon ever previously forged by man had had anything approaching this amount of death-dealing capacity. The invention of the atomic weapon produced an instantaneous change in the nature of war. A five-thousand-years-old wicked institution that had always been cruel and devastating had now become suicidal. It was evident that, in any future war in which the belligerents on both sides possessed and used the atomic weapon, the distinction between victor and vanquished—a distinction that had made victory so desirable—would be obliterated. Both sides would be prostrated; no victor would emerge.

Attitudes to war in the atomic age

The intellectual understanding of this revolutionary change in the character and consequence of war spread with remarkable rapidity all over the world among people who were conscious of public affairs. Such people, though no doubt they are a minority, are the minority that decides what turn the conduct of public affairs shall take. It might therefore have been expected, on first thoughts, that the understanding of the revolutionary significance of the invention of the atomic weapon would have been followed by a revolutionary change of policy—for the sake of self-preservation, if not in virtue of a change of heart of the kind that was so potent a factor in bringing about the abolition of slavery, and is still so potent a factor today in the current struggle against racial discrimination in Southern Africa, the United States, and Britain. Yet, so far, mankind has, on the whole, been behaving since 1945 as if we were still living in the pre-atomic age.

The two post-Second-World-War super-powers, the United States and the Soviet Union, are still playing the dangerous game of power-politics—a game that has wrecked one civilisation after another since it was started by the Sumerian city-states in the third millennium B.C. Meanwhile, many of the minor states of the present-day world—and there are now about 125 local sovereign states on the surface of this small planet—are following suit to the two super-powers in continuing to use war—and this, in some cases, with most unfortunate success—as an instrument of national policy. The danger of the game of international power-politics is that it leads, inevitably, to "confrontations". There have been at least four of these between the Soviet Union and the United States between 1945 and 1967—over Berlin, over Korea, over Cuba, and over the Middle East—and there is also a current confrontation between them in Vietnam which is not the less dangerous for being covert, and which is all the more dangerous because it might involve China too.

Russia and America obviously both intend to refrain from waging an atomic war with each other. Indeed, they intend to abstain from fighting each other even with "conventional" weapons, since both parties are aware that a war between them that began in the old style would almost inevitably end in an atomic holocaust. Of the two, the United States is today probably in the more dangerous mood. Russia has had the experience of being invaded and devastated twice over within the memory of many Russians still alive. No part of the United States has been invaded and devastated since the Civil War of 1861-5, and "the Old South", which was crushed and crippled in that war and which is still smarting under the memory of it, is also today the most warlike section of the United States—presumably because it is the most backward and most ill-educated one. Moreover, with the signal exception of the overthrow of the Confederacy, the military history of the United States has, so far, been an unbroken "success story". It began with a victory over Britain; the catastrophic overthrow of the Confederacy was a famous victory for the Union; and the victorious North has set the tone of American society ever since. It is therefore peculiarly difficult for the American people today to admit that they may have made a mistake and that it might be advisable for them to think again and to change their policy. In the atomic age this current state of mind in America is dangerous, not only for the people of the United States, but for the whole human race.

The war in Vietnam is the first colonial war that has been fought with troops that are conscripts, not professionals and not *ad hoc* volunteers. Algeria, till France renounced her sovereignty over it, was nominally part of metropolitan France. However, the Algerian war was a colonial war in truth, and it is significant that the French conscripts sent by the French Government to Algeria contributed notably to making a continuance of the war impossible by revolting against the commission of the atrocities that a war of repression necessarily entails.

Today a majority of middle-aged American citizens appear to be as willing as any Canaanites or Aztecs ever were to sacrifice their sons on Moloch's altar. The question is whether the rising generation of male American citizens is going to submit to being sacrificed by coercion.

Meanwhile, since 1945, the human race has been living under a threat of extinction that had not hung over it since man definitively got the upper hand over all other large beasts of prey on this planet. This happened perhaps about thirty thousand years ago, and, at that date, human beings can hardly have been conscious of the danger of extinction from which they were liberating themselves. Today, on the other hand, they are fully aware of the threat; they know that it comes now from themselves; and they also know that it is a far more formidable threat than the previous threat of extinction by sabre-toothed tigers, and even than the recently eliminated threat of extinction by bacteria (a threat that man may be going to revive in the form of bacteriological warfare).

In the United States since 1945 a new pseudo-science has sprung up which purports to prognosticate what the effects of an atomic war would be. It expresses its findings in statistics totting up the number of human lives that would be lost and the amount of human productions of all kinds that would be destroyed. These statistics may be near the mark or may be wide of it; but, when the practitioners of this pseudo-science go on to discuss how many millions of deaths would be "acceptable", they are betraying the falsity of their claim to be scientific by trespassing on the field of the unknown and the unknowable. There is no precedent in past human experience for even a guess at the intensity of the feelings of horror, grief, fear, and, above all, guilt that ritual murder on the atomic scale would bring to the surface of a human being's consciousness from the dark and deep abyss which the progress of the genuine science of psychology is revealing to us.

8. Increased Longevity and the Decline of Infant Mortality

by Arnold Toynbee

THROUGHOUT the whole course of human history so far in the world as a whole, death from disease in civilian life in peace-time has been as familiar as death by violence in war. It is only within living memory, and this, so far, only in a small fraction of the human race, that the administration of public health and the medical care of individual human beings have progressed to a degree at which premature death from "natural causes" (i.e. disease)—in infancy, in early childhood, and at every successive stage of life before the attainment of the traditional full life-span of "three score years and ten"—has been reduced to a point at which death, under peace-time conditions of life, has become unfamiliar.

The "developed" fraction of the human race is, of course, the fraction in which death by violence in war has been quite as familiar as it has been at most times and places in the past since the institution of war was invented. The number of the survivors of the combatants in the First World War must, in 1968, still run to millions; the number of the survivors of the combatants in the Second World War certainly runs to millions more. Many of these ex-soldiers who are still alive today will have killed fellow human beings—in some cases in an impersonal way, by dropping bombs from aeroplanes or by firing shells from cannons, but also in some cases in hand-to-hand fighting with bayonets, hand-grenades, and flame-throwers. Many more will have seen other men being killed by other hands, and will have seen corpses on battlefields.

Since 1914, the conduct of war has become progressively more atrocious, as has been noted in the previous chapter.[1] The napalm and the "anti-personnel" bombs that are being used today in Vietnam—and this against civilians as well as against combatants—are more fiendish weapons than any that had yet been devised or even imagined by the date of the outbreak of the First World War. In civilian life too in our time, genocide has been practised in cold blood by the Nazis, first in Germany itself and then in the other European countries that the Germans conquered temporarily during the Second World War. The Germans' mass-murder of civilians, non-Jews as well as Jews, is comparable in scale with the genocide committed by the Mongols in the 12th and 13th centuries of the Christian era and by Timur Lenk in

[1] "Death in War", p. 148 ff.

the 14th century. In the Western world as a whole, however, peace-time behaviour has become progressively more humane since the later decades of the 18th century. Thus, on the whole, the gulf between peace-time Western conduct and experience and war-time Western conduct and experience has been widening in our time till it has now perhaps become wider than it has ever been at any other time or in any other society.

This heightening, in the contemporary West, of the perennial contrast between war-time conditions and peace-time conditions has manifestly produced psychological strains and tensions in contemporary Westerners' souls. At the same time, the effect of war-time views of death on peace-time views of death has perhaps been smaller than might have been expected. One of the features of the institution of war is that it suspends, "for the duration", a number of fundamental peace-time tabus; but, in suspending them, it does not abrogate them; they revive (though by no means always intact) with the return of peace. This is, no doubt, one of the reasons why the war-years of a human being's life-time seem to him, in retrospect, to belong to a different series from the peace-years. At least, this appears to be how their past life looks to most Westerners who have lived through the two world wars. The war-years seem in retrospect unreal in some sense even to Westerners who were then combatants, and, *a fortiori*, to the majority who were then still civilians. It has also been noted that children in the United States who watch hostilities actually in progress on the television screen are conditioned to think and feel about the genuine killing that they are viewing as if it were play-acting—as so much of what they view on television actually is. Accordingly it is probably true—paradoxical though this may sound—that, in this present-day Western society that has waged two unprecedentedly genocidal world wars and has invented the atomic weapon, death is less familiar today than it is among the non-Western majority of the human race and than it was, till recently, in the West itself.

The decline of early mortality

Till recently in all societies, the West included, human beings did not dream of the possibility of defying and defeating the prodigality of Nature. Like rabbits, humans bred up to the biological limit as a matter of course, since the procreation of the maximum number of children was the only known means of enabling the race to survive in conditions under which the number of casualties "from natural causes" (leaving deliberately inflicted war-casualties out of account) was also at a maximum. Parents assumed, almost as a matter of course, that only part of their numerous progeny would live to attain adult age. Children were aware that brothers and sisters of theirs had died before they themselves had reached the age of consciousness, and the survivors lived on to lose other brothers and sisters who had been their playmates.

The experience of becoming orphans before becoming adults was also far more common in the West a few generations ago than it is today; and the death of grandparents was still more familiar—partly because the average expectation of life was then appreciably shorter than it has now come to be in the West, and also because family solidarity was then still strong in the West—as, happily, it still is in the rest of the world down to the present moment. In the West, as elsewhere, till not very long ago, grandparents had a place in their children's and grandchildrens' home as a matter of course. The personal relationship between grandparents and grandchildren was close, and the grandchildren felt the loss when their grandparents died in the course of nature.

This unsought automatic education of children in familiarity with death was harsh (and is harsh, for it is still part of a child's normal experience among the non-western majority of mankind). At the same time, there is a sense in which this harsh experience was and is salutary; for every human being is going to die sooner or later, and it will be less difficult for him eventually to face his own death, when he realises that this has become imminent, if, since childhood, he has been familiar with death as one of the normal facts of our human condition. Being human, he may nevertheless resent death as an outrage against human dignity, but at least he will recognise that death is an outrage which is a matter of inexorable fact, and that every human being has to come to terms with it. The penalty for unfamiliarity with death in childhood, and even in early adult life, is that death becomes unthinkable and unmentionable, as it has come to be in the United States today.[1]

Social problems connected with longevity

Like the reduction of the rate of infant mortality, the lengthening of the expectation of life in old age has been one of the notable triumphs of modern Western medical science; and this, too, has its nemesis. The prolongation of life has been achieved in the West just at the time when the age-old tradition of family solidarity has been breaking down there, and also in a period of progressive monetary inflation. The traditional household provided a place for all living members of the family of all generations. It included not only parents and children but also maiden aunts; and, though a spinster's life might be forlorn in a society in which professional careers were not yet open for women, the aunt's life did have its function, reward, and satisfaction in a household in which there were grandparents, as well as a bevy of children, to be looked after; for this was, and is, too arduous a job for one woman—the wife and mother—to cope with single-handed. In the present-day Western world the normal family is limited to a small number of children and

[1] See above, "Changing Attitudes Towards Death in the Modern Western World", p. 131.

their parents. It no longer includes maiden aunts to help in the house; unmarried women are now employed, like men, in non-domestic work.

In some families the wife and mother herself now does part-time professional work—partly in order to supplement her husband's earnings in a period in which the rise in prices is constantly running ahead of the rise in wages, and partly because the relative social prestige of being a married woman and a spinster has now been reversed. The spinster has changed from a dependant, living in her married sister's or brother's house, into a professional woman who is earning her living like a man. In her new role, the spinster puts the wife and mother out of countenance. The once proud wife and mother now tends to feel inferior if she is nothing more than that. A household that no longer includes maiden aunts, and in which the wife and mother herself may be chafing if her domestic work has to be her full-time occupation, evidently no longer has any room for grandparents. These must now fend for themselves as best they can.

Under these novel conditions, the lengthening of the expectation of life is far from being an unmixed blessing. Old people nowadays in the West have to bear the double burden of loneliness and anxiety.

The anxiety is financial. In a period of inflation, a fixed pension buys less and less; most middle-class pensions from non-governmental sources are fixed once and for all; governmental pensions are raised from time to time, as the cost of living continues to rise; but they are seldom adequate, and there is usually a time-lag between the rise in the cost of living and the consequent raising of the pension-scale. Most of the former wage-earners who have reached and passed the age of retirement from the work on which they had previously been employed are unable to find new openings for earning money as freelances, even if they still have the physical health, the energy, and the wits to continue to take an effective part in the world's work. Those who do both find new openings and retain the capacity to take advantage of them are a fortunate minority; yet their exceptional good fortune is bound to be a wasting asset. "Though men be so strong that they come to four score years, yet is their strength then but labour and sorrow."[1]

Old people in the present-day world are lonely because they no longer have an assured place, as a matter of course, in a household that also includes middle-aged people and children. Thrown back on their own resources, the old drop out of the world in losing contact with the generations that represent the present and the future. The old are lonely even if they are married and if both members of the married couple are still alive. They are lonelier if they are unmarried. They are loneliest of all if they are widows or widowers.

When the psalmist comments that the strength of men and women who have reached the age of 80 is "then but labour and sorrow", the reason that he gives for extreme old age being sorrowful is: "so soon

[1] Psalms 90, 10 (Book of Common Prayer).

passeth it away, and we are gone." This statement, which was universally true till recently, reads ironically today. If a present-day Western old person for whom the prolongation of life is becoming an increasing burden could still count on death's being near, this prospect would not cause him sorrow; it would give him relief. Unfortunately, medical science has now become adept at keeping human beings physically alive in biological circumstances that would have killed them off inevitably not so very long ago. Consequently a present-day Western human being can no longer count, even at the age of 80, on being released in the near future from an ordeal that is becoming increasingly hard for him to bear. Deprived, as he now is, even at 80, of the sure prospect of an early death, he must pin his hopes, instead, on an early onset of senility; for senility does still perform the merciful service that death is being frustrated from performing by the marvellous progress of medical skill. Like death, senility extinguishes both anxiety and loneliness; for senility can eclipse consciousness as effectively as death does.

Responsibilities arising from a lower death rate

The lengthening of the expectation of life and the reduction of infant mortality confront human beings with the necessity of making previously impracticable and inconceivable choices and decisions, and this enlargement of the field of human action is an addition to the burden of human responsibility.

The progress of science that has reduced infant mortality has simultaneously produced contraceptives; and these two achievements, between them, have now imposed on Western parents the duty of family planning. Instead of begetting the biological maximum number of children, parents now have to decide what is the social optimum number. This is the number that will give each child that is deliberately brought into the world the greatest opportunity of leading the best possible life—the best possible in the spiritual sense of the words, subject to the consideration that there is a minimum standard of material well-being, short of which a human being is unlikely to be able to achieve his full spiritual potentialities.

Manifestly the choices involved in family planning are difficult. Yet they are not so difficult as the problems that are raised by Western man's recently acquired longevity.

Arthur Hugh Clough, in his poem *The Latest Decalogue*, expands the sixth commandment to read:

Thou shalt not kill, but need'st not strive
Officiously to keep alive.

The poem was written as a satire on man's hypocritical evasion of duties to which he pays lip-service. The poet cannot have suspected that, within a century of his own death, his quip was going to become a serious moral problem.

Suicide

The plight of old people in the 20th-century Western world had been anticipated, by more than two centuries, in Swift's imaginative intuition of the plight of his imaginary Struldbrugs; but there is a crucial difference between the Struldbrugs' problem and 20th-century Western man's. The Struldbrugs were immortal. Neither they themselves nor any other human being had the power to release the Struldbrugs from their immortality by bestowing on them the boon of death. Longevity, however, is not immortality, to whatever length longevity may be prolonged by present-day medical ingenuity. It is within an old man's power to commit suicide; it is within his physician's power not to strive officiously to keep him alive; more than that, it is within his physician's power to put a patient who is miserable out of his misery—a service that any merciful-minded human being would perform unhesitatingly for any non-human living creature for which life had come to be no longer worth living. Here are three choices, and the patient's choice is a less difficult one than the two that nowadays confront the patient's physician.

It has been noted already[1] that Western man's current inhibition against committing suicide is a Christian superstition that is an anachronism in a post-Christian society. Yet, even if it were granted (and this issue is still a controversial one in the West) that suicide is a basic human right—at least for a human being to whom life has become a burden—there might be good grounds for holding that the exercise of this right should be subject to consideration and endorsement by responsible public authorities. Before giving their consent, the authorities ought to satisfy themselves that suicide is the patient's firm and well-considered choice, and that it is not the desperate whim of a mood of melancholia that might pass. Above all, they must be satisfied that the patient is not contemplating suicide under pressure from other people—and this is a contingency against which the public authorities would have to be on their guard; for anyone who is both old and incapacitated is inevitably a burden on society in general and on his own nearer relatives in particular; and, if he happens to be a man of property, his relatives might have a positive as well as a negative interest in his dying sooner rather than later.

Supposing, however, that the patient has become senile before death has overwhelmed him, the burden of making the choice between keeping him alive and letting him or making him die would fall, not on the patient himself, but on his physician; and, for the physician, the choice would be difficult and the responsibility would be heavy.

[1] See above, "Traditional Attitudes Towards Death", p. 73.

This problem is already exercising the minds and consciences of medical practitioners. Sooner or later, the problem will have to be faced, not only by the physicians, but by the public and by the civil authorities. It would be impolitic and unfair to leave the whole burden to be borne by the physicians unaided. Sooner or later, they will have to be authorised to exercise this formidable choice according to rules worked out, for their guidance, by society in co-operation with the physicians themselves.

9. Death in Twentieth-century Fiction

by Eric Rhode

WILLIAM EMPSON's poem *Ignorance of Death* has the best description I know of the quandary writers find themselves in when faced with this subject. Empson begins by gently mocking various attitudes taken up by some of the populist followers of Marx and Freud. He then goes on to argue:

> Because we have neither hereditary nor direct knowledge of death
> It is the trigger of the literary man's biggest gun
> And we are happy to equate it to any conceived calm.

Inevitably this demolition undermines just about every literary attitude possible and leaves Empson with little to say for himself:

> . . . I feel very blank upon this topic,
> And think that thought important, and proper for anyone to
>   bring up,
> It is one that most people should be prepared to be blank upon.

This argument is effective, even though we may want to question its conclusion. The image of the literary man as a hunter has force. We are very conscious nowadays of how, when a character dies, the author brings about his death: Agatha Christie, say, plots her murders. Any attempt to grieve over these deaths has to be very delicately handled if it is not to appear hypocritical.

Some Victorian authors, above all, killed for effect. A good death-bed scene encouraged piety. (Though no one has satirised this piety more cogently than a Victorian, Lewis Carroll, with his Walrus and Carpenter weeping over the oyster-shells.) It allowed for a moral lesson. It strengthened social and religious values by rallying the faithful and troubling the doubters. But some of these great Victorians had other motives besides those of coercing their readers. Many of them believed in their god-like power to circumscribe the totality of things, even the unknowable experience of death; and they assumed much, not least an after-life. Dickens' treatment of little Nell's death is an often quoted example of this omnipotence. In *Dickens and the Twentieth Century* Gabriel Pearson writes of *The Old Curiosity Shop*:

> "Though the death-scenes are usually singled out for their offensive exploitation of emotion, it is not so much these (they occupy little

space) but the total conception of the child as heroine, martyr, angel and child-bride of the underworld that repels . . . so much significance is being read into her, and all unsupported by anything she does or suffers."

But even if Dickens had substantiated Nell's death and genuinely conveyed her suffering, wouldn't we still feel worried about it? What are his motives in choosing the death of *a child*? In part, probably, because he knew his readers enjoyed such a scene. But there was another motive, I think, which Dickens hints at a few pages after Nell's death, when he refers to the apparent suicide of wicked Quilp.

"He was left to be buried with a stake through his heart in the centre of four lonely roads . . . It was rumoured afterwards that this horrible and barbarous ceremony had to be dispensed with . . . But even here, opinion was divided . . ."

As well it might be. The attack on Quilp is so obvious: it had to be qualified. It is as though Dickens had partially realised how a fictional death can be a pretext for vindictiveness. And this is where our complaint against some of the Victorians must mainly lie: too often their choice of victim is, by too nice a coincidence, the usual object of perverse fantasy or erotic resentment. In this sense, there is little to choose between the deaths of Dickens's little saints and those of Dostoievski's prostitutes.

But literary effect can take a different form. What are we to make of, say, Othello's self-pity in his final grandiose speech? F. R. Leavis has argued that it was consciously planned as a revelation of Othello's egotism: but this sounds like special pleading. The impact of Othello's rhetoric at this point is so strong and so uncriticised by the rest of the play that, in the theatre at least, we may feel it to be a denial of death. Shakespeare, I would suggest, sympathises with the role-playing of his hero; his blank verse is remote from Empson's "blankness". But of course we cannot know what Shakespeare's sympathies were. What we can be sure of is that it is only now, in the 20th century, a critic has felt the need to point out the incompatibility of a certain tragic style—the rhetoric of Seneca—in dealing honestly with the experience of death.

This point is made at length in Tom Stoppard's play, *Rosencrantz and Guildenstern are Dead*, where Hamlet's deliberations are commented on wryly by a very modern Guildenstern. "No, no. It's not like that. Death isn't romantic . . . death is not anything . . . death is . . . not. It's the absence of presence, nothing more . . . the endless time of never coming back . . . A gap you can't see, and when the wind blows through it, it makes no sound."

Stoppard's play catches perfectly a current mood—downbeat,

L

cheekily diffident, blank. No one had done more to establish this mood in contemporary writing than Philip Larkin.

Hours giving evidence
Or birth, advance
On death equally slowly.
And saying so to some
Means nothing; others it leaves
Nothing to be said.

But these responses, like Empson's "blankness" are too easy, too civil. Empson may put forward an argument which undermines most previous treatments of death, but he only manages to replace it with another kind of sentimentality. You would think that this unknowable event which so deeply influences our consciousness and feelings calls for more than a polite reticence. Maybe: yet many thinkers and writers of this country seem to share Empson's reservations. Wittgenstein's view in the *Tractatus* that "Death is not an event in life. Death is not lived through" is closely linked to his conclusion that "Whereof one cannot speak, thereof one must be silent." The abrupt, casual announcements of death in the novels of E. M. Forster imply, I think, a desire only to describe known areas of experience. Wisdom lies in knowing our limitations.

Our reluctance to mourn publicly with funeral rites and black crêpe —a decline in custom which Geoffrey Gorer has charted in *Death, Grief and Mourning*—is probably related to our disinclination at present to treat death ceremoniously in fiction. But removed from the realms of feeling, reduced to a series of facts and statistics about corpses, death becomes a subject for black comedy and macabre elaboration. This inhibiting of the imagination is sometimes ascribed to our paralysing fears of a nuclear holocaust, or to our unworked-through guilt about the concentration camps: the massacres of this century are, it appears, too much for the mind to contemplate. I do not know if, or how, this theory can be tested.

Yet death and mourning need not be tabu subjects in fiction, as Tolstoy's *The Death of Ivan Ilyich* shows. Tolstoy does not strike attitudes. He makes no explicit comment on Ivan's death. His story reads like a series of observations: the art (and the artist's comments) lie in the ordering given to these observations. This honesty is what we might hope for from a good documentary like, for instance, *A Very Easy Death*. Simone de Beauvoir felt very deeply about her mother's death, yet she did not allow feeling to distort her powers of observation and logic. She gathered her evidence and arrived at a consistent conclusion: for her, death was an outrage, degrading and unnatural.

Tolstoy comes to a different conclusion, yet for the most part he uses the same method. In one way, however, *The Death of Ivan Ilyich* is unlike a documentary: it has the freedom to refract experience through the facets of various minds. The first part of the story is concerned with Ivan's colleagues, and their shrewd, smart reactions to the news of his death. Tolstoy's narrative is perceptive, often to the point of cruelty. Ivan's devoted son is observed as being very much like his father: "His eyes were red with weeping and he had the look seen in the eyes of nasty-minded boys of thirteen or fourteen." The narrative then moves back in time and takes on an unexpected warmth as it reviews Ivan's life briefly. Up to this point the evidence, as documentary, is irreproachable; but the third part, which tells of how Ivan felt in the process of dying, is less surely based.

"It occurred to him that what had appeared utterly impossible before—that he had not lived his life as he should have done—might after all be true. It struck him that those scarcely detected inclinations of his to fight against what the most highly placed people regarded as good, those scarcely noticeable impulses which he had immediately suppressed, might have been the real thing and all the rest false."

These observations are convincing. We can imagine how the experience of dying allows a man to remember his life in a disinterested fashion. We can accept, too, that though the truth is painful, its evasion may cause an even greater agony. But then, as Ivan dies, Tolstoy begins to make at least one unacknowledged assumption.

"And all at once it became clear to him that what had been oppressing him and would not go away was suddenly dropping away on all sides. He felt full of pity for them [his family], he must do something to make it less painful for them, release them and release himself from this suffering. 'How right and simple,' he thought. 'And the pain?' he asked himself . 'What has become of it? Where are you pain?'
He began to watch for it.
'Yes, here it is. Well, what of it? Let the pain be.'
'And death? Where is it?'
He searched for his former habitual fear of death and did not find it. 'Where was it? What death?' There was no fear because there was no death either.
In place of death there was light."

Tolstoy assumes that a voluntary renunciation of the world will bring us into harmony with the total renunciation that is death. (An assumption close to that of a play Tolstoy found disagreeable, *King Lear*.) The trouble with this austere conclusion is not that it asks too much of us, but that it is too facile. We recall that Ivan never loved anyone: but what if he had, and what if he had found the world immensely beautiful? How would we feel about the ending to this story if it had been about the death of, say, John Keats? To renounce falsity is one thing, but to renounce voluntarily the whole world—on the grounds that it would be selfish not to—is, rather, to destroy the good with the bad.

Still, we do not go to fiction for a comprehensive insight into what it means to die. What we look for, hopefully, is a formal consistency. *The Death of Ivan Ilyich* is so masterly that we are likely to be convinced by its final pages: but what convinces us is a perfection of style, one man's vision fully embodied, not the sense of its being the last word on the subject. We can be just as much convinced by the Prince of Salina in Giuseppe di Lampedusa's *The Leopard* (1958) who remembers, while dying, the joys life brought him—joys which crystallise into an unexpectedly pleasing image of death.

> "Suddenly amid the group appeared a young woman: slim, in a brown travelling dress and wide bustle, with a straw hat trimmed with a speckled veil which could not hide the sly charm of her face . . . It was she, the creature he yearned for, coming to fetch him; strange that one so young should yield to him; the time for the train's departure must be very close. When she was face to face with him she raised her veil, and there, chaste but ready for possession, she looked lovelier than she ever had when glimpsed in stellar space.
>
> "The crashing of the sea subsided altogether."

This vision, an eroticised form of Mariolatry, is at the furthest extreme from Tolstoy's puritanism; yet in its own way it is almost as persuasive as Ivan's renunciation. It seems that since our last moments can not be predicted, all we can do when dying is to project our own fears and wishes in to the unknown. The writer wins our confidence by giving experience contours which we feel to be true to our sense of life. If he then goes on to put forward a construction on our death-bed thoughts and sensations, the most we can expect from him is consistency. But this extrapolation requires uncommon tact. The impulse to change stance, or to simplify, or to transfigure death symbolically has to be resisted. Even so considerable an artist as Virgina Woolf could fail in this, as we see in the concluding paragraph of *The Waves* (1931):

> "And in me too the wave rises. It swells; it arches its back. I am aware once more of a new desire, something rising beneath me like a proud horse whose rider first spurs and then pulls him back. What enemy do we now perceive advancing against us, you whom I ride now, as we stand pawing this stretch of pavement? It is death. Death is the enemy. It is death against whom I ride with my spear couched and my hair flying back like a young man's . . . I strike my spurs into my horse. Against you I will fling myself, unvanquished and unyielding, O Death!
>
> "The waves broke on the shore."

To see death metaphorically, vaguely, as a mediaeval joust reduces it to something the mind can contain: so Mrs. Woolf, by providing death with a structure, seems to diminish its terror. In fact her metaphor is incongruous, even grotesque, to an extent that suggests that she has seized on an imagery and rhetoric unrelated to feeling. But how can words be adequate to this experience, how can man find a verbal structure or mythology that reflect it truthfully? *Sons and Lovers* (1913) reveals one way of solving this problem, in the scene where D. H. Lawrence writes about the death of Paul Morel's mother. Lawrence encourages us to identify with Paul—who, in fantasy, thinks of himself as the dead woman's lover:

"She lay raised on the bed, the sweep of the sheet from the raised feet was like a clean curve of snow, so silent. She lay like a maiden asleep. With his candle in his hand he bent over her. She lay like a girl asleep and dreaming of her lover . . . She was young again . . . She would wake up. She would lift her eyelids. She was with him still."

The comparison of an elderly woman's corpse with a sleeping maiden would seem as mawkish as Mrs. Woolf's metaphor if it had remained unqualified. Lawrence, however, shows Paul's fantasy to be a delusion:

"He bent and kissed her passionately. But there was a coldness about the mouth. He bit his lip in horror. Looking at her, he felt that he could never, never let her go. No! He stroked the hair from her temples. That, too, was cold. He saw the mouth so dumb and wondering at the hurt. Then he crouched on the floor whispering to her:

" 'Mother, mother!'

"He was still with her when the undertakers came, young men who had been at school with him."

The transformation of a dead mother into a sleeping maiden could only be achieved, for a short while, in one man's mind. Yet its comfort had to be felt before he could be pierced by a sense of loss. The blanket of mythology was needed so that, when it was torn away, the shock of reality could chill him (and us) more intensely. The final sentence is the most poignant, with its hint that Paul and his generation are now alone in being responsible for the world.

The remarkable ending to James Joyce's short story, *The Dead* (1914), has the opposite effect, to its own derogation. It cocoons us beautifully from any sense of loss or isolation, by a resorting to a Virgilian mythology and the pleasures of mellifluence. Gabriel and his wife lie in bed. She has just told him about her first love, Michael Furey, who died young.

"Generous tears filled Gabriel's eyes. He had never felt like that himself towards any woman, but he knew that such a feeling must be love. The tears gathered more thickly in his eyes and in the partial darkness he imagined he saw the form of a young man standing under a dripping tree. Other forms were near. His soul approached the region where dwell the vast hosts of the dead. He was conscious of, but could not apprehend, the wayward and flickering existence. His own identity was fading out into a grey impalpable world: the solid world itself, which those dead had one time reared and lived in, was dissolving and dwindling.

"A few light taps upon the pane made him turn to the window. It had begun to snow again. He watched sleepily the flakes, silver and dark, fall obliquely against the lamplight. The time had come for him to set out on his journey westward. Yes, the newspapers were right: snow was general all over Ireland. It was falling on every part of the dark central plain, on the treeless hills, falling softly upon the Bog of Allen and farther westward, softly falling into the dark mutinous Shannon waves. It was falling, too, upon every part of the lonely churchyard on the hill where Michael Furey lay buried. It lay thickly drifted on the crooked crosses and headstones, on the spears of the little gate, on the barren thorns. His soul swooned slowly as he heard the snow falling faintly through the universe and faintly falling, like the descent of their last end, upon all the living and the dead.''

This is a remarkably fine piece of writing. Yet it is almost too fine, for it appears to have little regard for the needs of mourning. Perhaps this is what was wanted. The snow may fall over Ireland, and Michael Furey may be buried in the graveyard, but Gabriel lies snugly in bed with his wife. His grief, in fact, is as indulgent as the piety of Carroll's Walrus and Carpenter. It is unclear whether Joyce intended to make this point or not, though the implied pun in Furey's name does point up George's lack of passion, and George does seem to represent Ireland's apathy ("snow was general all over Ireland"). But the contrast between the two men is not really felt. The dead are no more than shades, and shades are powerless to hurt or to influence. They, and the aloofly viewed falling snow, are about as substantial as a film image. In *Ulysses* (1937) Joyce was to write about death more sardonically. Yet Bloom's ruminations at Dignam's funeral are, in their own way, as sentimental as Gabriel's.

"Rtststr! A rattle of pebbles. Wait. Stop.

"He looked down intently into a stone crypt. Some animal. Wait. There he goes.

"An obese grey rat toddled along the side of the crypt, moving the pebbles. An old stager: great grandfather: he knows the ropes. The grey alive crushed itself under the plinth, wriggled itself in under it. Good hiding place for treasure.

"Who lives there? Are laid the remains of Robert Emery. Robert Emmet was buried by torchlight, wasn't he? Making his rounds.

"Tail gone now.

"One of those chaps would make short work of a fellow. Pick the bones clean no matter who it was. Ordinary meat for him. A corpse is meat gone bad. Well, and what is cheese? Corpse of milk."

This is an Edgar Allen Poe nightmare in spite of its comic surface and it has, deliberately, all Poe's limitations as an approach to death. Idiomatic, naturalistic, humorous, it establishes the modern note. But this is to anticipate, for I would like us to look first at one other author from before the First World War, whose writing about death has a rare, possibly unique, quality.

Some of Thomas Hardy's poems on death are examples of Empson's literary man at his worst: poems in which Hardy becomes the Imminent Will working out patterns of fate with a morose-seeming glee. His lines on the loss of the *Titanic, The Convergence of the Twain*, are typical of this formula. The catastrophe is distanced and dehumanised. It becomes something to be gloated over.

> Over the mirrors meant
> To glass the opulent
> The sea worms crawl—grotesque, slimed, dumb, indifferent.
>
> Jewels in joy designed
> To ravish the sensuous mind
> Lie lightless, all their sparkles bleared and black and blind.

Unobserved by man, the qualities of objects become interchangeable. The mirrors take on an unreal life and become like jewels, while the jewels become like dulled mirrors. The universe reveals a bizarre process at work (inevitably described as "sinister"), the forces of nature, alien to man. It is an idiosyncratic, brilliant view of a catastrophe, as inhuman as the processes it sets out to describe.

But Hardy could also evoke incomparably the experience of death and mourning. With *Veteris vestigia fiammae* (1913), the twenty-one poems written after the death of his first wife, he created a sustained invocation in which, as R. P. Blackmuir said in *Language as Gesture*, "all that was personal—the private drive, the private grief—was cut away and the impersonal is left bare, an old monument, mutilated and weathered, of that face which only the personal hides . . . a style reduced to anonymity, reduced to riches." Of no poem is this more true than *The Walk*.

> You did not walk with me
> Of late to the hill-top tree
>   By the gated ways,
>   As in earlier days;
>   You were so weak and lame.
> So you never came,

And I went alone, and I did not mind,
Nor think of you as left behind.

I walked up there today
Just in the former way;
   Surveyed around
   The familiar ground
   By myself again:
   What difference then?
Only that underlying sense
Of the look of a room on returning thence.

Any comment on this perfect poem sounds superfluous. But I would like to make one tangential point. Hardy shows us, I think, that you cannot really write "about death", you can only write about a personal experience of mourning. Indeed, the psychoanalyst Melanie Klein has suggested that this experience of mourning is at the basis of all creativity —an idea which Dr. Hannah Segal, the Kleinian analyst, has developed at length in her essay "A Psychoanalytic approach to Aesthetics".[1] No artist had a greater insight into the creative process than Proust, and Proust's insight, she believes, is bound up with his capacity to mourn: that is, his capacity to restore, at whatever the cost in pain, internal figures felt to be destroyed by himself.

"In the last volume of his work Proust describes how at last he decided to sacrifice the rest of his life to writing. He came back after a long absence to seek his old friends at a party, and all of them appeared to him as ruins of the real people he knew—useless, ridiculous, ill, on the threshold of death. Others, he found, had died long ago. And on realising the destruction of a whole world that had been his he decides to write, to sacrifice himself to the re-creation of the dying and the dead. By virtue of his art he can give his objects an eternal life in his work.

"What Proust describes corresponds to a situation of mourning: he sees that his loved objects are dying or dead. Writing a book is for him like the work of mourning in that gradually the external objects are given up, they are reinstated in the ego, and re-created in the book . . . Proust reveals an acute awareness of what I believe is present in the unconscious of all artists: namely, that all creation is really a re-creation of a once loved and once whole, but now lost and ruined object, a ruined internal world and self. It is when the world within us is destroyed, when it is dead and loveless, when our loved ones are in fragments, and we ourselves in helpless despair—it is then that we must re-create our world anew, reassemble the pieces, infuse life into dead fragments, re-create life."

We can see this process at work in Hardy's *The Walk*—where the poet

[1] *New Directions in Psychoanalysis*, Tavistock.

tries to recognise that the outside world continues to exist without his dead wife, yet also tries to reinstate his wife as an internal figure. Hardy goes for a walk alone, but doesn't mind, because he is able to anticipate her welcome on his return. After her death, he has to return to an empty room. Yet he doesn't address the poem to another person. Timidly, hesitatingly, even with a slight rebuke, he continues to converse with his dead wife, and with an intimacy that would be embarrassing to us, the intrusive reader, if it were not untouched by self-pity. The poem is a partial victory against helpless despair; its strength depends on Hardy's implicit belief that the internal presence of his wife cannot die. At the same time the victory is only partial. The loss is terrible. The empty room has to be lived with. Any hope of seeing his wife again as an actual presence has to be relinquished.

Hardy is submerged by the experience of mourning, by reality itself. He is unable to defend himself against pain by aligning himself with the destructive, over-ruling forces, be they of Nature or of the gods. He cannot be, as in his poem about the *Titanic*, an Olympian spectator. He is in no position to create a mythology out of his pain.

It was slightly different for some of the First World War poets. Isaac Rosenberg, for instance, had an exceptional courage in bearing pain, and no man could have exposed himself more to the horror of war. This anguish, and the need to preserve sanity, drove him into finding some positive confrontation to the meaningless slaughter. He sought for more than a political remedy, an answer from the politicians back home. The war was evil, profane; it called for a metaphysical response. And so, almost inevitably, Rosenberg was compelled in *Dead Man's Dump* to contrast brutal images of wheel-crushed faces and crunched bones with an imagery that conveyed the sacredness of life ("soul's sack, God-ancestralled essences").

> The wheels lurched over the sprawled dead
> But pained them not, though their bones crunched;
> Their shut mouths made no moan.
> They lie there huddled, friend and foeman,
> Man born of man, and born of woman;
> And shells go crying over them
> From night till night and now.
>
> Earth has waited for them
> All the time of their growth
> Fretting for their decay:
> Now she has them at last!
> In the strength of their strength
> Suspended—stopped and held.
>
> What fierce imaginings their dark soul lit?
> Earth! Have they gone into you?

Somewhere they must have gone,
And flung on your hard back
Is their soul's sack,
Emptied of God-ancestralled essences.
Who hurled them out? Who hurled?

Rosenberg doesn't linger over the nightmarish aspects of war. You sense rather how he is straining to give the outrage a meaning by relating it to the values of a comprehensive myth. He doesn't allow the impact of death to reduce all values to nothing. The imagination could grasp the terrors of the battlefield if it were allowed to expand and to take in the biblical imagery of the Judeo-Christian tradition. Hell is no longer a metaphor. A gas attack or a louse hunt are indistinguishable from the Dance of Death. In *Strange Meeting* Wilfred Owen can assume the visionary powers of Dante or of Keats (in the second *Hyperion*) without forcing the poem. We are far from Joyce's shades. But we are far, also, from his unruly rat. The horrors of war are to be touched on, briefly, for the main concern isn't with them but with what might have been.

Yet this tension between the sacred and the profane was not to last, and Gabriel's swoon and Bloom's rat were to become typical of the mainstream of post-war writing. We revert to an old romanticism, fashionably glossed by surrealist techniques. Death is seen to resemble the state of falling asleep, of dreams and dream images, of fragmentation and irresponsibility. This fragmentation is often evasive, though much of this kind of writing is richer than a mention of Cocteau's *Orphée*, or of Ionesco's *Amédée* and *Exit the King*, might imply. Even so intelligent a poet as Randall Jarrell, in *The Death of a Ball Turret Gunner* (1945), can reduce the implications of death to nothing more than a violent shock.

From my mother's sleep I fell into the State,
And I hunched in its belly till my wet fur froze.
Six miles from earth, loosed from its dream of life,
I woke to black flak and the nightmare fighters.
When I died they washed me out of the turret with a hose.

The dream of life gives way to the nightmare of war: but how can the dream and nightmare be understood if they remain unrelated to a non-dreamlike state of mind outside them? Keith Douglas's *Vergissmeinnicht* (1943) has the same sort of fragmentation.

But she would weep to see today
how on his skin the swart flies move;
the dust upon the paper eye
and the burst stomach like a cave.

For here the lover and the killer are mingled
who had one body and one heart.

And death who had the soldier singled
has done the lover mortal hurt.

Douglas was influenced by Rosenberg, yet his response to the violence
done to the dead man is not one of outrage. At most it is one of regret.
The loving woman may weep, but there is no sense of profanity, no
relating of the event to a wider vision of what life could be. The final
stanza sounds like Gray's *Elegy*. Its pity is luxuriant, even patronising,
and has the same falsity as Gabriel's sorrow for Michael Furey. In
retrospect, the brutal description of the corpse appears to be an attempt
to compensate for the poet's failure to identify with the lovers. (Imagine
how differently Douglas might have thought of his own epitaph.)

Fragmentation of this kind is characteristic of our culture and, like
the slivers of a broken mirror, it is often inseparable from a sharp-edged
violence. In popular fiction this violence may be admitted quite freely:
in the novels of Mickey Spillane and Ian Fleming, human beings—or
rather puppets representing those things we hate and fear—become as
expendable as cans. The result is, as Geoffrey Gorer calls it, a pornography of death. To some extent, this pornography has always been
with us. But Gorer believes it to be on the increase. "While natural
death becomes more and more smothered in prudery, violent death
has played an ever-growing part in the fantasies offered to mass
audiences—detective stories, thrillers, Westerns, war stories, science
fiction and eventually, horror comics."

But Hardy's poem about the sinking of the *Titanic* shows us that
another kind of dehumanisation is possible, in which the experience of
death is ritualised from purely an aesthetic point of view. This ritual is
liable to be convolute and surreal and, as in T. S. Eliot's *The Waste Land*
(1922), to owe something to the Jacobeans.

> The corpse you planted last year in your garden,
> Has it begun to sprout? Will it bloom this year?
> Or has the sudden frost disturbed its bed?
> Oh keep the Dog far hence, that's friend to men,
> Or with his nails he'll dig it up again!

Dream fragments are woven together in a way that heightens their
unreality. An emblem for this process would be a decomposing corpse
which still resembles the living body, even though it is already being
transformed into something else: the decaying horse's head in Gunter
Grass's *The Tin Drum* "from which small light-green eels were darting
furiously", or, in Peter Redgrove's *Corposant* (1961):

> . . . she rises shrieking from the bone-dry bath
> With bubbling wrists, a lamp and steaming breath,
> Stretching shadows in her room till daybreak
> The rancid larder glimmering from her corpse

Tall and wreathed like moulds or mists,
Spoiling the market value of the house.

In *Second Skin* (1963), John Hawks, a connoisseur of this style, has a
boy play the cello outside the bathroom where his father is about to
commit suicide. "I played with no thought of him, really, but he must
have gagged a little to himself in there, choked a little like a man cough-
ing up blood for the first time as he tried to decide how best to use the
nickel-plated weapon." The boy, it appears, wants to deter his father.
But the effect of the scene is quite different: it is as though he were
leading his father on in a *danse macabre*. "So I played on, phantom
accomplice to his brutal act, and all the while hoping, I think, for
success and pleased with the song." We are reminded of Nero, fiddling
while Rome burned. The artist and death become identified. Death, the
artificer, transmutes his victims into something rich and strange, as does
the artist. So Hawks, in *The Cannibal* (1948):

"There the Merchant, without thoughts of trade, dressed in grey,
still fat, had died on his first day at the front and was wedged, still
standing upright, between two beams, his face knocked backwards,
angry, disturbed. In his open mouth there rested a large cocoon,
protruding, alive, which moved sometimes as if it were alive. The
trousers, dropping about his ankles, were filled with rust and tufts
of hair."

Certainly, at all levels of society there is an unease about the kind of
funeral rites or good manners that should attend a decease. Empson's
"blankness", though it has its attractions, is probably too hard to
maintain when under the stress of grief. In fiction, attempts at "blankness" usually come out as a rather unfeeling impersonality. Gorky may
be able to recall his father's corpse with some shallowness (in *My
Childhood*), but then he is reconstructing the beady-eyed view of a small
boy.

"His feet were bare and the toes were strangely distended, while
the fingers of his hands, resting on his breast, were curled in . . . All
the light had gone out of his still face. But what scared me most was
the snarl his open mouth showed with the teeth bared."

It asks too much of us to remain blank. Impersonality must seem a
shallow response when we compare it to the fullness of Paul Morel's
sorrow, or to the beautiful image Pasternak gives to Yuri Zhivago of his
buried mother sinking deeper and deeper away from him beneath the
ground as the snow falls. It is also liable to tip over into the terrifying or
the comic[1]—or both, as in the ending to Wallace Stevens's *The Emperor
of Ice-Cream* (1923).

[1] As for the comic, see Thomas Mann's *The Magic Mountain* (1924). After a stately description of Joachim's handsome corpse, Mann has the silly, likeable Frau Stöhr demand,
in a slip of the tongue, that the Erotica symphony should be played over his grave.

If her horny feet protrude, they come
To show how cold she is, and dumb.
Let the lamp affix its beam.
The only emperor is the emperor of ice-cream.

This social unease about funeral rites plays into the hands of the satirist, and Roman Catholics like Evelyn Waugh and Muriel Spark have taken full advantage of it. But this satirical tone can be directed towards high ritual also: an agnostic like H. G. Wells can take genial pleasure in showing us how the mourners at the solemn funeral of Mr. Polly's father kept being distracted. "The funeral in the rather cold wind had proved wonderfully appetising . . ." Indeed most comedy about death is less about death than about the proprieties surrounding it. W. H. Auden and William Plomer both find a grim humour in contrasting the gentility of certain women with their ugly deaths, and Joseph Kesselring's *Arsenic and Old Lace* depends on the oddity that two refined old ladies should be mass-murderers who bury their victims with a prayer-book ceremony.

But often this comedy, which seems to be about death, is really based on a denial of the experience of mourning. Such a negativism, made into a fine literary device, characterises much of Samuel Beckett's writing. Malone in *Malone Dies*, for instance, is an old man who relishes the arid, stony nature of his existence. He is incapable of love and so has nothing to lose by dying. At times he tries to imagine an after-life: but it is, at best, a hell similar to his present state. The only vitality he can find in himself refers to language and to verbal games. He likes to tell himself lugubrious, droll stories about moribund characters. Yet as much as he tries to bring these figures back to life, they remain depleted. Malone's fate is a tragic one, though he doesn't realise it. He is controlled by envious, destructive voices in himself that parody all feeling. They mock him and, by implication, mock all of us.

"I shall soon be quite dead at last in spite of all. Perhaps next month. Then it will be the month of April or of May. For the year is still young, a thousand little signs tell me so. Perhaps I am wrong, perhaps I shall survive Saint John the Baptist's Day and even the Fourteenth of July, festival of freedom. Indeed I would not put it past me to pant on to the Transfiguration, not to speak of the Assumption."

But these destructive voices cannot totally defeat Malone. An element of hope remains. Life continues to flicker in him, and he continues to tell his drab stories. The besieged fortress won't fall. This precarious balance between hope and utter despair is the principal source of irony in *Malone Dies*.

The narrator in Italo Svevo's *The Confessions of Zeno* (1923) is less given over to despair and so more capable of fighting it. The chapter on the death of his father is genuinely a comedy about death, unique in tone. Like Adolphe in Constant's novel, Zeno is a confused and vacillating egoist. But like Adolphe also, he is determined to be truthful about himself, however much it may damage his self-esteem. As his father dies, he struggles to respond appropriately to the gravity of the situation. He loves his father, and his father exists in the novel as a credible and whole human being—we can understand why Zeno should dread his loss. But Zeno's mind wanders. The knowledge of death and mourning is a voyage into alien seas which he will do anything to postpone. He finds himself plagued by his hatred of doctors, his hypochondria, his resolution—frequently made, and just as frequently broken—to give up cigarettes. These trivia oppress his mind; they take on the same seriousness as his anxieties about death. He is horrified by his weakness: at the same time he is conscious of how ludicrous he is being. He tries to make his (and our) amusement seem natural by assuming a matter-of-fact voice. He tries to be civil, to take up an Empsonian stance. Literary artifice is allowed to distance the incipient hysteria. But he is too honest to his feelings to maintain this position. In dying, his father falls and strikes him across the face. As a rational and civilised person Zeno is convinced this blow was unintended. Yet he cannot stop the incongruity of this accident—that it should occur at a moment of most blinding pain—from embittering his grief.

Malone and Zeno are lonely stoics; in this sense they are typically figures of our time. Society provides them with no protection against the impact of death. They reject its forms of mourning and they reject the religious consolations of a former century. They try to get by on irony alone. But is there a no more positive way in which agnostic men can face the thought of dying?

Two novels by Albert Camus—*The Outsider* (1940) and *The Plague* (1947)—concern themselves heroically with this problem. Meursault in *The Outsider* is a man who, unlike Malone, is capable of enjoyment. He lives in and for the world. But at his mother's funeral and at the prospect of his impending execution for a gratuitous murder he feels nothing but indifference. As Camus shows, this indifference is a source of contentment: it brings Meursault into harmony with what he believes is the "benign indifference" of the universe. In *The Outsider* "blankness" is given a metaphysical perspective.

"I couldn't feel an interest in a dead girl. This seemed to me quite normal; just as I realised people would soon forget me once I was dead. I couldn't even say that this was hard to stomach; really, there's no idea to which one doesn't get acclimatized to in time."

Meursault is less a stoic than someone who is numb to the needs of mourning; and society, in the form of the law courts and the press, feels obliged to label him a monster. But Camus is writing about more than one exceptional case. He brings together the moral questionings of Gide (the gratuitous murder) and the moral implications of the Hemingway style to build up a composite picture of a hero of our time. We are asked to identify with Meursault. The universe is shown to be indifferent; men are shown to be like robots.

"I saw some Arabs lounging against the tobacconist's window. They were staring silently in the special way these people have—as if we were blocks of stone or dead trees."

As for the European journalist in court: "What held my attention were his eyes, very pale clear eyes, riveted on me, though not betraying any definite emotion. For a moment I had an odd impression, as if I were being scrutinised by myself."

Yet in spite of its power, *The Outsider* doesn't convince as a portrait of a new kind of man. Like Sartre's *La Nausée*, it remains a study in one man's psychopathology: it covers only one small aspect of ourselves. *The Plague* is more ambitious. A whole city—Oran—and not one intelligence is at its centre. There is a wider range of response than in *The Outsider*: and most of the people who die, or learn to live with death, are less unusual than Meursault. The plague itself is universalised, related to many previous catastrophes and tyrannies. Camus sees it as a form of test. It can turn men into animals or drive them into extreme types of behaviour; yet it can also, like the experience of being tortured by the Gestapo, reveal admirable qualities. Men can die in ways that Camus thinks of as virtuous.

Specifically, he admires those who refuse to find a reconciliation in death, those who resist death with defiance, and those whose thoughts remain to the end with the living:

"The egoism of love made them immune to the general distress and, if they thought of the plague, it was only in so far as it might threaten to make their separation eternal. Thus in the very heart of the epidemic they maintained a saving indifference, which one was tempted to call composure. Their despair saved them from panic, thus their misfortune had a good side. For instance, if it happened that one of them was carried off by disease, it was almost always without having had time to realise it. Snatched suddenly from his long, silent communion with a wraith of memory, he was plunged straightaway into the densest silence of all. He'd no time for anything."

Camus gives us an example of each of the three ways of dying that most impress him. The priest Paneloux almost defeats the plague virus in himself by the intensity of his faith. "Even at the height of his fever Paneloux's eyes kept their blank serenity and when, next morning, he was found dead, his body drooping over the bedside, they betrayed nothing. Against his name the index-card recorded: 'Doubtful case'." The writer Tarrou fights death by refusing to compromise with it through evasion or self-pity. But the most significant death of all is that of a child—significant because, though the child has no conscious philosophy, he is able to fight death as stubbornly as any adult.

"They had already seen children die—for many months now death had shown no favouritism—but they had never watched a child's agony minute by minute, as they now had been doing since daybreak. Needless to say, the pain inflicted on these innocent victims had always seemed to them to be what in fact it was: an abominable thing. But hitherto they had felt its abomination in, so to speak, an abstract way; they had never had to witness over so long a period the death-throes of an innocent child.

"And, just then, the boy had a sudden spasm, as if something had bitten him in the stomach, and uttered a long, shrill wail. For a moment that seemed endless he stayed in a queer, contorted position, his body racked by convulsive tremors; it was as if his frail frame were bending before the fierce breath of the plague, breaking under the reiterated gusts of fever. Then the storm-wind passed, there came a lull and he relaxed a little; the fever seemed to recede, leaving him gasping for breath on a dank, pestilential shore, lost in a languor that already looked like death. When for the third time the fiery wave broke on him, lifting him a little, the child curled himself up and shrank away to the edge of the bed, as if in terror of the flames advancing on him, licking his limbs. A moment later, after tossing his head wildly to and fro, he flung off the blanket. From between the inflamed eyelids big tears welled up and trickled down the sunken, leaden-hued cheeks. When the spasm had passed, utterly exhausted, tensing his thin legs and arms on which, within forty-eight hours, the flesh had wasted to bone, the child lay flat, racked on the tumbled bed, in a grotesque parody of crucifixion."

We are far here from the notion of the writer killing off his characters for literary effect. The quality of this passage has the power to suggest that Camus had observed the death of a child and later felt compelled to record the experience, however searing the recollection of it might have been. Its authenticity can be gauged by comparing it to the self-regarding account of another small boy's death—Nepomuk, in Thomas Mann's *Doctor Faustus*. Mann's literary, indulgent attitude to this death is evident from a note made in his diary after reading this chapter to his family. "I read this sweet and fearful episode. It is probably the most poetic moment the novel attains, and I read it with an emotion which the listeners obviously felt. We spoke a great deal about the ethereal and heartbreaking incident."

Camus, on the other hand, is identified with his subject. He doesn't attitudinise or beautify. Death is a total outrage, no pretext for a fine style. In this, Camus is in agreement with Simone de Beauvoir.

PART THREE

Frontiers of Speculation

1. Perspectives from Time, Space and Nature

by Arnold Toynbee

In a previous section[1] it has been noticed that, in the once Christian Western world since the 17th century, the progress of physical science has reduced man's stature and has diminished his importance in Western man's eyes. Science has revealed to us first that our planet, then that our sun, and finally that even our galaxy is not the centre of the physical universe, as our Christian ancestors had believed our planet to be. Science has also revealed to us that, though our ancestors became human perhaps a million years ago, and were not created in 4004 B.C., one million years is as infinitesimally short a span of time as five or six thousand years on the time-scale of the age of our solar system and the vaster time-scale of the physical universe as a whole. These progressive scientific discoveries have made man seem puny and insignificant. This was the effect of them on Pascal's mind, though, in his generation, modern science was still in its infancy and though Pascal himself rallied, sophisticatedly but decidedly, to his ancestral Christianity.

However, one characteristic of modern science is that it is perpetually on the move and is constantly gathering speed. As it forges ahead, it keeps on revising its picture of the universe; and, as this picture changes, our impression of man's place in the universe changes with it. In our time, science has made two major new discoveries. In the field of physical nature we have become aware of relativity; in the field of psychology, science has laid bare, in the human psyche, the abyss of the unconscious beneath the thin crust of consciousness and will. Both these discoveries are still too recent for us to be able to forecast their eventual effect on our view of man's place in the universe; but already we can perhaps venture on two guesses. These two discoveries will not restore man to the central position that he has occupied in the Zoroastrian-Jewish-Christian-Muslim scheme of things. At the same time, they may not leave man looking quite so puny and insignificant as he looked from the 17th till the 19th century.

The theory of relativity has made us aware that an astronomer observing motions in the physical universe, like an anthropologist observing behaviour in a human tribe, is something more than a mere observer; he is an actor as well; for his observation produces an effect, not only in his own mind, but on its object. The tribe's behaviour changes when it comes under the anthropologist's eye. The mutual

[1] "Changing Attitudes Towards Death in the Modern Western World", p. 122 ff.

relations and relative speeds of the heavenly bodies change when these come under the eye of an observer perched on any one of them. In fact, the observer is not only an actor; he is an actor who plays a creative part in the drama of which he is a spectator. The physical universe has no centre and no fixed points. The star on which the astronomer happens to find himself stationed is on the move itself while he is observing the motions of other stars within his ken. Any star habitable by an astronomer is as good—or as bad—an observation-post as any other. There may be innumerable stars habitable and inhabited by astronomers in a physical universe that may be infinite; and, since even those habitable stars that are nearest to each other may be myriads of light-years distant from each other, an astronomer on any one of them may be, like Alexander Selkirk, "monarch of all he surveys", though he may be only one of many such monarchs scattered about in the universe. Man on his planet is one monarch who surveys the universe, and, in surveying it, modifies it and thus, in a sense, creates it. The discovery of relativity has not restored to man the centrality and uniqueness with which he was credited in the pre-Copernican and pre-Newtonian picture; but it has at least put him on an equal footing with other possible denizens of the universe who may share with man his capacity for playing the role of a creator in the act of taking observations. Thus, unless and until science takes yet another dramatic turn, we, in our generation, can feel rather more sanguine about man's position in—and action on—space-time than our parents and grandparents could in the light of their generations' scientific knowledge.

If the discovery of relativity has slightly re-enhanced our estimate of man's significance in the physical universe, the discovery of the sub-conscious abyss of the human psyche has revealed that, in the psychic medium, a single human being is a universe in himself.

We are still as far as ever from understanding the nature of the relation between the psychic and the physical aspect of reality. We know merely that these two aspects coexist not only in man but in every other species of living creature on this planet, and it is possible that they may coexist in everything in the universe. In all forms of life on earth, the coexistence of a psychic and a physical component seems to be a necessary enabling condition for the maintenance of life itself. At any rate, the earthly life of a terrestrial living creature comes to an end when its psychic and physical elements part company.

The human brain is the human psyche's physical instrument, vehicle, installation, or apparatus. We do not really know what we mean by these and other words which we use as labels for a relation which we do not yet understand. We do know, however, that, as a physical structure, a human brain is comparable to the whole physical universe in the number of its constituents, in the speed of their movements, and in the complexity of these movements' interrelations. We also know that there is a correlation between the brain and the psyche in their respective structures and capacities, each in its own medium.

As for the exploration of the human psyche, the pioneers who, in our time, have broken through the crust of consciousness and will into the underlying abyss of the subconscious and the irrational have already sounded depth below depth without having yet come within sight of anything that looks like rock-bottom. (In Western languages, it is virtually impossible to describe the psychic universe otherwise than in physical terms used metaphorically. The speakers of Western languages have, for the most part, so far, been extroverts; so these languages have developed only a meagre psychic vocabulary hitherto.)

Meanwhile, the deeper the level of the psychic abyss that our explorers of the psychic universe plumb, the less personal the character of each successively explored level turns out to be. Though the surface through which the psychologists make their borings is a personality, the lowest of the levels that they have reached already appear not to be the private property of this particular personality or of any other. The lowest-lying psychic materials that the psychologists have succeeded in dredging up to the level of consciousness so far seem to be samples of a "collective unconscious". How far does this collectivity extend? Is it common to all human beings only? Is it common to all living creatures on this planet? Is it common to the whole of the universe in its psychic aspect? If each of these questions in turn were to receive an affirmative answer, we should be coming near, in terms of investigation, to the Hindu intuition "Thou art That"—the "Thou" being the dweller in the innermost of a human soul and the "That" being the Ultimate Spiritual Reality behind the universe. In terms of action, we might find our intellectual discoveries in this psychic field inclining us to follow the Buddha's prescription of strenuous spiritual exercises for reducing the self to the point of attaining nirvana—a state of extinguishedness in which selfhood has been burnt away, leaving intact, but now cleansed, the underlying Spiritual Reality on which selfhood, in the Buddha's belief, is an unfortunate excrescence.

Elsewhere in this book,[1] it has been pointed out that the Hindu philosophers' intuition and the Buddha's prescription anticipated, by about 2,500 years, the pioneer work of the first generation of Western psychologists. But, of course, the discovery of Ultimate Spiritual Reality and of the path by which a human being may find his way towards it by spiritual action has not been an Indian monopoly. Mystics nurtured in a number of different philosophies and religions at many different times and places have converged from many quarters on the same point by means of the same kind of spiritual travail.

The similarity of the findings of modern Western psychologists, Hindu philosophers, and mystics of many schools points to an answer to the riddle of the sequel to death. These findings suggest that death's

[1] See p. 71.

sequel is neither annihilation nor personal immortality, but is a re-merger in an Ultimate Spiritual Reality from which the human personality that lives and dies has temporarily detached itself by a *tour de force*—purchasing a partial independence from its source at the cost of a partial alienation from it.

If this is the truth, the intuition of it has been shared with the philosophers and the mystics by the poets. This is what Euripides is intimating when he puts the question:

"Who knows if to be alive is not really to die, and if dying does not count in the nether world as being alive?"[1] "Who knows if this experience that we call dying is not really living, and if living is not really dying?"[2]

In the mouth of Euripides, this question is significant; for Euripides was a leading exponent of the rationalism that, in his generation, was being adopted by a sophisticated minority in the Hellenic world as a sub-stitute for traditional religion.

It is equally significant to see the same intuition finding vent in poems written in the Western world since the rise of modern Western science. Two English examples are a poem by Henry Vaughan (1621-1695) and a more famous poem by William Wordsworth (1770-1850). The theme of these two poems is the same. It is an expansion of the theme that is implicit in Euripides' question. Life in the form of a human personality on earth is an offshoot of a different and better kind of life on another plane. Life on earth is also a trajectory, in which the mundane zenith, a human being's so-called "prime of life", is actually the spiritual nadir. The child retains recollections of its true home that fade when the grown man, at the height of his powers, becomes engross-ed in "the cares of this world".[3] When, however, the supposed zenith has been passed, and life's trajectory is now descending through old age towards death, childhood's temporarily obscured awareness of our true home may be recaptured. Vaughan has called his slighter poem, appropriately, *The Retreat*. Wordsworth, bemused by his ancestral Christian tradition, has called his mightier ode *Intimations of Immortality*, though, in truth, both his and Vaughan's and Euripides' intimations are, not of immortality, but of nirvana.

The essence of Vaughan's short poem is conveyed in three couplets:

Happy those early days, when I
Shined in my angel-infancy,
Before I understood this place
Appointed for my second race . . .
O, how I long to travel back
And tread again that ancient track.

[1] Euripides from his lost play *Polyidus*.
[2] Euripides from his lost play *Phrixus*.
[3] Mark, iv, 19

The essence of Wordsworth's longer poem is difficult to convey without quoting every word; for this poem is profound, and the lofty level of its inspiration is sustained from beginning to end. I make the following extracts from it at my peril.

Our birth is but a sleep and a forgetting;
The soul that rises with us, our life's star,
    Hath had elsewhere its setting
    And cometh from afar . . .

O, joy that in our embers
Is something that doth live,
That Nature yet remembers
What was so fugitive . . .

The memories for which the poet raises his "song of thanks and praise" are:

    Those shadowy recollections
    Which, be they what they may,
Are yet the fountain-light of all our day,
Are yet a master-light of all our seeing;
    Uphold us, cherish, and have power to make
Our noisy years seem moments in the being
Of the eternal silence; truths that wake
    To perish never . . .

Hence, in a season of calm weather
    Though inland far we be,
Our souls have sight of that immortal sea
    Which brought us hither,
    Can in a moment travel thither,
And see the children sport upon the shore
And hear the mighty waters rolling evermore.

Wordsworth must have been very familiar with Vaughan's poem; he may have known Euripides' lines. It seems unlikely that he was influenced by Indian philosophy; yet, in his intimations, the Indian note is not only unmistakable; it is predominant.

The Ultimate Reality may indeed be "the eternal silence" of a nirvana that is the prelude to birth as well as the sequel to death. Yet, if nirvana is ultimate and is also blissful, why has its silence ever been broken? Why emanation, why creation, why *maya*, why karma? Plotinus spent a lifetime in exercising his subtle mind on this question without finding a satisfying answer. Marcion saw in creation the act of a malevolent god, but he was also aware of the presence and the power of love, and he imagined the intervention of a second god, a saviour god, to account for that.

If the truth about life and death is obscure, the reason for life and death is still more enigmatic. "Verily we are Allah's, and to Him do we return".[1] If we translate into non-personal terms the Prophet Muhammad's vision of Ultimate Reality as a divine person, and if we substitute for this anthropomorphic image of Ultimate Reality Wordsworth's simile of an "immortal sea", we might think of a human person—which is the only kind of person that we know—as being a wave that rises and falls, or a bubble that forms and bursts, on the "immortal sea's" surface. Like a wave or a bubble, a human person is ephemeral in himself; yet, also like a wave or a bubble, a person may be a temporary form assumed by something that is abiding. The person who lives and dies in a psychosomatic organism on this planet may be a manifestation of Eternal Spiritual Reality. But, if this is what we are, we have to live and die without ever knowing in what relation we stand to the Ultimate Reality that is the source and destination of our being. In our ephemeral human life on earth, are we accidents that have no meaning in terms of this reality from which, as persons, we are temporarily differentiated? Or are we truants, who have alienated ourselves from the source of our being by a perverse *tour de force* that we cannot sustain beyond the brief span of a human life's trajectory? Or is a human life on earth a mission on which a "Thou" that is identical with the "That" has been seconded from the Eternal Reality for some purpose (in human terms) which does have some significance?

We do not know. We awake to consciousness in a situation that is, and remains, a mystery to us. This is a hard price to pay for being human. Yet would any human being have rejected the offer of life if he had been warned in advance of its hardness and had been given the option of declining to be born?

[1] *Qur'an*, Surah ii, verse 151. Cp. ii, 43; vi, 60; x, 4.

2. Attitudes to Death in the Light of Dreams and other 'Out-of-the-body' Experience

by ROSALIND HEYWOOD

THIS CHAPTER and the following one on "Death and Psychical Research" are both concerned with the questions: What is death? Why do so many Westerners fear it? Is the idea that "mind" and body die together any less of an assumption than that some spark of "mind" survives the death of the body? Is there a chance that certain "out-of-the-body" experiences, which often reduce the fear of death in those who have them, may be indications that it does not lead to extinction but to a wider life?

However impersonally these questions are asked, to ask them at all implies an attitude, that the nature of death is not yet settled. To the orthodox materialist such an attitude is childish folly, for he *knows* that mind must die with body since they are but two aspects of the same thing. To imagine anything else is no more than sentimental wishful thinking. What point can there be in considering evidence to the contrary, however plausible? There *must* be some other explanation for it. But evidence does not cease to exist because it is ignored, and there are a number of what may at least be regarded as hints and clues that the nature of death is still an open question. The difficulty is to study them apart from wishful thinking—either way, for some people long for oblivion as others do for survival. How are we to be sure that we do not interpret the hints and clues in accordance with our wishes?

The fear of death

It may help to begin by trying to disentangle the various aspects of the fear of death. One is clearly the useful biological instinct to survive, which drives a rabbit to flee from a fox, and a man to evade an oncoming car, even if he is on his way to jump over Westminster Bridge. Another is fear of the process of dying. There are hints that, when it comes to the point, this is less painful than is widely assumed. In a recent American survey, doctors and nurses reported that "fear was not a dominant emotion among the dying", and that in their experience "elated moods occurred in about one in twenty dying patients".[1] This elation can be

[1] Karlis Osis, *Deathbed Observations by Doctors and Nurses*, Monograph, Parapsychology Foundation, New York, 1961.

very moving. I remember being in charge of a dying patient who was delirious and in great pain. Suddenly he became calm and his face lit up. "Oh," he cried joyfully, "The Light! the Light! Oh, there's Annie —and John!" I am in no position to say whether he did see Annie and John, but he certainly had the experience of doing so, and it made him die happy.[1]

But one must not paint too rosy a picture. Sometimes the fear of death endures till near the end. Canon John Pearce-Higgins told me of how he had been able to help a frightened man to face his impending death with greater calm. "But when I was called back, at night, for a second visit," he said, "a huge night sister fixed me with a menacing stare and said, 'Now, Padre, no talking to the patient about death. They can't take it.' "

Death today may be harder to "take" for two reasons. It is less familiar in everyday life than it used to be; fewer of the young die, and the old are usually whisked off to hospital, instead of departing surrounded by their own families and seen out by priests who express no doubt about what they will find on the other side. The decay of religion has made death even more of an unknown quantity; the materialist goes, with nothing to cling to, into the dark and annihilation. It is hard to discover to what extent annihilation, as such, is dreaded on the mental level by the average healthy person. At the beginning of the century the American Society for Psychical Research put out a questionnaire entitled "Human Sentiment in regard to a Future Life", and the answers indicated far less enthusiasm for the idea of survival than had been expected. A few years ago I was told that a distinguished critic had refused to review a scholarly book weighing the evidence for survival on the ground that even did it contain watertight proof of it, his readers would not be interested. And an editor was reported as being so shocked at the idea that he thought it would be his duty to censor any account of such proof in his paper. When I asked a Freudian analyst his view of such an attitude he replied that it was only those people's way of repressing their own fear of death.

Nowadays that fear may well be increased by the shadow of the great mushroom which the old have hung over the human race as a whole. And it does not seem very odd that some of the young should try to escape from that shadow and the raucous, ruthless and, so the old often tell them, meaningless world which lies beneath it. Nor, perhaps, is it odd that they take whatever means of escape come to hand, from psychedelic drugs to transcendental meditation, especially when they find that those means sometimes at least lead to temporary bliss.

One indication that the fear of death is widespread, but repressed, is that in personal life its mention is so often tabu. To say of some future project, "Well, I'm 73, I don't have to bother about that," brings the

[1] There are reports of many such experiences both in Dr. Osis' monograph and in an earlier book by the physicist, Sir William Barratt, entitled *Deathbed Visions*, Methuen, 1926.

almost certain reply, "Don't be so morbid!" In his recent book, *Death, Grief and Mourning in Contemporary Britain*, Geoffrey Gorer points out that as only a minority of British people practise religion or pray, the majority have no guide as to how to behave in the face of death. In consequence, a number of people end up either in preoccupation with trivialities or the apathy of despair.

Another symptom of repressed anxiety about death may be the widespread interest in violence and destruction—at a safe distance, in a book, a film, or Vietnam. Anxiety must find a safety valve somehow. A popular newspaper recently portrayed the bloody corpse of a man who had just been shot in a quiet English suburban street, and underneath the photograph was a neighbour's comment: "I was stunned. I thought that sort of thing only existed in books or films."

Who are the priests' successors?

To some extent the psychiatrist and analyst have taken over the task of helping the anxiety-ridden to face their certain death—excluding, perhaps, the school of thought which allays anxiety with pills and electric shocks, but does not necessarily seek for its cause. As everybody knows, that great man, Freud, was the first to lay bare the widespread hidden anxiety about death, which he took to imply extinction. In a sense the Freudian outlook may almost be said to have turned traditional religion with its emphasis on survival upside-down. This, for instance, is how Dr. Ernest Jones, Freud's influential friend and follower, saw the picture:

"I would say that in the realms of thought and action the distinction between men who believe that mental processes or beings can exist independently of the physical world, and those who reject this belief, [is] the most significant of all classifications: and *I should measure any hope of further evolutionary progress by the passage of men from one class to the other.*" (My italics, R. H.)[1]

The idea of Thanatos, the death instinct, which Freud also originated, has become almost as much part of the mental climate as his idea of Eros, the life instinct (which of course includes sex). But Dr. Stafford Clark has pointed out that in fact he did not develop the concept of Thanatos as he did that of Eros, but left its "source . . . its impetus, its . . . objects relatively undiscussed".[2] And here we may leave it too, for the majority of psychologists never accepted it and most of his own successors now seem to look on the concept as a defence on Freud's own part against the torture of *not knowing* . . . better believe the worst and have done; whereas we are assuming in this chapter that the answer to death may not yet have been found.

[1] Ernest Jones, *Free Associations*, Hogarth Press, 1959, chapter 3, p. 59.
[2] David Stafford Clark, *What Freud Really Said*, Macdonald, 1965, and Pelican Books, 1966.

In our search for clues to that answer we turn to Jung. It will be remembered that, in contrast to Freud's sombre materialism and concern with the individual psyche, he widened the scope of his own psychology to study each psyche in relation to what he postulated as the great collective unconscious of mankind, and, even further, to the infinite. He wrote in his autobiography, "The decisive question for man is: 'Is he related to something infinite or not?' . . . Only if we know that the thing which truly matters is the infinite can we avoid fixing our interest upon futilities."[1]

Dreams and death

Like Freud, Jung made a profound study of dreams, but for him they revealed far more than the individual's attitude to death; they were linked with universal primordial images, which were the source of all our unconscious thoughts, including those of life after death. In his view such thoughts were also universal. Might there conceivably be subconscious knowledge behind them? From personal experience Jung came to think that at least part of the psyche is not subject to space and time; hence "the unconscious has better sources of knowledge than the conscious mind, which has only sense perception to guide it". In consequence, "we are dependent for our myth of life after death upon the meagre hints of dreams and similar spontaneous revelations from the unconscious". But he added a warning. "We cannot attribute to these allusions the value of knowledge, let alone proof. They can however, give the probing intellect the raw material which is indispensable for its vitality."

Jung clearly felt that his own probing intellect had been given a good deal of raw material. "Not only my own dreams, but also occasionally those of others, helped to shape, revise and confirm my views on life after death." He did not particularly wish for such a life, but he said that as ideas about it came to him unbidden he was not prepared to repress them out of prejudice.

Like the rest of us, Jung found it hard to conceive what life after death might be like—"We cannot visualise another world ruled by quite other laws"—but he still looked on the question of a future existence as being, for most people, "so urgent, so immediate and also so ineradicable   that we must endeavour to form some sort of view about it."[2]

For him this view had to be more than a belief. "A belief to me," he wrote, "is only the phenomenon of belief, not the content of a belief. This I must see revealed empirically in order to accept it."

[1] Carl Jung, *Memories, Dreams, Reflections,* Collins, and Routledge and Kegan Paul, 1963. The following quotations from Jung are all taken from this book, mainly from the chapter "Life after Death".

[2] That the question of *post-mortem* existence is ineradicable is illustrated in Edgar Hertzog's book, *Psyche and Death* (Hodder and Stoughton, 1966). This compares myths about death from prehistoric times onwards with unconscious attitudes which resemble them as revealed in dreams today.

Here are two examples of dreams—his own—which influenced Jung's outlook.

"I had another experience of the evolution of the soul after death when—about a year after my wife's death—I suddenly awoke one night and knew that . . . I had spent a whole day with her. She was engaged on studies of the Grail. That seemed significant to me for she had died before completing her work on this subject. Interpretation on the subjective level, that my anima had not yet finished with the work she had to do, yielded nothing of interest; I know quite well that I have not finished with that. But the thought that my wife was continuing after death to work on her further spiritual development —however that may be conceived—struck me as meaningful and held a measure of reassurance for me."

Of course, Jung did not allow himself to take this dream literally. He commented on it that

"ideas of this sort give a wrong picture . . . like the construction of a four dimensional model out of a three dimensional body . . . Mathematics goes to great pains to create expressions for relationships which pass empirical comprehension. In much the same way it is all-important for a disciplined imagination to build up images of intangibles by logical principles and on the basis of empirical data, that is, on the evidence of dreams."

The following dream illustrates Jung's preoccupation with the problem of the Self and the Ego, the Self conceived as existing outside physical time and space. (If so, might this mean beyond physical death?) In the dream he entered a small hillside chapel and was surprised to find no image of the Virgin on the altar, but instead a wonderful flower arrangement. In front of the altar sat a Yogi in deep meditation, and Jung saw that he had Jung's own face. At this he woke up, profoundly frightened, and thought, "Aha, so he is meditating me. He has a dream and I am it." And he felt that when the Yogi awakened, he himself would no longer be.

"The aim of this dream," wrote Jung, "is to reverse the relationship between ego-consciousness and the unconscious, and to represent the unconscious as the generator of the empirical personality. This reversal suggests that in the opinion of the 'other side' our unconscious existence is the real one and our conscious world . . . an apparent reality constructed for a specific purpose, like a dream which seems a reality as long as we are in it."

When searching for reasonably short dreams relating to death from some further source, there leapt into my mind two of my own from the far past which had made so deep an impression on me that I had never forgotten them. Being personal, I record them with diffidence, but they have the advantage that in the first case my knowledge of theories about the unconscious was certainly nil, and in the second, to the best of my recollection, if not nil it was embryonic.

The first dream illustrates subconscious preoccupation with the idea of death in a young child, for it came repeatedly at the age of six. Night after night my sister's high chair turned into a devil, chased me across the nursery floor, and caught me. At that I died—and awoke shaking with a terror which I kept to myself. No good waking Nanny to tell her that one had died. She would only say, "Nonsense, child! Shut up and go to sleep." How many children do the same?

In the second dream (I was now grown up) I found myself standing at the back corner of a very large schoolroom. It was filled with rows of seats, all occupied by sad-looking men in black overcoats and bowler hats, and in front of them on a bier lay a majestic figure in white priestly robes. As I watched, the men all got up and filed sadly past the figure and out at the far door—and as they disappeared the figure itself began swiftly, revoltingly, to turn green and horrible, to decompose. I wanted to fly, but I couldn't. To leave that poor decomposing "thing" quite alone would be too cruel. So, fighting sickened revulsion, I ran across the schoolroom, bent down and kissed it, crying, "I love you, I love you!" At that, instantly, it became fresh, clean, alive, wholesome, happy, and said, "You see, I was deserted by humanity." Then I woke up, deeply moved and with the sense of having experienced something of importance, though I had no idea what it was. It may be of psychological interest that only when the dream floated into my mind as apposite for this paper did a possible interpretation dawn on me.

Much is being learnt about dreaming nowadays, and research in America has shown that it is necessary even from the physiological point of view. A contemporary psychiatrist, Dr. Colin McGlashan, has recently asked an interesting question: What is the dreaming mind?, in contrast to the usual one: What does it do? He suggests that one of its functions is to be an instrument of liberation, which can release new forms of awareness, and he likens it to "a file smuggled into the space-time cell where man lies captive; a cell whose walls and ceiling are our five senses and whose warders are the inflexible concepts of logic".[1] That file, he thinks, might help man to escape, not into a cosy heaven, but into a world which is fluid, ambiguous, paradoxical, and of which, indeed, he is afraid. One gets a picture of a child, poking one toe into an unknown turbulent sea.

Out-of-the-body experience

The idea of dreaming as an instrument of liberation into a wider world leads on to a more or less related type of experience which may also be one of those revelations from the unconscious which Jung looked

[1] Colin McGlashan, *The Savage and Beautiful Country*, Chatto and Windus, 1966, p. 122.

on as containing possible clues to the nature of death. This experience is of the apparent temporary release of consciousness from the physical body, into what, non-committally, may be called ultra-physical realms. But how, is the obvious question, does that differ from ordinary dreaming? So far the only answer is that many experients insist that it does: surroundings seem to exist in their own right and to be more coherent and rational than in "ordinary" dreams; also consciousness feels enhanced and the sense of "reality" even greater than in physical existence. And this holds, they say, not only during the experience but when it is looked back upon later. William Gerhardi declared that if the whole world told him that his out-of-the-body experience had been a dream, he would remain unconvinced.[1] Perhaps the answer is that, as Jung, McGlashan and others have suggested, not all dreams are "ordinary", mere subjective fantasies, but that from both sleep and waking consciousness men can pass into other realms of being.

Of course, when people claim to have had out-of-the-body experience the outside enquirer has no means of proving that they are not suffering from delusions or simply romancing, for they go forth alone with no companion to confirm their tales and no mundane events to mark their journey. And yet such great men as William James have dared to envisage that certain types of such experience may bring more information about man's total environment and his own nature than any other line of exploration.

Delusion or exploration, out-of-the-body experience seems to be an enduring factor in human nature, since it has been reported down the ages and throughout the world, quite often by outstanding people, independently and in very similar terms. Some pre-scientific cultures took such reports at their face value to indicate the actual existence of another world which the soul goes to inhabit after death and which the living can visit, either in dream or in an altered state of consciousness induced by training, ritual or psychedelic drugs. In some remote communities these beliefs still hold, and regular "travellers" are looked up to as guides and seers. Obviously in our sophisticated materialist culture such beliefs would go underground, but according to Jung they still persist in the unconscious, and, if so, that may help to account for the fact that apparent out-of-the-body experiences are still reported by some educated persons who are ready to brave the laughter they can evoke. Recent pilot studies hint that they may be less rare than is assumed, though to confirm this is not easy since more diffident experients fear that their mention might lead to the psychiatrist's couch. At the same time, the extent to which they are now being sought artificially through drugs suggests that, as well as providing an escape from fear and suffering, they may also fulfil a need for wider contact with reality than that supplied by the sensory experience which today

[1] William Gerhardi, *Resurrection*, Cassells, 1934. A vivid account of Gerhardi's experience is given in this book.

is usually assumed to be all there is. Take a television interview with the young pop singer, Marianne Faithfull, in February 1968. When asked what she felt about drugs she replied, "Drugs are the doors . . . you just see a crack. I think LSD was important. I know so many people that before they took it were such a drag, and when they took it they really opened up. Then of their own accord they stopped. Nearly everybody has stopped taking LSD."

What had she seen through the crack? she was asked. "Something I think we've forgotten about completely, something like God; something calming. You realise that the state we should be in is perfection, that we're not in it; and that the reason we're here is to find it."

Later she was asked if she feared death. "I think it's very important to stay in the world and do things," she answered, "but I think it's a beautiful thing, death."

Marianne Faithfull felt that she had only peeped through a crack in the door. It is not surprising that people who have had the further experience of passing through that door are brought right up against the sixty-four thousand dollar question: Is the wider reality they find on the other side an illusion, or is it another aspect of the totality?

Whatever the answer, such experience is still worth considering here because of its marked effect on the attitude to death of a number of people who have it. To take three examples: Tennyson's experience made death seem to him a "laughable impossibility"; Koestler's made it a vaguely annoying irrelevance, and a lifetime of such experiences have apparently caused it to seem so unimportant to the mathematician, Professor J. H. M. Whiteman, that in a whole book devoted to examining them he does not mention it even once: his interest is entirely concentrated on exploring the more intense and inspiring Reality which he feels they have opened up. Whatever experients mean by Reality, which they usually write with a capital R, it is a word often used to describe out-of-the-body experiences; hence one may guess that, were these universal, death would be taken for granted as the gateway to a larger life. That, of course, does not mean that it would be so. Universality of experience could mean universality of delusion. Were we all drunkards we might all experience pink elephants, and even were death such a gateway, that would not necessarily imply the continuance of the narrow self-regarding type of consciousness natural to the physical personality. "The loss of personality," said Tennyson of his experience, "seeming no extinction but the only true life."

Irrespective of whether out-of-the-body experience is real or illusory, in this chapter the term will be taken to cover both the type in which the experient feels himself to be what, for want of a better phrase, I will call a spark of consciousness which is unaware of any body, and the type in which he seems to himself to have moved out of his ordinary body into another non-physical one, which is more mobile and more responsive—some people feel it can float through walls and so on—but which still has a shape and is located at some definite point in space.[1] Often the experient himself seems puzzled. Saint Paul said of the occasion when he felt himself snatched up into the "third heaven": "Whether it was in the body I know not, or out of the body I know not: God knoweth." The term will also be taken to cover the whole range of such experience, including transient psychical impressions as of standing beside one's physical body and seeing it asleep on its bed against its normal background, "travel" in varying surroundings, and also mystical illumination. It is next to impossible to convey the feeling of mystical experience to people who have not had it. In a wide sense, perhaps, it could be called a profoundly enhanced sense of meaning, of values, but it does not come to the saintly idealist only. Sometimes the physical world vanishes, but not always; in what is called nature-mysticism it is seen transfigured, having become the outermost sheath of an inner Reality on which the mystic's attention is focussed, and which, so he tells us, appears more uplifting and meaningful the nearer the "centre" is approached. There seems to be every degree of illumination, from a simple sense of what Rudolf Otto called the numinous—he looked on this sense as the germ of mystical experience—to the transcendant visions of the greatest seers.

It is very hard for the non-mystic to attempt to describe the likenesses and differences between psychical and mystical experience, especially as they may occur concurrently. Perhaps the nearest one can get is to say that the first seems to be more like awareness of form, however fluid, the second of essence, of content, of meaning. One thing, at least, seems pretty clear, that in both cases language evolved to deal with physical phenomena, perceived through the senses, will be inadequate and misleading. For instance, if those words so often used, "another world" mean anything, it may not be "a different place" in the sense that France is a different place from England, but another aspect of the totality. The phrase "ultra-physical realms" may perhaps be safer, as less tied to the ideas of space and visual perception. Again, what may be called the progress towards greater Reality, of which so many mystics and, indeed, psychics speak, is sometimes described as "upward" and sometimes as "inward", and the overtones of physical travel in both words will probably mislead the non-mystic and non-psychic as to what is meant. But what others are available?

Before reading examples of out-of-the-body experience it is as well to be clear about one's own reactions to the idea itself. In those who assume that man's only means of communication with his environment or his fellows is *via* the senses, that reaction will probably be something

[1] Different people describe different kinds of body. Looked at from the physiological standpoint the kind experienced might perhaps vary with the stimulation of the different sense organs and areas of the brain concerned with conscious, semi-conscious or unconscious experience of the orientation of the body. Sometimes a person will speak of having experienced another *physical* body. In most cases this might well be a subjective hallucination with a physiological cause, and thus of little evidential value.

N

like "just a dream", or "merely subjective", or "probably pathological and anyway meaningless". Or, if we are feeling very tolerant, "perhaps psychologically true". Moreover, apart from their views as to what can or cannot be, for people who lack any such experience even to *imagine* more real-seeming realms than our own, much less envisage that they might be real, is about as easy as to imagine a donkey which can trot two ways at once.

Reactions to the two following quotations can give a clue to one's own basic attitude. In the first a physicist, Professor Denys Wilkinson, speculates about interpenetrating universes; in the second a psychologist, William James, gives his conclusion about the nature of consciousness—a conclusion which was forced on him by his own study and experience.

Professor Wilkinson: "Perhaps there do indeed exist universes interpenetrating with ours; perhaps of a high complexity; perhaps containing their own forms of awareness; constructed out of other particles and other interactions than those we know now, but awaiting discovery through some common but elusive interaction which we have yet to spot."[1]

William James: "One conclusion was forced upon my mind at that time [by his experiences when taking nitrous oxide. R. H.] and my impression of its truth has ever since remained unshaken. It is that our normal waking consciousness, rational consciousness as we call it, is but one special type of consciousness, whilst all about it, parted from it by the filmiest of screens, there lie potential forms of consciousness entirely different. We may go through life without suspecting their existence; but apply the requisite stimulus and at a touch they are there in all their completeness, definite types of mentality which probably somewhere have their field of application and adaptation. No account of the universe in its totality can leave these other forms of consciousness quite disregarded. How to regard them is the question—for they are so discontinuous with ordinary consciousness. Yet they may determine attitudes though they cannot furnish formulas, and open a region though they cannot give a map. At any rate they forbid a premature closing of our accounts with reality."[2]

It is a fairly safe bet that most people will take Professor Wilkinson's speculations in their stride, having learnt to swallow the astounding ideas that sub-matter may vanish and reappear, exist without weight or mass, and travel backward in time. But many have also learnt to smile at such ideas about "extended" consciousness as those of William

[1] Denys H. Wilkinson, F.R.S., "Matter and Sub-Matter", *The Listener*, July 31st, 1960, p. 96.
[2] William James, *The Varieties of Religious Experience*, Gifford Lectures, 1901-2, Longman's Green (1937 edition), p. 378.

James, and this makes it very difficult for them to enter imaginatively into the state of mind of people whose attitude to death has been changed by what they believe to be out-of-the-body experience. The best plan, therefore, seems to be to read a few representative reports simply as raw material, and, if possible, with T. S. Eliot's "complete simplicity which costs not less than everything". After having done so, we can ask the question: Do those reports merely describe the subjective side of certain physiological states, or may they tell us something about ultra-physical aspects of man's environment in which his consciousness might possibly continue after death?

Examples of out-of-the-body experience

Here, as examples of raw material, are some experiences which were directly induced by the immediate presence of death. The first was reported by the late Lord Geddes, who was a physician and a professor of anatomy, in an address to the Royal Medical Society in Edinburgh. At the time, 1937, he said that he withheld the name of the experient for professional reasons, but it is now widely believed to have been himself.

"On Saturday, November 9th, a few minutes after midnight, I began to feel very ill and by 2 o'clock was definitely suffering from acute gastro-enteritis . . . By 10 o'clock I had developed all the symptoms of very acute poisoning . . . pulse and respirations being quite impossible to count . . . I realised I was very ill and very quickly reviewed my whole financial position: thereafter at no time did my consciousness appear to me to be in any way dimmed, but I suddenly realised that *my* consciousness was separating from another consciousness which was also me. These for purposes of description we could call the A and B consciousnesses, and throughout what follows the ego attached itself to the A consciousness. The B personality I recognised as belonging to the body, and as my physical condition grew worse . . . I realised that [it] was beginning to show signs of being composite, that is, built up of 'consciousnesses' from the head, heart, viscera, etc. These components became more individual and the B consciousness began to disintegrate, while the A consciousness, which was now me, seemed to be altogether outside the body, which it could see. Gradually I realised that I could see not only my body and the bed in which it was, but everything in the whole house and garden, and then I realised that I was not only seeing 'things' at home, but in London and in Scotland, in fact wherever my attention was directed it seemed to me; and the explanation I received, from what source I do not know, but which I found myself calling my mentor, was that I was free in a time dimension of space, wherein 'now' was in some way equivalent to 'here' in the ordinary three dimensional space of everyday life. I next realised that my vision included not only 'things' in the ordinary three dimensional world, but also 'things' in these four and more dimensional places that I was in. From now on the description is and must be entirely metaphorical because there are no words which really describe what I saw or rather appreciated. Although I had no body I had what appeared to be perfect two-eyed vision, and what I saw can only be described in this way, that I was conscious of a psychic stream flowing with life through time, and this gave me the impression of being visible, and it seemed to me to have a particularly intense irridescence. I understood from my mentor that all our brains are just end-organs projecting as it were from the three dimensional universe into the psychic stream and flowing with it into the fourth and fifth dimensions. Around each brain, as I saw it, there seemed to be what I can only describe in ordinary words as a condensation of the psychic stream . . ."

The experient then goes on to describe the differently coloured little clouds of condensation which were attached to various people he knew, and then he says,

"I saw A enter the bedroom. I realised she got a terrible shock and I saw her hurry to the telephone; I saw my doctor leave his patients and come very quickly, and heard him say, or saw him think, 'He is nearly gone.' I heard him quite clearly speaking to me on the bed, but I was not in touch with the body and could not answer him. I was really cross when he took a syringe and rapidly injected my body with something, which I afterwards learned was camphor.[1] As the heart began to beat more strongly I was drawn back and I was intensely annoyed because I was so interested and just beginning to understand where I was and what I was 'seeing' . . . Once I was back all the clarity of vision of anything and everything disappeared and I was just possessed of a glimmer of consciousness which was suffused with pain.

"It is surprising to note that this dream, vision or experience has shown no tendency to fade like a dream would fade, nor has it shown any tendency that I am aware of to grow or to rationalise itself as a dream would do. I think that the whole thing simply means that but for medical treatment of a peculiarly prompt and vigorous kind I was dead to the three dimensional universe. If this is so and if in fact the experience of liberation of consciousness in the fourth dimensional universe is not imagination, it is a most important matter to place on record . . .

"Thus ends the record. What are we to make of it? . . . Was it a dream or does it record a symbolic vision of one aspect of reality translated into inadequate words? I do not know . . ."

[1] Readers will remember Jung's out-of-the-body experiences during illness and that he too was given camphor injections.

Later, when analysing this and some other experiences, Lord Geddes says that he regards it as a valuable symbolic impression of man's body-soul as it disintegrates in death, but he emphasises that "the whole adventure, if such it were, took place on the plane of Nature. It is thus to be sharply differentiated from the records of the spiritual adventures of the mystics."[1]

The above experience was due to severe illness. The following occurred to a very fit mountaineer during his struggle to climb back to safety, after having shot over the edge of a precipice. He writes:

"I found myself hanging on the rope a few feet below the crest of the ridge. I turned, snatched at the rocks and clawed my way back. I had fallen altogether about 20 feet and the rope . . . had held . . .

"During the time I was doing this a curious rigidity or tension gripped my whole being, mental and physical . . . It was an overwhelming sensation and quite outside my experience. It was as though all life's forces were in process of undergoing some fundamental evolutionary change, the change called death . . . I know now that death is not to be feared, it is a supreme experience, the climax, not the anti-climax of life.

"For how long I experienced this crescendo of power I cannot say. Time no longer existed as time . . . Then suddenly this feeling was superseded by a feeling of complete indifference and detachment, detachment as to what was happening or likely to happen to that body. I seemed to stand aside from my body. I was not falling for the reason that I was not in a dimension where it was possible to fall. I, that is, my consciousness, was apart from my body and not in the least concerned with what was befalling it."

The author then speculates as to what brought about this state of mind, the partial dissolution of the physical and spiritual caused by the assumption that death was inevitable, the mental effect of intense strain, or what? "It is not within my province," he concludes, "to discuss that which only death can prove; yet to me this experience was a convincing one; it convinced me that consciousness survives beyond the grave."[2]

The next case is taken from a letter appearing in the *Sunday Times* of March 25th 1962.

"During the war in the Western Desert, I was knocked unconscious by bomb blast and had the peculiar sensation of being out of my body viewing the scene from a point about 20 feet above the ground . . . I could hear the aircraft as it came in on another attack and the voices of my companions. I could see the dust clearing away from the explosion that had knocked me unconscious and my own body lying there on the gravel.

---

[1] Lord Geddes, P.C., G.C.M.G., K.C.B., M.D., "A Voice from the Grandstand", *The Edinburgh Medical Journal*, N.S., (IVth), Vol. XLIV, p. 367, 1937.
[2] F. S. Smythe, *The Spirit of the Hills*, Hodder and Stoughton, 1935.

"... I remember the thought, ' I've got to get back ', and then ... I was back in my body consciously trying to force my eyes open. An odd thing was that, although I could hear perfectly while I was unconscious and could tell my comrades what they had said during that period, when I recovered consciousness I was stone deaf and remained so for two weeks afterwards ...

"This experience has convinced me that there is a part of the person that survives after death ... I am certain that when I do eventually die, or rather when my body dies, part of me will carry on, to where or to do what I do not know."

In the S.P.R. *Journal* for March 1948 can be found records of similar experiences in similar circumstances, and in the *Journal* for June 1957 is another, contributed by Professor F. J. M. Stratton, F.R.S., which occurred to a physician friend of his after an air crash. While apparently out of his body the physician had observed certain events near some hàngars which were out of sight of where that body was lying, and the details he gave on returning to consciousness were confirmed as correct. He himself commented that one interesting effect of the experience was the "removal of any fear of death, because of the extraordinarily pleasant experience of what one felt and became aware of when one was apparently detached from one's body". He added that he felt no further interest in his body, but had an "intense feeling, 'Why are these people bothering about my body? I am entirely content where I am.' " And he was completely happy as to what was going to happen to him.

Finally, a few extracts from the report by a very puzzled American soldier about his own experience after fainting at the onset of an attack of pneumonia. He had been about to catch a train to go for his medical training and on apparently coming round from his faint he realised that he would probably miss it. "What happened next," says his report, "I understand no more than I ask you to ..." What did appear to him to happen was that he leapt out of bed to dress and then saw what seemed to be himself lying on the bed and wearing his fraternity ring. At that, terrified, he fled from the room. No one took any notice of him and eventually he felt he must get back to his body. When with some difficulty he found it, a sheet had been drawn over the face, but he recognised his ring on the hand. "This is what we human beings call death," he thought, "this splitting-up of the self." At that he experienced the room as "flooded with the most total compassion I have ever felt. It was a presence so comforting, so joyous and all-satisfying that I wanted to lose myself for ever in the wonder of it ..." Then he went on a far journey, packed with experience—and then he woke up in bed. Later on his doctor told him that he had apparently died but that a shot of adrenalin had brought him back to life.[1]

[1] From an account by S. Smith in *The Enigma of Out-of-the-Body Travel*, Helix Press, New York, 1965, p. 146.

Those experiences were induced by crisis situations, but crisis is not the only source of out-of-the-body experience. It can occur to dedicated persons such as Yogis and saints after spiritual training, but is looked on by them as a kind of by-product, not its goal: that is enlightenment. It can also be induced by drugs, drink, anaesthetics and hypnosis and it sometimes comes spontaneously to ordinary healthy persons in a waking state. This can happen, for instance, in response to beauty. If I may be personal, when young I once had the experience of being swept by a surge of splendid music out of my body into new and wonderful surroundings. I do not of course know what actually happened, beyond that, so I am told, my body became inert, but I do know what I experienced and its apparent reality.[1] Incidentally when "out" I gave no thought to whether or not I had a body: I was far too interested in my new surroundings.

Some people have learnt, as they believe, to step out of the body when its suffering becomes too great to be borne. Madame Julia de Beausobre achieved this during long confinement in the Lubianka prison, and a sober head teacher told me that when a prisoner of war in Japan he too had learnt to do it when things became too bad.[2] He said he had been able to teach most, but not all, of his fellow prisoners to do the same.[3]

Incidence of spontaneous out-of-the-body experience

Now to turn to the question of how widespread today is spontaneous out-of-the-body experience? This is easier to ask than to answer since some experients have never heard of such a thing, so when it comes to them personally they look on it as unique, subjective, possibly abnormal and in any case better not mentioned. There are a few hints, however, that it may be less rare than is assumed. Apart from the reports of it amassed by such bodies as the British and American Societies for Psychical Research and continental researchers, cases are quoted and discussed in books written since the last war by Stephen Findlay,

[1] Dr. Charles C. Tart of the Department of Psychology, University of California, has recently done a pilot physiological study of a subject who reported repeated out-of-the-body experiences. The preliminary indications were that these occurred in conjunction with a "non-dreaming, non-awake brainwave stage, characterised by . . . slowed alpha activity . . . and no activation of the autonomic nervous system". *Journal*, American S.P.R., January 1968.

[2] Julia de Beausobre, *The Woman Who Could Not Die*, Chatto and Windus.

[3] A scientist friend who kindly read the typescript of this paper commented on the above passage:

[This type of] out-of-the-body experience seems common in vivid visualisers, especially in children, non-bookish adults and females. With their eyes fixed on the distance and sight, as it were, switched off, they visualise the room from some quite different angle, as they might in a day-dream, but with abnormal vividness, and so picture themselves as another might see them. When I was being publicly scolded in class I had no difficulty in escaping to a far corner of the ceiling, whence I could look down with amused pity at the poor little boy on the bench below. My visual powers faded in early adolescence, and after that I never had such experiences again. It appeared to be a common schoolboys' trick, since we took it for granted when discussing our mishaps with each other.

Marghanita Laski, Professors R. C. Zaehner and W. T. Stace, and Drs. Raynor Johnson, F. C. Happold and Louisa Rhine. Dr. Robert Crookall has collected reports of hundreds of such experiences and classified them according to family resemblances, and a well-known American sociologist, the late Professor Hornell Hart, made a long-term study of them. He came to the conclusion that the resemblance between conscious apparitions of the living, which he accepted as probably being due to out-of-the-body travel, and apparently purposeful apparitions of the dead, provided evidence pointing toward survival which could not be ignored. (See note to the succeeding chapter, page 227.)

A number of modern authors have written accounts of out-of-the-body and mystical experience, some of them autobiographical. Among them in the last century were Wordsworth, Emily Brontë, George Eliot, George Meredith and Tennyson, and in this century, Arnold Bennett, D. H. Lawrence, Virginia Woolf, Warner Allen, Bernard Berenson, John Buchan, William Gerhardi, Koestler and Hemingway. After he had been badly wounded Hemingway wrote to a friend a delightfully unportentous account of an experience very like those quoted earlier in this chapter. "I felt my soul or something coming right out of my body, like you'd pull a silk handkerchief out of a pocket by one corner. It flew around and then came back and went in again and I wasn't dead any more."[1]

A slight clue to the incidence of out-of-the-body experience was obtained by Professor Hornell Hart. In 1952 he asked 155 students at Duke University, North Carolina, the following question: "Have you ever actually seen your physical body from a viewpoint outside that body, like standing beside the bed and looking at yourself lying in bed or like floating in the air near your body?" What seems a surprisingly large proportion of the students, 30 per cent, answered "Yes", but this was reduced to an overall 20 per cent by a smaller proportion of affirmative answers from two other groups. Of the students who had had such experience, over 70 per cent had done so more than once. In 1966, fourteen years later, an English investigator, C. E. Green, asked a similar question of 115 undergraduates at Southampton University, and again in 1967 of 350 at Oxford. At Southampton about 19 per cent answered "Yes", and at Oxford no less than 34 per cent. Green reports that in both enquiries "no significant difference was found between Arts and Sciences students, or between men and women, or between undergraduates from State or public schools". On the whole the undergraduates who later described their experiences in detail seemed to assume that these were exceptional and did not appear to have any explanation for them. A hint of the limiting effect of the contemporary mental climate on what an experient is able to make of out of the body experience may perhaps be found in the account of one undergraduate,

[1] Quoted by S. Smith in *The Enigma of Out-of-the-Body Travel*, Helix Press, New York, 1965, p. 22. Hemingway made use of this experience in Chapter 9 of *A Farewell to Arms*.

". . . 'Me' disappears . . . and there is a feeling of the world consisting merely of waves of energy all connected, my brain included. It is almost a religious experience—although I am not a Christian, nor do I believe in God." This subject said that he had such an experience about once a month and when asked what emotions accompanied it he replied, "Awe, wonder and delight, but terrible fear once or twice."[1]

Repeated out-of-the-body experience

We can now turn to the experiences of people who believe that they have learnt to leave the body almost at will and have written accounts of the process and their travels. It is not always easy to disentangle what actually appeared to happen to the experient from his subsequent interpretation of it, or to make allowances for the extreme difficulty of describing apparently ultra-physical happenings in language and images evolved to deal with physical ones. This applies, of course, just as much if the phenomena are subjective.

Of those who have recorded their repeated "excursions" with care during this century the best known are a Frenchman, who called himself Yram, an Englishman, Oliver Fox, and an American, Sylvan Muldoon.[2] On the whole their "travels" have been on what Lord Geddes called the plane-of-nature. For this they use the traditional term, astral, which is perhaps a pity as in the eyes of outside enquirers it has sometimes been debased by purveyors of easy uplift. Very recent accounts come from Professor J. H. M. Whiteman, who, being a physicist and a mathematician, seeks to make them as objective as Darwin's reports from the Galapagos Islands. They are of particular interest because they cover the whole range from psychical or plane-of-nature experience to heights of mystical insight. He claims to have had these experiences since boyhood and to have learnt to analyse and control them. He calls them by the non-committal name of Separations and up to the time of writing his book about them had recorded about 2,000.[3]

Professor Whiteman makes the startling contention that it is no good trying to establish the reality of what he calls "inner" phenomena by study of their occasional secondary effects in the "outer" world. They demand "a new view of science substantially different from that of either the physical sciences or dogmatic behaviourism." His aim is to put forward a workable scheme "for the study and explanation of the mental phenomena and processes or any other kind of awareness with

[1] C. E. Green, "Exosomatic Experience and Related Phenomena", *Journal*, S.P.R., September 1967.
[2] Yram, *Practical Astral Projection*, Rider and Co., translation from the French, *Le Medecin de l'Ame*. Oliver Fox, *Astral Projection: A Record of Out-of-the-Body Experiences*, University Books, New York, 1962. Original English edition, undated, some time in the 1930s. Sylvan Muldoon and Hereward Carington, *The Projection of the Astral Body*, Rider, 1929, and a number of subsequent books.
[3] J. H. M. Whiteman, *The Mystical Life*, Faber, 1961.

which parapsychology and mysticism are concerned, *on the basis of evidence in their own fields.*"[1]

Here once more is a case of having to learn to do the works before you can hope to know the doctrine. Whiteman, of course, is only one of a long line of mystics who are convinced that there exists an actual and rational ultra-physical or, as he calls it, "inner" Reality, to which we belong even more than we do to the physical world, and which is perceptible to all students who will make the effort to acquire the technique of passing across the unending motorway stream of their own thoughts and fantasies. The intensity of his conviction is brought home by the down-to-earth fashion in which he describes ultra-physical experience.

a. The objects of perception, understanding and feeling are organised in such a way as to constitute the phenomena of a world that is not physical.
b. The human or other form in which these faculties seem to be placed is also situated in that world.[2]

His attitude to dreams seems to be that they can be fantasies, and can also present irrational and uncontrolled pictures of actual "inner" realms, but that from them one can learn to pass over into rational "inner" experience.

Like other mystics Whiteman sets no more store by psychical than by physical experiences as such; they are both means of making contact with an environment; what matters to the mystic is the goal which all experience can serve, a closer approach in love and awe to the Centre of things. Yet he does seem to think that psychical experience may indicate the beginning of struggle towards spiritual enlightenment, that to find oneself looking down, say, at one's sleeping body may hint that a humble first step has been taken inward towards what, again non-committally, he calls the Source. Take the following two extracts from his book about his own experiences. The first describes a psychical separation, the other a moment of mystical illumination.

"Waking up during the night I was aware of lying on my front in bed. Nevertheless I rose in a separated form and stood on the floor feeling joyful at being in a form more properly corresponding to my mind or real nature than any physical form . . ."[3]

[1] Extracts from an unpublished paper which Professor Whiteman has kindly allowed me to quote.
[2] J. H. M. Whiteman, *The Mystical Life*, Faber, 1965, p. 48. Whiteman uses the word "phenomena" in the original sense of "appearances".
[3] *Ibid.*, The opposite reaction is shown by a woman whose experience is quoted by C. E. Green in "Analysis of Spontaneous Cases", *Proceedings* S.P.R., 1960, p. 143. She reported: "When I got up with the intention of getting back into bed to my surprise and a feeling of horror, I saw my own body stretched on the bed asleep—at any rate completely motionless . . . I was compressed back into that body as a picture into its frame . . . When I had recovered my composure I could think of no rational explanation of what had occurred, but I went over each impression and movement very carefully so I should not give a garbled account of what had taken place."

The second extract comes from a long account of a mystical experience which occurred before Professor Whiteman had studied the many similar experiences in mystical literature. Throughout the day preceding it he had been specially conscious of what he describes as an attitude of Obedience towards the Divine Wisdom. Then he writes:

". . . The separation did not begin from a dream state; but during the night I became fully awake to the quality of this directed obedience . . . Almost immediately the separated form was drawn upwards, quickly, as if through a great distance . . . All at once, without any further change, my eyes were opened. Above and in front, yet in me, of me and around was the Glory of the Archetypal Light . . . a creative light of Life itself, streaming forth in Love and Understanding and forming all other lives out of its substance . . ."

After some attempts to describe his then state of consciousness and his impression of the Source, which, like all descriptions of mystical experience in physical terms and images, end in paradox, the account concludes:

"But now understanding and obedience began to wane and obscurity of mind insensibly took hold, *because of the encroachment of self* . . . Then presently consciousness settled again in the physical body." (My italics. R. H.)[1]

Here we are back with Plotinus:

"Many a time it happened [to me]—lifted out of the body into myself, becoming external to all other things, beholding a marvellous beauty, assured of community with the highest order, acquiring identity with the divine . . . Yet there comes the moment of descent."[2]

As is well-known, similar mystical experiences can be quoted by the hundred from the Upanishads, Milarepa, Plotinus and St. Paul onward, and irrespective of culture, sophistication and religious belief, and one and all seem to convey, whether rightly or wrongly, a sense of meaningful Reality far beyond the most concrete of mundane events. Take Koestler's description of his own repeated experience after his capture by Franco's troops while working for the Left in Spain. When it first occurred he was in solitary confinement under sentence of death, but from death, he says, it took all its terror. His description of it ends: "Then I was floating . . . in a river of peace . . . It came from nowhere and went nowhere . . . Then there was no river and no 'I'. The 'I' had ceased to exist."[3]

Mystic after mystic has tried to describe this joyful loss of "I"-ness, which seems the only true life, but to the uninitiated it appears merely illogical. Who but "I" can notice that there is no "I"? Perhaps there is a clue to the paradox in Whiteman's remark, "But now understanding

[1] *Ibid.*, pp. 35-6. [2] *Enneads* IV, viii, 1, McKenna's translation.
[3] Arthur Koestler, *The Invisible Writing*, Hamish Hamilton, Collins, 1954, p. 352.

and obedience began to wane and obscurity of mind insensibly took over because of the encroachment of self." And perhaps "self" could be the B (body) consciousness mentioned by Lord Geddes? Whatever the answer, the experience clearly startled the fiercely logical intellectual, Koestler; in fact, he says, it laid the ground for a change of personality. His comments after writing the passage quoted above are very interesting.

"It is extremely embarrassing to write down a phrase like that when one has read *The Meaning of Meaning* and nibbled at logical positivism and aims at verbal precision and dislikes nebulous gushings. Yet mystical experiences, as we dubiously call them, are not nebulous, vague or maudlin; they only become so when we debase them by verbalisation. However, to communicate what is incommunicable by its nature one must somehow put it in words, and so one moves in a vicious circle. When I say the 'I' had ceased to exist I refer to a concrete experience that is verbally as incommunicable as the feeling aroused by a piano concerto, yet just as real only much more real. In fact its primary mark is the sensation that this state is more real than any other one has experienced before, for the first time the veil has fallen and one is in touch with 'real reality', the hidden order of things, normally obscured by layers of irrelevancy. . . . The 'I' ceases to exist because it has by a kind of mental osmosis established communication with and been dissolved in the universal pool. It is this process of dissolution and limitless expansion which is sensed as the 'oceanic feeling', as the draining of all tension, the absolute catharsis, the peace that passeth all understanding."[1]

Later he adds that the experience was meaningful, "but not in verbal terms". Verbal transcriptions that come nearest to it are: "The unity and interlocking of everything that exists." He also says that it filled him "with *direct certainty* that a higher order of Reality existed and that it alone could invest existence with meaning".

Koestler is a writer who takes infinite pains to say exactly what he means. But can the above mean anything to people whose whole attention is always fixed on information brought them *via* the senses, which can be described in verbal terms? Or are they in the position of the Tierra del Fuegans when the *Beagle* anchored off their shores—that they did not even notice it because their imagination could not encompass so vast a ship. How much shall we be able to notice, it is being asked, if we meet entirely new things when travelling in space?

Artificially induced out-of-the-body experience

The natural tendency to dismiss reports of seeming ultra-physical realities as no more than fantasy is encouraged by the fact that they

[1] *Ibid.,* p. 353.

come not only from psychics and mystics but also from the mentally ill and the takers of drugs. For instance, in *Wisdom, Madness and Folly*, his remarkable account of his own mental illness, John Custance gives vivid descriptions of even at times transcendent phenomena, and in *The Doors of Perception*, Aldous Huxley, with eyes sharpened by mescalin, describes the outer world as seen transfigured by something very like the mystic's inner light. But it could also be said, perhaps, that this variety of witness supports the argument that ultra-physical aspects of reality are not merely subjective creations of the experient, but exist in their own right.

Here are three accounts of out-of-the-body experience induced by psychedelic drugs. The first describes an apparently changed relation to space, the second to time, and the third seems to approach the mystical in type.

The first occurred in 1955 to an English anthropologist, Colin Turnbull, when he was in India studying Sanskrit. Early on the day commemorating the god, Krishna, he visited the home of the Professor of Philosophy at Banaras University, where he partook with enthusiasm of the delicious traditional sweets and soft drinks with which that occasion is honoured, having no idea that they contained bhang (hemp or marihuana). Later on he went to spend the afternoon at the ashram of Sri Anandamai, a revered religious teacher, and there, after various physical symptoms and a growing sense of peace and well-being, he felt as if his consciousness had left his body entirely. He writes: "It was not only that the body had no feelings, it was rather that I had no use for it any longer. I felt completely free." Then, feeling quite clear-headed, he had the experience of travelling up through the clouds and away over the Himalayas, where he looked down on that tremendous landscape in an apparently normal fashion. Eventually, though with regret, he returned to his body on the terrace at Banaras. He comments that "during the experience the whole world around me seemed to be more full of life than it had ever been before and full of those qualities that the Hindu scriptures proclaim to be the highest of all—truth, goodness and beauty." Later he spoke to Sri Anandamai about it.

"I told her how it had been nothing like a dream or a fantasy but had seemed a very real and therefore *not a very extraordinary experience*. She . . . said that what I had seen was real, that it had been good for me to see it, but she added a caution that many Hindu sages and aspirants used bhang in order to achieve a dissociation between the mind and the body, but that it was highly dangerous. The only safe way was the traditional way of training both mind and body together, until the demands of the one upon the other became minimal."[1] (My italics, R. H.)

Under bhang, Colin Turnbull appeared to experience a new freedom

[1] *The Drug Experience*, edited by David Benn, Orion Press, New York, 1961, p. 106 et seq.

in relation to space. Under similar drugs the same sense of freedom can come in relation to time, much as it came to the experient quoted by Lord Geddes at the point of death. Christopher Mayhew's account of experiencing under mescalin at 3 p.m. events which in fact took place at 3.30 is well known. His conviction that this actually happened did not lessen with time, as is shown by the following comment, written, he says, after brooding about the experience for several months.

"I still think that my first astonishing conviction was right that on many occasions that afternoon I existed outside time . . . By 'I' in this context, I mean, of course, my disembodied self, and by 'experienced' I mean learned by a special kind of awareness which seemed to comprehend, yet be different from seeing, hearing, etc. . . . I count this experience, which occurred when I was wide awake and intelligent, sitting in my own armchair at home, as the most astounding and thought-provoking of my life."[1]

This sort of out-of-the-body experience does not fade from memory like the ordinary dream. I have seen a letter from the late Lord Geddes, written 19 years after his lecture mentioned earlier, in which he said that the experient still found the experience quoted in it as impressive as he had done at the time. Like that experience, which was of feeling "free in a time dimension of space wherein 'now' was in some way equivalent to 'here' ", Mr. Mayhew's may also have been a fleeting direct awareness of aspects of the space-time continuum which in ordinary life only mathematicians approach indirectly by means of equations. They do not experience them as they experience a flash of lightning. And even to the non-mathematician the kind of experience we are considering here may seem less unthinkable when we remember that modern physics looks on the space-time frame as something overlaid by the observer on the external world. We must never, said Eddington, lose sight of its fictitious and arbitrary nature.

Richard Jeffries, the mystically minded farmer's son, reached this concept a century ago without the aid of mathematics or drugs. "I cannot understand time," he wrote, "It is eternity now. I am in the midst of it. There may be time for the clock . . . there is none for me."[2]

Our third example of drug-induced experience took place in 1957. It is described by the experient, a New York psychologist, in a letter to Miss Susy Smith, and it has semi-mystical overtones.

"I felt as if I were almost completely detached from my physical body . . . [It] was just a dead weight that I was aware of, as if I were looking down on it from a great height. The experience was one of height and light . . . I seemed to be a pin point in space, space all around me in every dimension, space filled with light, not a blinding

[1] *The Observer*, October 26th 1956.
[2] Richard Jeffries, *The Story of My Heart*.

light but a radiant light and space that was not just empty space but space pregnant with meaning, a meaning that I could not comprehend but which I felt very distinctly, space that was peopled, perhaps, with some knowing force."

The psychologist went on to say that the most outstanding characteristic of the experience was clarity of mind.

"When I say the mind I certainly mean the higher mind, the 'I' in capitals. It was this 'I', this most real part of the Me which I felt soared on this flight . . . utterly awake, utterly sensitive, far more sensitive than in the usual state to forces around me and certainly beyond the spectrum which I in the usual state could be aware of. Certainly I brought back from this experience even greater conviction of the preservation of this 'I' beyond that thing which we call physical death. I felt so completely separate from and so distinct from my physical self that it would seem utterly incomprehensible or illogical that this 'I' should become extinct when this worn out carcase of mine gives up in the end."[1]

One more example of artificially induced mystical-type experience may be added here, because the cause of it is not a drug but an anaesthetic, nitrous oxide, and also because the experient, Mr. R. H. Ward, makes an interesting comment on the strain such experience may put on the physical body.

". . . I knew, I understood, I actually was far more than I normally knew, understood and was. I put it in this way because I had no impression of suddenly receiving new knowledge, understanding and being. Rather I felt I was rediscovering these things, which had once been mine, but which I had lost many years before. While it was altogether strange, this new condition was also familiar; it was even in a sense my rightful condition. Meanwhile, what was becoming unreal, slow and clumsy was the ordinary world I was leaving behind . . ."[2]

The rest of Ward's description, although of interest, is too long to quote in full. After an impression of flight upward through what he calls "a region of ideas", he reached what seemed to him a state of

"complete and spontaneous lucidity, where there was not the slightest need to 'think'. One simply knew; and one knew, not merely one thing here and another there, and all of them quite unknown to ordinary consciousness; one knew everything there was to know. Thus one knew that everything was one thing, that *real knowledge* was simultaneous knowledge of the universe and all it contains, oneself included. It was perfectly true, what one had read in the books; in

[1] Susy Smith, *The Enigma of Out of the Body Travel*, Helix Press, New York, 1965, pp. 134-5.
[2] R. H. Ward, *A Drug Taker's Notes*, Gollancz, 1957, p. 27.

reality (as opposed to the comparative unreality in which we live) the All is the One."[1]

Ward had a number of such experiences, both spontaneous and under anaesthetics and psychedelic drugs, and they induced him to make the following comment:

"It is impossible not to suppose a relationship, which I believe we in no way understand, between experiences which reach a certain point in the rising scale of consciousness and the death of the body; there is perhaps a point in that scale beyond which the body cannot continue to live."[2]

But it is vital to remember that not all drug-induced visits to apparent ultra-physical realms are visits to "heaven". Sri Anandamai was right enough in saying that they can be very dangerous. Even some of the non-addictive psychedelic drugs, it is now thought, can do physical damage to genes, and taken in the wrong mood and with undesirable companions, psychologically they can lead to "hell" and, on occasion, to suicide. I have myself seen a well-known author take the dark path under mescalin and I do not wish to repeat the experience. In the light of such known risks, there may be powerful reasons, over and above the desire to escape, why so many people want to go on "trips". To use a very homely analogy, suppose we picture our total environment as something like an onion, and our senses as bringing us no more than snippets of information about its outermost sheath, of which our bodies form part. But our spiritual sustenance would have to seep out from its central core. In the past, perhaps, one way in which this sustenance could reach our conscious selves was through religious ritual and prayer, but for most people nowadays these are no longer living activities. It may be, then, that part of their psyche is starved and confined in a mental and emotional straight-jacket. And it may have been to such basic starvation that Jung was referring when he said that lack of a religious outlook was at the root of all his elder patients' troubles. If so, it may be no more odd that occasional disaster fails to deter the young from taking dangerous "trips", in search of what they hope may be food and freedom, than that thirsty animals risk being shot to get at a water-hole.

What is out-of-the-body experience?

So much for raw material. These few examples of seemingly out-of-the-body experience can be duplicated by the thousand, from the plane-of-nature experience of the poor woman who could not wait to get back to the body she saw in her bed, to the mystical illumination

[1] *Ibid.*
[2] *Ibid.*, p. 26.

which makes the experient forget all about the body with its self-regarding "I", in his joyful adoration of what seems to him the spiritual Source of All. What are we to make of them? Are they no more than fantasies, the subjective side of physiological disturbances, or even due, so some might say, to errors of early training in hygiene; or are they hints that in man is a spark of consciousness which can function free of the physical body in life and may continue to do so after death? But personal survival is a secondary question; the one that matters is: Can there be a "higher order of Reality" which "alone invests existence with meaning", as Koestler put it, and can men have out-of-the-body experience which leads to greater awareness of it?

To illustrate the question, take Colin Turnbull's mainly plane-of-nature experience. It is known that something like an out-of-the-body experience can be induced by artificial stimulation of the sense of orientation situated in the inner ear (the semicircular canals). This experience is like that of being whisked up in an express lift; the body seems to be left behind; and it can even become a sense of floating freely in space, devoid of gravity. Certain drugs will cause this disturbing stimulation, probably by increasing the local blood pressure. They can also induce vivid hallucinations. This at once brings the question to mind: Did the bhang cause disturbances of the ear and brain of which Turnbull's impression of free flight was merely the subjective side? Yet—is it wise to assume that the abnormal origin of an experience must always destroy its validity? Would it be better to ask: Could the bhang have induced a brain state which enabled his consciousness to escape and actually fly over the Himalayas? This last is hard to swallow. But the question may still be wrongly phrased. The idea of time as an ever-rolling stream seems to be a kind of thought-model created by man to stand for a quite different reality. May his idea of space be another such model? Would this kind of question be better: Did the drug temporarily release the mind from the body so that it could experience certain *relations* which our habitual thought-model translates as travel in space? Both this question and the previous one may be absurd, but at least they help us to remember that some of the difficulties in this subject may be because the way we think forces us to ask the wrong questions. Another thing to remember is that not all out-of-the-body states need to be lumped together. They may have a different explanation and different significance in different cases.

To get back to the basic questions: Is there a higher order of Reality? And do men ever have out-of-the-body experience of it? These, of course, can be answered Yes, or No, on the plane of belief, without overmuch concern for evidence either way. Or they can be pushed aside—leave all that to the experts and get on with life—though in getting on with life every man gives his own answer by his choice of aims and priorities. Or the views of experts can be sought. What do the scientists and philosophers say? Do they look on the physical world as a closed one, or do they agree with the great mathematician Hermann Weyl that it is being made by modern science to "appear more and more as an open one . . . pointing beyond itself"? In particular, what is their view of the nature of man?

First, let us remind ourselves of the physicalist view. This is how it has recently been put by a psychologist, Dr. Hudson:

> "Current physiological research provides increasing confirmation of the simple monistic doctrine that consciousness is no more than an epiphenomenal by-product *generated* by the physicochemical processes of the brain, and dualism a needless multiplication of hypothetical entities." (My italics, R. H.)[1]

The summing up of the problem by the philosopher Gilbert Ryle has passed into the language. "There is," he said, "no ghost in the machine." And, in an early book his fellow philosopher, A. J. Ayer, fairly wiped the floor with the poor mystic.

> "We do not deny *a priori* that the mystic is able to discover truths by his own special methods. We wait to hear what are the propositions which embody his discoveries, in order to see whether they are verified or confuted by our own empirical observations. But the mystic, so far from producing propositions which are empirically verified, is unable to produce any intelligible propositions at all. And therefore we say that his intuition has not revealed to him any facts. It is no use saying that he has apprehended facts but is unable to express them. For we know that if he really had acquired any information, he would be able to express it. He would be able to indicate in some way or other how the genuineness of his discovery might be empirically determined. The fact that he cannot reveal what he 'knows', or even himself devise an empirical test to validate his 'knowledge', shows that his state of intuition is not a genuinely cognitive state. So that in describing his vision the mystic does not give any information about the external world: he merely gives us indirect information about the condition of his own mind."[2]

Although Professor Ayer himself has since modified this view, it still represents an outlook—presumably based on 19th century physics—which is so widely accepted that, as Sir Alister Hardy puts it, "for a growing proportion of the population the idea of a spiritual side to the universe, distinct from the material, is regarded as a myth surviving from a pre-scientific age".[3] On the other hand, their own revolutionary discoveries have caused some of the greatest 20th century physicists, Eddington, Jeans, Heisenberg, for instance, to consider that outlook far too limited; and as regards the nature of man, an increasing number of

[1] Quoted by Sir Cyril Burt in *Journal* S.P.R., December 1967.
[2] A. J. Ayer, *Language, Truth and Logic*, Gollancz, 1936, pp. 118-119.
[3] Sir Alister Hardy, F.R.S., *The Divine Flame*, Collins, 1967.

eminent neurophysiologists seem flatly to disagree with Dr. Hudson's opinion that the brain generates consciousness and there is no more to be said. Even thirty years ago Sherrington came to the conclusion that physics and chemistry could not explain mind, and in his 1963 Eddington Memorial Lecture, the famous brain specialist, Sir John Eccles, made the same point.

"Contrary to the physicalist creed, I believe that the prime reality of my experiencing self cannot with propriety be identified with brains, neurones, nerve impulses or spatial temporal patterns of impulses . . . I cannot believe that the gift of conscious experience has no further future, no possibility of another existence under some other intangible conditions. At least I would maintain that this possibility of a future existence cannot be denied on scientific grounds."[1]

It may be noted that Eccles looks on the view that consciousness must cease at death as a *belief*, not a known fact, also that he refers to the physicalist view as a *creed*.

Among neurophysiologists the adventurous attitude seems to be growing, for in 1966 there appeared the report of an International Symposium on Brain and Consciousness at which a whole cluster of stars, Lord Adrian, Dr. Wilder Penfield, and Professors Sperry, W. H. Thorpe and Gomes, also rejected the physicalist view that the brain is capable of *generating* consciousness.[2] This swing from orthodoxy stems from their own researches, as Sir Cyril Burt has pointed out.

"What is now known of the chemistry of the nerve cell and the physics of nerve conduction indicate that the processes involved, alike in the parts of the nervous system which are accompanied by consciousness and in the parts which are unaccompanied by consciousness, differ in no essential way from a muscle cell; there is no unique physical or chemical process specifically associated with the emergence of consciousness. The structure of the brain is indeed amazingly complex, but it suggests a mechanism designed to *detect* or *transmit* conscious activity rather than to generate it." (My italics, R. H.)[3]

There are also adventurous spirits among distinguished philosophers. Compare the view that no aspect of reality can exist beyond that which can be verified by our empirical observations with that of C. D. Broad. Broad has no religious belief and has never had any kind of religious or mystical experience. He says that it is on intellectual assessment of the evidence alone that

[1] J. C. Eccles, *The Brain and the Unity of Conscious Experience*, Cambridge University Press, 1963, pp. 42-3.
[2] J. C. Eccles (ed.), *The Brain and Conscious Experience*, Springer, Heidelberg, 1966.
[3] Cyril Burt, *Journal S.P.R.*, December 1967, p. 190.

"I am prepared to admit that such experiences occur among peoples of different races and social traditions and that they have occurred at all periods of history. I am prepared to admit that, although the experiences have differed considerably at different times and places and although the interpretations of them have differed still more, there are probably certain characteristics which are common to them all and suffice to distinguish them from all other kinds of experience. In view of this I think it more likely than not that in religious and mystical experience men come into contact with some Reality or aspect of Reality which they do not come in contact with in any other way."[1]

Broad, we note, was more cautious than Ayer. He *thought* it more likely than not that religious and mystical experience can bring man into contact with some further aspect of Reality; Ayer *knew* that, were this so, the mystic would be able to express and demonstrate it to our satisfaction. His failure to do so was assumed to be his own fault and in no way due to the rigidity of our language or any limitation of understanding or awareness on our part. This view has the support of big battalions, but sometimes a voice is raised to query it. In March 1961, Philip Toynbee wrote in the *Observer*

"It seems to be the almost inevitable assumption of certain rationalist thinkers that the 'normal' state of our minds has some sort of experiential priority to all others, and that all 'abnormal' experiences must ultimately be related to it. But it is surely a pure fluke of nature that our senses operate as they usually do. We are right to give a practical priority to the normal modes of apprehension, simply because we must live within the laws of these modes for nearly the whole of our time. But if, for example, the mescalin taker sees a world of fantastic and unfamiliar colours, if he *experiences* a reversal of the normal progress of time, then no evidence of the normal senses can effectively be used to dissuade him of these realities. Experience itself should always be distinguished from the intellectual conclusions which are drawn from it."

So the experts speak with divided voices. The first group know that the brain generates consciousness and that experience which cannot be verified empirically by physical means must be "subjective". (Ought we laymen to take this as implying that man's knowledge of the working of the physical brain is fairly complete and that his intellect, even at this early stage of his career as *homo sapiens*, is already capable of comprehending all there is?)

Like Hermann Weyl, the second group are prepared to leave a door open. They do not pretend to have discovered the exact nature of the

[1] C. D. Broad, *Religion, Philosophy and Psychical Research*, Routledge and Kegan Paul, 1953, pp. 172-3.

"prime experiencing self", but they do not feel in a position to identify it with brains, neurones and so on. To the psychologist, Sir Cyril Burt, it seems more like an organ for detecting or transmitting conscious activity than for generating it, and the philosophers, Broad and H. H. Price, are even prepared to take a fresh look at Bergson's view, that it is essentially an organ of limitation, its function being to canalise *attention* onto those parts of the exterior world which may be biologically useful to man. It may help, perhaps, to remind ourselves of Bergson's view. He called the brain the organ of *attention à la vie* and he thought that its nature is to cause man to perceive all exterior things as divisible objects which he can take to pieces and remake to suit himself, and that from this arises the mechanistic interpretation of nature. But it may be, he suggested, that unconsciously man perceives—and remembers—far more than he realises and that potentially he may be capable of perceiving anything anywhere. (This was long before the days of the fuss about subliminal advertising based on the discovery that we perceive far more of the here and now than we consciously realise.)

If Bergson was on the right track, it becomes thinkable, perhaps, that when, through shock, illness, training, drugs, or a personal idiosyncrasy, the brain slackens in its job of holding attention fixed on the here and now, even in life some factor in man may occasionally escape into other realms of being. Broad calls this possible factor by the non-committal name of psi-component, and although they both wish it otherwise, he and Professor H. H. Price think that such a component *may* persist after death and that some sort of non-physical medium *may* exist in which it could function. This concept does not seem far away from the traditional astral plane of the occultists.

To describe the arguments which led these eminent philosophers to so unorthodox a hypothesis is beyond the scope of this chapter, but some analogies suggested by Broad may help us to escape from the bad habit of *assuming* uncritically that the very idea of a factor in man which can function without a physical body must be hopelessly at variance with the information acquired through the physical sciences. We need no longer suppose, he says, that, although a surviving psi-component may be bodiless, it is necessarily unextended and unlocalised, for we are nowadays well accustomed to such phenomena as electro-magnetic fields which cannot be called bodies in the ordinary sense, but which still have definite properties and dispositions. And he uses the analogy of a piece of broadcast music which may be said to exist on the waves of a transmitting beam; perhaps, he says, the notion that no part of a psi-component can persist after the destruction of its associated body is equivalent to imagining that nothing corresponding to the performance of an orchestral piece could exist anywhere in space after the station that broadcast it had been destroyed.[1]

[1] These ideas are taken from Professor C. D. Broad's *Myers Memorial Lecture*, "Persona Identity and Survival", published by the S.P.R.

What conclusions can we draw?

When conservative scientists and philosophers insist that there is no escape from a closed world, and others, equally eminent, think that it may well be open-ended, we laymen are left to make up our own minds as to whether death is more likely to be extinction or the gateway to further life.

One crucial ground on which the two groups appear to part company is that the open-enders seem prepared, though with due caution, to consider material which differs in kind from that which can be verified or falsified by direct observation on the physical level. The conservatives, apparently, are not. But if further aspects of reality do exist and are not taken into account, wrong conclusions may be drawn even about what has been observed. This holds at any level of sophistication. Take the witch doctor who was asked for cases when his magic *never* failed. In the light of his own knowledge he replied, logically enough, "Every so often a black beast tries to devour the sun, but in a few minutes my magic will *always* drive him away." And equally logical were the experts who declared that Marconi would never be able to communicate from Cornwall to Newfoundland by radio. This was perfectly obvious, because radio waves go straight and the world is round. It was obvious, but it was wrong, for they spoke before the Heaviside layer had been discovered. If logic has inadequate premises on which to work, the conclusions it draws may be very wide of the mark.

The theory that the higher forms of life are hierarchical in structure may help us here. It has often been put forward in the past and has recently been brought back into prominence by Professor Michael Polanyi, Arthur Koestler and others. It suggests the possibility that although the view that nothing exists but the physical world may be a convenient assumption at certain levels of consciousness, at other levels it may be quite inadequate. "The hierarchical structure of higher forms of life," says Polanyi, "necessitates the assumption of further processes of emergence." And again, "The logical structure of the hierarchy implies that a higher level can come into existence only through *a process not manifest at lower levels*, a process which thus qualifies as an emergence." (My italics, R. H.)[1]

Back in 1901, in his Gifford Lectures, *The Varieties of Religious Experience*, William James quoted a speculation by a Canadian psychiatrist, Dr. R. M. Bucke, which could perhaps be looked on as an extension of the hierarchical pattern.

> "Cosmic consciousness in its more striking instances is not simply an expansion or extension of the self-conscious mind with which we are all familiar, but the super-addition of a function as distinct from any possessed by the average man as self-consciousness is distinct from any function possessed by one of the higher animals."

[1] Michael Polanyi, *Tacit Knowing*, English edition, Routledge and Kegan Paul, 1967.

Whiteman's hypothesis also fits into the pattern: the study of the kinds of awareness with which parapsychology and mysticism are concerned must be carried out on the basis of evidence in their own fields; direct physical evidence of ultra-physical events is impossible; the best to be hoped for would be indirect proof that something unknown, somewhere unknown, had precipitated a particular physical event. Clearly this last would not get us far towards *understanding* the nature of consciousness in ultra-physical conditions. "Knowledge of ultimate things is not to be reached by mere reasoning. They demand experience," said the Buddha, long ago.

All the same, the outside enquirer who wants to find out if changes of consciousness can provide any clues as to the nature of death has to do what he can. And over and above the intangible nature of the hints and clues experienced by sensitives and mystics, he has also to reckon with the fact that, when it comes to interpretation of their experiences, such temperaments are often inclined to lack the orderly minds of scientists like Professor Whiteman. In any case interpretations are always coloured by the culture the experient lives in. Apuleius believed he once found himself in the presence of the goddess Isis; Bernadette's friends were convinced she had seen the Madonna; for a Buddhist nun it might have been Kwan Yin. Coldly reported, in each case the actual experience, whatever caused it, was probably of a female presence which stood as a symbol of love, wisdom and compassion. A further difficulty for the enquirer who is trying to understand ultra-physical experience from the outside is that mystics and sensitives are liable to feel suffocated by a mundane outlook. "God us keep/From single vision and Newton's sleep," cried the mystical genius, William Blake, being apparently unable to see that the greatest mystic might envy Newton's insight. On the other hand, the down-to-earth temperament is inclined to label all mystics woolly-headed, forgetting that few tycoons could equal Plotinus, St. Paul, St. Teresa of Avila or St. Augustine for worldly toughness and competence. Communication between visionary and enquirer is not easy.

We have already struck another basic difficulty of communication which arises even when the most logically minded experients try to share their ultra-physical experiences with those who lack them: that the language they have to use is designed to deal with physical events and is therefore a very unsuitable tool. This comes out in Koestler's embarrassed struggle to make his own experience sound intelligible. He could not escape paradox. Yet among themselves experients agree that the ultra-physical conditions they think they encountered seemed normal enough at the time; it is only the use of words which renders them paradoxical. Even in psychedelic experience, what may be called the "either-ors", such as here or there, then or now, in or out, up or down, can seem quite inapplicable, and first-class intellects may find themselves faced with this problem without the aid of drugs.

I can only say, there we have been: but I cannot say where,
And I cannot say how long, for that is to place it in time,

wrote T. S. Eliot in *Four Quartets*. And again,

. . . neither from nor towards;
At the still point, there the dance is
And neither arrest nor movement. But do not call it fixity.

As far as we can judge, the experience of the modern poet had much
in common with that of the mediaeval mystic, St. John of the Cross.
This is how he described one of his own mystical explorations.

I entered in, I know not where,
And I remained, though knowing naught,
Transcending knowledge with my thought.

Of when I entered I know naught
But when I saw that I was there
(Though where it was I did not care)
Strange things I learned, with greatness fraught.
Yet what I heard I'll not declare
But there I stayed, though knowing naught,
Transcending knowledge with my thought.[1]

Looked at from the "either-or" point of view, these poems do not
make sense. Is that a hint that, beyond the realm of space-time as we
know it, "either-or" thinking *alone* may not be enough? May it even
force us to ask the wrong questions about what lies beyond death,
questions which, as the Buddha put it about ultimate things in general,
do not fit the case? Take, for instance, that very puzzling pair, subjec-
tive-objective. Can that be a pseudo-dichotomy created by the nature of
the physical brain and the words we use? Professors Gardner Murphy
and H. H. Price have both speculated that at a subconscious level
psyche is less cut off from psyche than physical body is from physical
body; we are less encapsulated, as Murphy put it. Ouspensky said somewhere that at times he was projected into a world of complicated
mathematical relations where the antithesis we know between subject
and object was broken, and it almost seems as if certain poets, artists and
musicians of today are seeking desperately to express their own fleeting
glimpses of such a world in terms of their own arts. In his book on
Mysticism and Philosophy Professor W. T. Stace has suggested that there
may be a state of consciousness which he calls trans-subjective, but he
says frankly that in his view mystical revelation transcends the intellect.
Perhaps this only applies if the intellect is looked upon as exclusively a
tool for analysis, and not as one also for intuitive synthesis, which seems
to be what any understanding of mystical revelation demands.

At this point I felt discouraged at the difficulties and misconceptions

[1] "St. John of the Cross", *Poems*, translated by Roy Campbell, Harvill Press, p. 31.

which always swarm like mosquitoes whenever attempts are made to reconcile our usual outlook with the idea that ultra-physical aspects of reality may exist and even at times be accessible to consciousness and throw further light on its nature. So I wrote lamenting this situation to a friend who is a distinguished scientist. I cannot resist quoting his reply, with its comment that physics is forcing the recognition that the physical world itself is becoming more and more of a mystery. Perhaps this may eventually make its possible extension less unthinkable, even to the conservative mind.

". . . But the logic of the natural sciences is inductive and based on probabilities. If your aim is to *prove* things, your probabilities must be very high (e.g. if you want to prove it is safe to go up in a rocket); but if your aim is to *understand* things, you may be content with very low probabilities. Current nuclear physics is full of such hypotheses; so is modern cosmology (continuous creation of matter and other miracles). The interpretation of psychical and mystical experiences should, I think, be strictly logical. But its premises need not be 'intellectual'. They might be intuitive—sheer hunches, revelations, etc.

The defect arises on the sensory plane. Our sense organs were evolved for survival as man-sized organisms on dry land. Hence vision and touch (really the muscular sense) are our dominant senses. Classical science requires us to think in terms of visible objects with tangible mass visibly moving in a space that can be visualised. The modern physicist is now everlastingly begging students *not* to visualise the universe or space, and *not* to think of particles as something tangible. Forget your sensory equipment; use only logical conceptions, and a particle may also be a wave! Hence, one technique for avoiding the rigidity of words, of which you speak, is to think in terms of mathematics (not necessarily quantitative measurement: there is also a mathematics of qualities). And since experience as such cannot in the last resort be literally described (science admits nowadays that it can only offer models) we should, where necessary, fall back on symbols, poetry and even myths."

We have been asking two questions: Does apparent out-of-the-body experience merely tell us that some people suffer from rather odd subjective fantasies, or is it as actual as that of mariners in the far past, who returned from a long voyage south with an absurd tale of the sun shining from the north? If the experience is actual, does it suggest that death may lead us into some wider reality?

From conservative thinkers the answer is unequivocal: as there is no ghost in the machine, it cannot survive its break-up. The more adventurous offer no positive proof of survival, but they do not ignore possible pointers towards it. We have noted two of these here: that the most recent research suggests that the brain may not generate consciousness, but rather be an instrument of which it makes use, and that the hierarchical structure of higher forms of life demands the assumption of further processes of emergence. Are we entitled to ask: Where must those processes stop? Is there any reason why consciousness should not emerge on to an ultra-physical level of reality where it can exist independently of a physical body? It is not widely realised that such speculation may be less crazy than it was in the light of 19th century science. Sir Cyril Burt said recently in another context: "If modern scientific knowledge affords no evidence for survival, it is equally true to say that it no longer furnishes any evidence against it."[1] If this is so, it means that the layman can now study material which seems to hint at survival, and even come down in its favour, without being swept into an intellectual dustbin as unscientific. And for those who feel that they must still stay on the fence, at least that affords a wider view than the closed world on the conservative side of it.

A somewhat ironical footnote should perhaps be added to this chapter—that the usual effect of higher mystical experience seems to be that the experient no longer cares at all whether or not he survives as a self-regarding unit. In the light of the glory he has glimpsed this seems a matter of total unimportance.

[1] Cyril Burt, *Article in International Journal of Neuropsychiatry*, October 1966.

3. Death and Psychical Research

by ROSALIND HEYWOOD[1]

The function and subject matter of psychical research

The function of psychical research, or, as it is often called nowadays, parapsychology, is to examine in a scientific spirit any faculty in man, real or alleged, which cannot be explained according to the known laws of nature. Under this heading come experiences which, on the face of it, suggest the continued existence of discarnate persons. In regard to death, then, the function of psychical research is to ask the question: Do such reported experiences provide scientifically valid evidence that some component of a human being can survive the death of his body? If not, what brings them about? From this stem two further questions: What kind of component could survive and in what kind of environment?

To the materialist and behaviourist, of course, such questions are plain nonsense. Mind and body are but two aspects of the same thing; any fool can see that one must cease to exist with the other. All the same, it seems hardly reasonable to ignore a number of phenomena which appear to suggest the contrary; either these should be accepted, or adequately explained away, or the question left an open one. Jung put the situation very fairly. "Although there is no way to marshal valid proof of the continuance of the soul after death," he wrote, "there are nevertheless experiences which make us thoughtful. I take them as hints and do not presume to ascribe to them the significance of insights."[2]

Christians, of course, and many members of such groups as the theosophists, hold it as part of their belief that the soul survives the body, but one quite large group, the spiritualists, go yet farther than that; they are convinced, not only that human personality as we know it does survive death, but that certain specially gifted persons whom they call mediums have the power to make contact with the discarnate almost at will. That this belief has a wide appeal seems indicated by the report from the main spiritualist centre in London that in 1966 it had registered over 100,000 visitors.

Although the approaches of spiritualists and psychical researchers could hardly be more different—the first are convinced they know what the second seek to discover—part of the raw material they deal with is

[1] As the writer of this and the preceding chapter is a member of the Society for Psychical Research, she would like it made clear that any views expressed in them are hers alone, and should not be attributed to that Society, which holds no corporate views.

[2] C. J. Jung, *Memories, Dreams, Reflections*, Collins, and Routledge and Kegan Paul, 1963, p. 289.

the same; hence they are sometimes confused in the public mind. It may make this chapter more intelligible to those not conversant with that raw material to begin by giving two typical and well-authenticated examples of it. The first is a spontaneous experience which the spiritualist would take at its face value, as coming from the discarnate, Jung would call a hint, and the psychical researcher would study exhaustively to find its most probable explanation. The experience was of an apparition coinciding with the sudden death of an airman who was on a routine, not a combat flight. The apparition was reported by the friend who saw him *before* he heard of the airman's death.

"The percipient was Lieut. J. J. Larkin, of the R.A.F., and the apparition was that of one of Lieut. Larkin's fellow officers, Lieut. David M'Connel, killed in an airplane crash on December 7th 1918. Lieut. Larkin reported that he spent the afternoon of December 7th in his room at the barracks. He sat in front of the fire reading and writing and was wide awake all the time. At about 3.30 p.m. he heard someone walking up the passage.

'The door opened with the usual noise and clatter which David always made: I heard his "Hello boy!" and I turned half round in my chair and saw him standing in the doorway, half in and half out of the room and holding the door knob in his hand. He was dressed in his full flying clothes, but wearing his naval cap, there being nothing unusual in his appearance... I remarked "Hello! back already?" He replied, "Yes, got there all right, had a good trip" ... I was looking at him at the time he was speaking. He said, "Well, cheerio!", closed the door noisily and went out.'

"Shortly after this a friend dropped in to see Lieut. Larkin and Larkin told him that he had just seen and talked with Lieut. M'Connel. (This friend sent a corroborative statement to the Society for Psychical Research.) Later on that day it was learned that Lieut. M'Connel had been instantly killed in a flying accident which occurred at about 3.25 p.m. Mistaken identity seems to be ruled out, since the light was very good in the room where the apparition appeared. Moreover, there was no other man in the barracks at the time who in any way resembled Lieut. M'Connel. It was also found that he was wearing his naval cap when he was killed, apparently an unusual circumstance. Agent and percipient had been 'Very good friends, though not intimate friends in the true sense of the word'."[1]

A second example of raw material suggesting on the face of it discarnate existence is the following case of a medium conveying information which was certainly not known to her, and appeared to be known at the time to nobody living. The medium was Mrs. Osborn Leonard,

[1] Summarised by Professor Gardner Murphy in *Three Papers on the Survival Problem* (American Society for Psychical Research, 1945), from a longer report in *Proceedings* S.P.R., Vol. XXXIII, 1923, pp. 151-160.

who was studied over many years by psychical researchers and whose integrity never seems to have been questioned, even by the sternest critics of spiritualism, if they knew her.[1] The sitter was Mrs. Hugh Talbot, and the purported communicator her husband, who appeared to be trying ardently to prove his continued existence. In the middle of his attempt to do this Mrs. Leonard suddenly began talking about a book, which she showed with her hands as being about eight to ten inches long, by four to five wide. She said, reported Mrs. Talbot:

" 'It is not exactly a *book*, it is not printed . . . it has writing in . . . there are two books, you will know the one he means by a diagram of languages in the front . . . Indo-European, Aryan, Semitic languages . . . A table of Arabian languages, Semitic languages.' It sounded absolute rubbish to me. I had never heard of a diagram of languages and all these Eastern names jumbled together sounded like nothing at all, and she kept on repeating them and saying this is how I was to know the book, and kept on and on, 'Will you look at page 12 or 13. If it is there it would interest him so much after this conversation.' "

Mrs. Talbot reported that the next day she found two old notebooks which had belonged to her husband and which she had never cared to open. A shabby black leather one corresponded in size to Mrs. Leonard's description.

"To my utter astonishment, my eyes fell on the words, 'Table o Semitic or Syro-Arabian Languages', and pulling out the leaf, which was a long folded piece of paper pasted in, I saw on the other side 'General table of the Aryan and Indo-European languages'. On page 13 of this notebook was an extract from an anonymous work entitled *Post Mortem*. It describes the sensations of a person who realises that he is dead, and of his meeting with his deceased relatives."[2]

Such puzzling yet apparently meaningful phenomena have been reported since history began and in every culture. The dream which frightened Caesar's wife, the test set by King Croesus for the Oracles, which the Pythia at Delphi passed with flying colours, and the biblical story of the Witch of Endor are typical examples. In the past they were given such labels as divination, second sight, or possession and were taken for granted as supernatural.

The pagan world tended to attribute many psychic, or, as they are now often called, "psi" phenomena to the gods. The Christian Church,

[1] A book has recently appeared by Professor C. E. M. Hansel, entitled *ESP: A Scientific Evaluation*, Scribner, New York, 1966. In this he expresses the opinion that as E.S.P. seems inherently impossible, all evidence for it is more reasonably attributable to fantasy or fraud. Hence, he seems to think, there never can have been an honest medium.
[2] Taken from a summary by Professor Gardner Murphy in *Three Papers on the Survival Problem*, American S.P.R., 1945, of a detailed investigation of the case reported in *Proceedings*, S.P.R. 1920-21, pp. 253-60.

whatever their origin, looked on them as supernatural and therefore awe-inspiring and not matters into which the faithful were encouraged to pry. Then, with the coming of the Age of Science, all was changed. By the educated the supernatural was no longer looked on as awe-inspiring but as non-existent. There was no room for such irrational nonsense in the orderly predictable universe postulated by Newton and his successors; to be scientifically respectable one *must* attribute all reports of it to fantasy or fraud. Nevertheless, here and there these "impossible" phenomena continued to crop up, as they had always done, and at last, in the second half of the 19th century, some study of them began to be made by a few independent-minded scholars and scientists who did not mind being laughed at. This study resulted in their asking the revolutionary question: Can there be quite so much smoke without any fire? What if supernatural phenomena do occur and are not supernatural after all, but normal and subject to natural law?

The technique and evolution of psychical research

It soon became clear that research into such phenomena by isolated individuals would not get far; it ought to be co-ordinated. Realising this, and stimulated by the success of some of his own experiments in thought transference, in 1882 the well-known physicist, Sir William Barrett, called a group of his colleagues together to found the Society for Psychical Research (the S.P.R.). It was a distinguished group, headed by the philosopher, Professor Henry Sidgwick, and including the scientist Lord Rayleigh and the scholars Frederic Myers, Edmund Gurney and the first two Lords Balfour.[1] Their declared object was to study *by the methods of science* all phenomena, real or alleged, for which a scientific explanation was not already known. (In those days these phenomena included hypnotism, now a benefit of the British national health service.) The study was to be undertaken, they insisted, *without prejudice or prepossession of any kind*. That this lofty standard of detachment was asking a good deal of human nature in a subject which sought to probe the depths of that nature itself, soon became only too clear. It does not become less so as the years pass.

For readers who have not enquired into psychical research it may be helpful to list the names given today to the various manifestations of the erstwhile supernatural, including those concerned with mundane events, for they can affect our assessment of ostensibly extra-mundane ones. The supernatural as a whole has become the paranormal, implying no more than that the natural explanation for certain phenomena has not yet been found. All such phenomena taken together have been

---

[1] They were soon joined by people of comparable stature, among them the scientists Sir Oliver Lodge, Professor J. J. Thomson, and Mrs. Henry Sidgwick, Principal of Newnham College, Cambridge. A similar society was founded in the U.S.A. with William James among its early members.

given the non-committal blanket name of "psi", and they divide into two categories, physical and mental. In the first, physical matter appears to be affected or even moved by unknown means, possibly mental, but the evidence for this is conflicting and would take too long to discuss here. The second category, mental psi, was labelled extra-sensory perception, or E.S.P., by the well-known experimentalist in the subject, Dr. J. B. Rhine of Duke University, U.S.A. E.S.P. stands for response to impressions which are not received *via* any of the known senses, and are then found to correspond with mundane events which can be distant in space and/or time. (The name is not, perhaps, ideal for it seems to imply that no physical means of communication can be involved, and that has not been proved.) For purposes of study E.S.P. has been further divided into four classes: telepathy (response to another person's mental state), clairvoyance (awareness of a distant objective event), precognition (non-inferential awareness of a future event), and retrocognition (awareness of a past event without the use of memory, testimony or inference). But this division need not imply that E.S.P. is other than a single faculty operating in different situations.

That E.S.P. of mundane events does occur has been confirmed repeatedly over the last thirty-odd years by scientists from various universities, who have demonstrated its existence in hundreds of prosaic experiments in England, the U.S.A., Russia, Czechoslovakia and else-where; but there are large numbers of people too wedded to mechanistic orthodoxy to be able to envisage it. They find it easier to suppose that the many respected scientists involved have *all* either been cheated in conditions they took great pains to make fraud-proof and error-proof, or have themselves deliberately cheated, apparently in order to produce evidence for E.S.P. which has brought them neither fame nor fortune.[1]

As already mentioned, the tracking down and confirmation of E.S.P. of mundane events has complicated the issue as regards evaluation of further E.S.P.-type phenomena which appear to have extra-mundane origins. The cause of this complication is perhaps best made clear by a brief sketch of the course into which psychical research was forced, partly by its own discoveries, *en route*, of unknown depths and complexities in human nature, partly by the highly sceptical climate in which it was undertaken.

The S.P.R. was founded at a time when the irresistible force of scientific discovery was crashing most fiercely against the great fortress of traditional belief. The scientists of the day were even convinced that

[1] See op. cit. by Professor Hansel. His gallant and very ingenious attempt to prove all the evidence for E.S.P. a fake takes us back to the days when the great chemist Lavoisier read a paper to the French Academy which proved that meteoric stones could not fall from the sky because there were no stones in the sky to fall. (Quoted by John Langdon Davis in *Man: Known and Unknown*, Secker and Warburg, 1960.) It is extremely difficult even for the most brilliant men to accept phenomena which run counter to their own basic assumptions.

they had reached the boundaries of knowledge. The Riddle of the Universe is solved, declared the scientist Ernest Haeckel. At the same time, in the realm of biology, the discoveries of Darwin and others had devastatingly undermined the religious belief that man was a spirit made in the image of God, temporarily dwelling in a mortal body.

This shattering attack on old beliefs by new science, which seemed to be reducing man to a mere mechanism, was the main stimulus which induced the founders of the S.P.R. to undertake their much mocked-at venture. It seemed to them just possible that psychical research might throw some light on what man's nature really was. This is how, some years later, Professor Henry Sidgwick described their attitude:

"When we took up seriously the obscure and perplexing investigation which we call psychical research, we were mainly moved to do so by the profound and painful division and conflict as regards the nature and destiny of the human soul which we found in the thought of our age. On the one hand, under the influence of Christian teaching, still dominant over the minds of the majority of educated persons, and powerfully influencing many even of those who have discarded its dogmatic system, the soul is conceived as independent of the bodily system and destined to survive it. On the other hand, the preponderant tendency of modern physiology has been more and more to exclude this conception, and to treat the life and processes of any individual mind as inseparably connected with the life and processes of the shortlived body that it animates . . . Now our own position was this. We believed unreservedly in the methods of modern science, and were prepared to accept submissively her reasoned conclusions, when sustained by the agreement of experts; but we were not prepared to submit with equal docility to the mere prejudices of scientific men. And it appeared to us that there was an important body of evidence—tending *prima facie* to establish the independence of soul or spirit—which modern science had simply left on one side with ignorant contempt; and that in so leaving it she had been untrue to her professed method and had arrived prematurely at her negative conclusions. Observe that we did not say that these negative conclusions were scientifically erroneous. To have said that would have been to fall into the very error we were trying to avoid. We only said that they had been arrived at prematurely . . ."[1]

Apart from some pioneering experiments in telepathy, the main subject matter of psychical research for a number of years was (1) spontaneous cases of apparent psi reported by the public, and (2) the activities of spiritualist mediums, which purported to originate with the dead. Since the E.S.P. process was assumed to be non-physical, and, according to the knowledge of the day, the brain was not the type of instrument which could have a hand in it, it was thought for some time

[1] Presidential Address, 1888, *Proceedings* S.P.R., Vol. V, p. 291.

that even to prove that E.S.P. of mundane events was a fact would indicate that the soul or spirit was separable from the body, and thus make the idea of survival more plausible. Over the years, thousands of apparent cases of E.S.P. were checked and corroborated, enough, indeed, in the view of Sidgwick and his colleagues, to convince their scientific contemporaries of its reality. But they were mistaken. The general opinion remained that of Professor Joseph Jastrow: "Telepathy is an egregious logical sin." No matter that there were thousands of cases. Take them separately, said the critics, and each one could be explained away as due to some such human weakness as bad observation, wishful thinking, unconscious inference, false deduction or faulty memory. And failing all of those, any one incident could always be ascribed to chance coincidence. Ten thousand leaky buckets, they insisted, can hold no more water than one.

The fiercely sceptical mental climate eventually canalised the main stream of psychical research into efforts to produce *experimental* evidence for E.S.P. of *mundane* events to which none of the above criticisms could apply, for in experiments the statements made by percipients could always be checked against their targets so that even the bogey of chance coincidence could be ruled out. (Herein lies the extreme difficulty of research into survival, that no statement made by the purported discarnate can ever be checked unless it is about a mundane event; thus the information it contains might always in theory have been discovered by some form of direct E.S.P. Some of the evidence might carry weight in a court of law, but nothing so far has been produced which would be watertight enough for a science laboratory.)

Ironically enough, although experimental evidence for E.S.P. of mundane events was finally produced, coercive enough for men of the stature of Professors C. D. Broad, H. H. Price, Sir Cyril Burt, Sir Alister Hardy and H. J. Eysenck to come to the conclusion that there was no escaping from it, it does not after all provide the hoped-for proof of the dual nature of man. That is because in the meantime the concepts of physics have basically changed. The building blocks of the universe are no longer regarded as solid little atoms, but as infinitesimal concentrations of intangible energy, and when it comes to the realms of the very large and the very small, classical notions about the nature of time and space, as well as of matter, no longer hold. At the same time, in the realm of the very small, the brain is being found to function as a chemico-electrical instrument of incredible delicacy and in a manner unthinkable when it was ruled out as being in any way involved in E.S.P. Hence, some researchers both in the West and the U.S.S.R. have recently envisaged the possibility that telepathy, for instance, may turn out to be some unknown form of linkage between brain and brain, rather than between mind and mind. If so, it need lend no support for the hypothesis of an independent mind or soul. But other researchers, probably the majority, still consider that E.S.P. of mundane events in general is a matter of minds, not brains alone—and if they are right it may still point towards the possibility of survival.

To go back to the early researchers. They soon discovered that sifting the evidence for spontaneous psi was an even harder job than they had expected and that many apparent examples of it could indeed be explained away as due to some such normal cause as the critics asserted. In particular they made one basic rule to which their successors have always adhered: that no E.S.P.-type experience must be considered evidential unless the percipient had reported it or taken definite action on it *before* he had received news of the related event by normal means. Scientifically necessary as is this strict procedure, it may give a distorted view of the actual incidence of E.S.P., because if the well-authenticated cases are genuine, it is improbable that all the similar cases, where for some natural reason authentication was not possible, should be spurious. Take the following summary of a close parallel to the apparition of Lieut. M'Connel, quoted above, which was told me after the Second World War by a matter-of-fact Flight Lieutenant who was extremely puzzled by his experience. His squadron was sent to intercept a wave of enemy bombers and after a ferocious dogfight the scattered pilots returned to base separately. My informant said that while walking towards the mess tent after landing he was joined by a fellow pilot, a red-headed man of very individual appearance. After a few heartfelt remarks about the violence of the dogfight the red-headed man turned away to his own quarters, and my informant went on to the mess tent and ordered a drink. While he was having it a third pilot came in and said that the man my informant appeared to have been talking to a few minutes before had been blown to pieces about an hour earlier. Had he mentioned the talk *before* the third man came in, the case could have been classed as evidential of *something* paranormal at least; as it stands, it is a "mere anecdote".

A useful clue to the frequency of E.S.P.-type experience is given in a recent book by Dr. Louisa Rhine, *ESP in Life and Lab*.[1] Here she traces the process that ends in the expression of E.S.P., and draws her illustrations both from the psychological data observed in experimental work over thirty years at Duke University, North Carolina, and from 10,000 examples of spontaneous E.S.P.-type experiences, many of them connected with deaths, which had been sent her by the general public. (It may perhaps reasonably be assumed that the cases sent to Dr. Rhine were only a fraction of those which actually occurred.) Psychologically the two groups are seen to have much in common.

Some psychological discoveries of psychical research

One result of their meticulous sifting of cases was that the early researchers anticipated some of Freud's revelations about the complex

[1] Collier Macmillan, 1968.

subconscious life of man, and as time went on this led them to realise more and more the extreme difficulty of obtaining evidence for survival which could not be attributed, even if not to normal sources, at least to E.S.P. of mundane events. For instance, they found that at hidden levels of the psyche man is extremely suggestible, a great dramatiser, and seldom if ever forgets; hence information believed in all honesty to come from the discarnate might have been obtained normally years before and consciously—but *not* subconsciously—forgotten. Some researchers came to think, too, that apparitions could be explained as visual hallucinations created unconsciously by the percipient himself in order to bring to his *surface* attention information which he had received telepathically at a deeper level, and which had been prevented, perhaps by some kind of biologically useful censorship, from emerging directly. (On one occasion, for instance, a lady read in a letter some news which was not in it but was afterwards found to be correct.) It was also realised that what one may call a telepathic "signal" seems, on occasion, to lie in wait in the subconscious until the percipient's mood and situation enable it to emerge; until, say, he goes home to bed after an evening at the theatre. These findings suggested the possibility that an apparition which purports to be of a recently dead man may in fact be a delayed hallucinatory dramatisation by the percipient himself of an earlier telepathic "signal" which he had subconsciously received from one about to die.

Psychical researchers, incidentally, have discovered by means of repeated widespread questionnaires that visual hallucinations are seen by about 10 per cent of normal persons at least once in their lives, and do not necessarily have any connection with drink, drugs or disease as is popularly supposed. Only a small proportion of these hallucinations turns out to correspond with actual events or persons, but it was found, unexpectedly, that of those which did, more of the persons "seen" were alive than dead. In other words, from the cool investigator's point of view, the simple apparition of a recently dead man, however convincing to the percipient, cannot be regarded as a sure sign of survival.[1]

The same ambiguity applies to "haunts", that is, to visual or other external hallucinations, or to inner emotional or mental impressions, which are *independently* experienced in a particular place by different persons at different times. Excluding normal explanations, such as water gurgling through pipes, rats gambolling in attics, white owls being taken for white ladies, and so on, that such experiences do occur can hardly be doubted by investigators who dispassionately study the

---

[1] It is perhaps fair to note that in *The Enigma of Survival*, Rider, 1959, Dr. Hornell Hart, who was Professor of Sociology at Duke University, North Carolina, for nearly twenty years, has pointed out that some people have had the experience of mentally "projecting" themselves to distant spots, and that their apparitions have been seen at those spots at the time they did so. He argued that as these *conscious* apparitions of the living have various features in common with apparitions of the dead, the possibility that the latter may represent *conscious* personalities who have survived bodily death cannot lightly be set aside.

evidence. But how to interpret them is another matter. (One of the toughest psychological problems in psychical research is the natural human tendency to interpret an experience in terms of one's own outlook.) For one thing, in the light of modern field theory it may not be necessary to rule out the hypothesis that a place can be permanently affected by some emotionally charged event which once took place there. For another, experiments as well as spontaneous cases suggest that E.S.P. seems to have a more flexible relation to time and space than sensory perception; thus, in the case of a "haunt", retrocognition could have been at work, or precognition of being told about it later on,[1] and there is always the possibility that a sensitive person visiting a traditionally haunted place may pick up the idea telepathically from living persons who know the tradition, and then experience the traditional event in an apparently exterior, but in fact self-induced, hallucinatory fashion. In other words, a haunting ghost may be an authentic experience, but once more need not imply the appearance of an actual discarnate entity.

At the same time, no researcher who is trying to live up to the standard of studying psi phenomena "without prejudice or prepossession of any kind" can ignore cases of unexpected apparent *intervention* by the dead which is both purposive and conveys information known at the time to nobody living. Whatever the explanation, there is *something* to be explained. A famous example of such intervention is known as the Chaffin Will Case, and the following summary of it was made by a lawyer and well-known psychical researcher, Mr. W. H. Salter, who investigated it exhaustively himself.[2]

"James Chaffin, a farmer in North Carolina, died in 1921 as the result of a fall, leaving a widow and two sons. In 1905 he made a will leaving his whole property to his third son, Marshall, who proved the will and himself died about a year later, leaving a widow and a son, a minor. In June 1925 the second son, James, began to have vivid dreams of his father appearing at his bedside and speaking. This vision may have been a 'borderland' experience, occurring between sleeping and waking. It was more realistic than pure dreams usually are but in an experience as informative as this the distinction is of little importance.

[1] In *Noted Witnesses to Psychic Occurrences*, Boston S.P.R., 1928, Dr. Walter Franklin Prince reports an experience of seeing a "ghost" of the future which was interpreted as of the past. An American singer, a quaker, David Bispham, was taken to visit an old bookseller who was a sensitive and who claimed to see one of Bispham's ancestors standing by him. He described the ancestor's appearance in detail: red brocade coat, lighter satin waistcoat, gold chain with locket, sword, grey hair, clean-shaven. Knowing of no such ancestor, Bispham did not think any more about the matter until eighteen months later he was offered his first engagement to sing in opera in England. This was to take the part of a French duke, and for it he had to shave off his beard and wear a grey wig and just the clothes described by the old man.

[2] *Zoar, or The Evidence of Psychical Research concerning Survival*, by W. H. Salter, Sidgwick and Jackson, 1961, pp. 45-6.

"The figure was dressed in a black overcoat which James had often seen his father wearing. [James said that] 'He took hold of his overcoat this way and pulled it back and said "You will find my will in my overcoat pocket" and then disappeared.'

"James went to his elder brother's house and found the coat, and inside the inner pocket, which was sewn up, a roll of paper with the words, 'Read the 27th chapter of Genesis in my daddie's old Bible'. James found the old Bible in a drawer in his mother's house and *in the presence of witnesses* [my italics, R. H.] found between two folded pages on which the 27th chapter of Genesis was printed, another will, dated January 16th 1919, whereby the Testator, 'after reading the 27th Chapter of Genesis', in which the supplanting of Esau by Jacob is related, divided his property equally between his four sons, and added, 'You must all take care of your Mammy.'

"The second will, though unattested by witnesses, was valid by the law of the State . . . Before probate, however, the Testator appeared again to his son, James, saying: 'Where is my old will?' and showing 'considerable temper'."

Such cases obviously carry more weight if they do not stand alone, yet, as has been said already, to find others which by good fortune are equally well-authenticated is hardly likely. Take the two following which may be as indicative of something paranormal as the Chaffin case, but which no serious investigator, particularly in the present mental climate, could treat as such.

The first was brought to my notice privately by a friend who knew the persons concerned and through whom I checked it as far as possible. One morning early in 1967 a man suffered a stroke and died the same evening. About five the next morning his sister-in-law heard the words, "Look after Mary" (his wife) loud and clear, and although she had not been told that the man had died, she woke her husband and said to him that she knew this must be so. A friend of the family also reported that in the early hours of the same morning she saw the man clearly and was asked by him to tell his wife how sorry he was that he had not put his affairs in order. The friend had not been told of his death and did not know the position of his affairs. But here the criticisms that can be made are obvious: both ladies had heard of the stroke, so were probably anticipating an early death. And it could be wondered whether, privately, the friend may have thought the man unbusiness-like? Her imagination could have done the rest.

A similar case is recorded in a recent American book.[1]

The singer, Tito Schipa, was given a room in an inn which was about to be sold, as the previous owner's will could not be found. He was disturbed during the night by noises and finally by the words "Look on the left wall." He did so and saw nothing, but as the dis-

[1] *ESP*, by Susy Smith, Pyramid Books, New York, 1962.

turbances went on he finally dragged a table to the wall, climbed on it and took down an oil painting. The missing will was stuck behind it. Unfortunately there is no authentication given for this anecdote and no means of knowing how much it may have gained by the passage of time, or from mouth to mouth; or, conversely, how many salient points may have been omitted. So, even if authentic, it is not "evidence".

Some psychological aspects of mental mediumship

It is now time to turn from spontaneous E.S.P. to the second phenomenon which suggests that the human personality can survive the death of the body: mental mediumship, an activity which can be evoked more or less to order and on which spiritualists mainly base their belief that contact can be made with the dead.[1]

It is best, perhaps, to begin by describing the bare facts of mental mediumship as seen by an investigator who sets out to study it with a critical but open mind. The most basic of these is that by speech or writing a man or woman can pass on to others information which seems to well up from some hidden region of the psyche, and to which, occasionally, he or she does not appear to have had access by sensory means. Such persons are also called sensitives, which is a more neutral name for those who have gifts of this kind without necessarily holding spiritualist beliefs about them. Since in our culture more women than men are mediums, from now on I shall refer to them as women.

In extreme cases mediums produce their information while in a trance, a condition in which the conscious personality has voluntarily handed over to another and quite different one. Spiritualists call this new personality a Control, because they believe it to be a discarnate spirit who has temporarily taken possession of the medium's body and who sometimes claims to have access to a wider sphere of knowledge than have embodied persons. The phenomenon is world-wide. In other cultures the Control can be non-human; for the Greek oracles or in Voodoo today, a god, for the Witch of Endor, a familiar spirit. But in all cases the medium purports to be a medium of communication between another state of being and our own, with the Control coming from the other side of the curtain, so to speak.

Most non-spiritualists, especially in the light of modern psychology, do not look on a Control as a discarnate spirit but rather as another facet of the medium's own personality. If that is so, since the evidence is excellent that she does on occasion produce information outside her own normal knowledge, she must presumably have acquired it either

---

[1] Spiritualists also claim that what they call physical mediums can produce material indications of survival, but as the evidence for this is controversial and bedevilled by much fraud it will not be discussed here. Nor will fraudulent mediumship in general, because although, being profitable, it is unfortunately widespread and reflects most unfairly on the many honest mediums, it clearly has nothing to do with what may be genuine evidence for survival and can of course be unmasked by the methods used in any other form of deception.

by some kind of E.S.P. of mundane events, or—the dispassionate investigator cannot rule this out—the facet of her personality which emerges in trance may be able to communicate with another order of being by some extended form of E.S.P. Of course, neither the spiritualist nor the psychologist may have the right answer here, for we may not be asking the right question, and we shall not get the right answer until we do.

The next point to be noted is that mediumship, even of the trance variety, is not a thing entirely apart from normal states. There are many degrees of dissociation. At the near end, for instance, we all go into day-dreams in which our attention is withdrawn from the outer world. Most of us, too, have known the solution to a difficult problem to emerge unexpectedly when we are thinking of something else. It is now an accepted fact that much, if not all, creative work is done by means of such sudden upwellings from the subconscious: hidden parts of the mind are constantly at work. And there also seems to be every degree of dissociation from the alert state in which the attention is actively fixed on the outer world to the deepest trance of mediumship. Take inspirational speech. A great preacher once said after an outstanding sermon that he had no idea what he was going to say until he heard himself saying it. In fact there seems to be some justification for the lady who declared that she could not know what she thought until she had heard what she said! A further step is automatic writing. Quite a number of people can do this. If they make a practice of holding a pencil resting on blank paper they will find that, irrespective of their conscious intention, eventually it will write more or less coherent, though seldom interesting, passages. In fact there is every degree of dissociation from day-dreaming to—in a very few people—total mediumistic trance, and in others, of course, to mental illness.

Much of what many mediums say in trance seems very much like the product of a kind of dream state, and is often neither coherent nor true to fact. One well-meaning medium whose skill I had been asked to test implored me repeatedly on behalf of my dead husband not to sit at home and mourn his loss, but to go out and play bridge, or something, to get away from myself. In spite of my telling her, frankly and emphatically, that my husband was very much alive and only too delighted when I had time to stay at home, her trance personality, like a damaged record, had apparently got stuck in a kind of "sorrowing widow" groove, and she still continued to beg me to cheer up and go out.

But the prevalence of mediocre and even dishonest mediums must not blind the investigator to those rare examples—the equivalent of great artists—who do at times seem able to make contact with events distant in time and space. And it is about them that he must ask: How and whence do they get their information? It is only reasonable to ask these questions "without prejudice or prepossession", that is, in the light of what appears to happen when a good medium goes into trance. And what appears to happen is that at first the Control personality, which is quite different from her normal one, takes over and may perhaps do no more than pass on messages from other purported discarnate communicators. But at times he (or she) may go further, by handing over, so he claims, to one of them. Then there may come a second remarkable change in the medium's voice, manner of speech and even vocabulary. It is *as if* some third personality, different from both the medium's normal one and the Control, were talking through her lips, and on occasion this personality appears to the sitter to have mannerisms and characteristics just like those of the person he purports to be. Many of these alleged communicators insist that the process of making contact with mundane conditions is hard and painful—like diving into a fog, one said—and that to transmit more than distorted and incoherent fragments through the medium is extremely difficult. This helps to account, it is claimed, for the banal triviality of so many purported communications, and indeed, seen with ordinary mundane eyes, to which the whole idea of extra-mundane communication is almost incredible, the plaint seems not entirely without reason.

Yet at times, with a first-class medium, the alleged communicators' performances can be very lifelike and convincing, and whatever second thoughts the investigator may have afterwards, it would show bias to rule out absolutely that what appears to be going on may be going on. Obviously though, he must envisage all alternative explanations, beginning with the simplest.

The simplest, of course, is that a medium may appear to be exercising E.S.P. when she is not. It has been found, for instance, that when she is in trance, submerged drama-loving levels of her psyche will serve up, as coming from the discarnate, snippets of information inferred unconsciously from the sitter's behaviour, age, sex or even carelessly revealing remarks. The normal consciousness of an honest medium is not to blame for this deception, because even if she realises what has been said or written by her trance consciousness, she *need have no idea of its source*.

Another alternative to genuine contact with the discarnate in a medium is unconscious memory. The late Dr. Eric Strauss, head of the Psychiatric Department at St. Bartholomew's Hospital, could himself do automatic writing, and on one occasion he produced a lengthy script, written in German upside down, and purporting to come from a long-dead German about whom consciously he knew no more than his name. Surprised, he looked him up in the encyclopaedia, to find that the script contained nothing that was not in it. In his opinion the simplest explanation of his performance was that he had once casually glanced at the article and quite forgotten consciously that he had done so. But it looks as if the subconscious never forgets.

The fact is that in all of us, even the most prosaic and least mediumistically minded, a certain subconscious level of the psyche seems to be a great dramatiser who loses no opportunity of showing off. Dreams make this clear enough. And, as Professor H. H. Price has pointed out, the more one is inclined to reject the survivalist explanation of medium-istic phenomena, the more one is bound to emphasise this subconscious dramatising power. For, as he says, sometimes it is possible to have a conversation with an alleged communicator. He makes suitable replies, agrees or disagrees, answers questions . . . It really is *as if* one were talking normally with a stranger. "If all this is just subconscious dramatisation on the medium's part," says Professor Price, "it is comparable with the late Miss Ruth Draper at her best."[1]

Whence does a medium get her information?

The next question is: suppose a medium produces a piece of informa-tion which she has acquired neither from the discarnate nor by sensory means, how could she have got hold of it? The simplest alternative seems to be by telepathy from somebody present; the next, telepathy from a distant living person; or she might even have seen clairvoyantly a distant document, such as a letter written by a dead person which no one living had read.

Here is a first-hand example. Soon after the Second World War I decided to test a medium by having an anonymous sitting with her and mentally asking the fate of a German friend, of whom I had heard nothing since 1938. He was a prominent man of great integrity, and I feared he must have been killed, either by the Nazis or the Russians. He soon appeared to turn up at the sitting, gave his Christian name, spoke through the medium in character and reminded me of various pleasant experiences which he had shared with my family in America, and I had forgotten. He then said he had been killed in grim circum-stances which he did not want to talk about. *After* the sitting I made enquiries as to his fate. He was eventually traced by the Swiss Foreign Office to a neutral country, and in reply to a letter from me he said that he had escaped both Nazis and Russians, had married, was living in two rooms and had never been so happy in his life. Here, then, it looks as if the medium, unknown to herself, was building a picture of the German from *my* subconscious memories and *my* fears as to his fate.

There is one famous case which also makes it clear that a medium cannot tell whether her information comes from an incarnate or a discarnate source. A medium being tested by a lecturer in mathematics at London University, Dr. S. G. Soal, produced for him as a communi-cator one Gordon Davis, a childhood friend whom he believed to have been killed in the First World War. Through the medium, "Gordon Davis" spoke of experiences they had shared in their youth and then went on to describe in some detail a house he said he had once lived in, including pictures, a black china bird on the piano, the outlook and so

[1]Script for a B.B.C. broadcast.

on. About eighteen months later Dr. Soal learnt that Gordon Davis had not been killed but was practising as an estate agent in Southend. So he went to see him, and was much surprised to find him living in the house described by the medium; but he had only gone there *after* Dr. Soal's sitting with her. They looked up his professional diary to find that at the time of the sitting he had been peacefully interviewing a client, quite unaware of his ostensible presence many miles away. This curious incident again highlights that perennial difficulty in survival research, the apparently elastic relationship of E.S.P. to time as it is mediated to us *via* the senses; for Dr. Soal's medium, like the old man who described David Bispham's "ancestor", spoke of events which had not yet happened as if they were in the past.

We now come to cases where the psychical researcher has to face the fact that a medium has apparently achieved the feat, either, as she believes, of getting information from the discarnate, or, at two or three removes, from living persons. Here is one occasion when the famous Mrs. Osborne Leonard did this in conditions where no possibility of leakage has been found, and when the details intended to prove the identity of the purported communicator were too many and specific to be reasonably attributable to chance.

Professor E. R. Dodds, at the time Regius Professor of Greek at Oxford, who, incidentally, does not believe in survival, asked Mr. Drayton Thomas, a Methodist minister, to take a proxy sitting with Mrs. Leonard. (In a proxy sitting, the sitter represents someone else and knows no details about the life of the deceased person with whom it is hoped to make contact.) The sitting was not even at second-hand, on behalf of Professor Dodds himself, but at third-hand, for a friend of his, a Mrs. Lewis. She wanted to try to get proofs of identity from her dead father, Mr. Macaulay, who in life had been a water engineer. All Mr. Thomas was told was his name, home town and date of death, presumably the essential minimum if the medium was to locate any one person among the countless millions of the dead. This minimum seemed to be enough for Feda, Mrs. Leonard's Control, since she set about identifying Mr. Macaulay right away. First she described his tools and drawing office, very well for a person who was not an engineer. Then she mentioned his great interest in saving water, particularly bath water. She gave his pet name, Puggy, for his daughter. She referred to his damaged hand, and so on. And she added one tiny item which seemed uniquely applicable to the Macaulay family. This was to give the names of some persons, who were now, she said, with Mr. Macaulay (these persons were in fact dead), and who had shared a specially happy period during his life on earth. One name puzzled her. "It might be Reece, R.E.E.C.E.", she said "but it sounds like Riss, R.I.S.S." She also added as further proof of identity that Mr. Macaulay had proposed to his first wife on a bridge.

All this meant nothing to Mr. Thomas and he sent the records to

Professor Dodds, who sent them on to Mrs. Lewis. She confirmed that all the items given were correct, including names, and added that her father's passion for saving bath water had been a family joke, also that during the happy period referred to, her schoolboy brother had hero-worshipped another boy called Rees and had said so often that his name was spelt R.E.E.S., not R.E.E.C.E., that to tease him his young sisters had taken to singing, "Not Reece but Riss". And Mr. Macaulay did propose to his first wife on a bridge.

Trivial though they are, such facts seem quite well adapted to pinpointing Mr. Macaulay, given a means of transmission as admittedly inadequate, distorted, sporadic and fleeting as that through a medium. But the question the psychical researcher still has to ask is: From where did they really come? Excluding deliberate fraud on the part of a respected minister and professor, from which they gained no advantage, and the improbable alternative that Mrs. Leonard hit on so many unusual items just by chance, he seems to be faced with an either/or. Either she extracted those items from the mind of a living person at several removes, or she somehow tapped the past of a person no longer living. But even if this last is the answer, it would not be watertight evidence for Mr. Macaulay's survival, because, as has been said already, repeated experiments as well as countless anecdotes suggest that E.S.P. sits more loosely to time than sensory perception. So this might have been a case of retrocognition, if not of telepathy from the living at several removes.

The Cross Correspondences: do they hint at discarnate planning?

Once more then, the researcher, as with spontaneous E.S.P.-type experiences, seems to be driven back to cases which apparently indicate continuing *intention* and *planning* on the part of discarnate persons as the material most suggestive of survival.

The best known example of such material is, perhaps, the series of mediumistic utterances, mostly in the form of automatic scripts, which are known as the S.P.R. Cross Correspondences. These scripts continued to appear for about thirty years, were studied in depth by expert investigators and seemed to them to show repeated evidence of design and intention. They are unique in having been produced not by one person only but by up to a dozen, some of them widely separated and some of whom never met. Yet over and over again the scripts showed every sign of being inter-related. They were also of higher quality and often more coherent than the productions of most mediums. Individual examples of their inter-related patterns are too long and elaborate to be quoted here, but their startlingly unexpected and apparently meaningful framework can be sketched,[1] and a summary given of the one most recently reported.

[1] Most of the original scripts were printed in the *Proceedings* of the S.P.R., with many

Round about 1900 the deaths occurred of three distinguished Cambridge scholars, Edmund Gurney, Henry Sidgwick and F. W. H. Myers. They had all been founder members of the S.P.R. and had all been profoundly concerned with the problem of whether or not the human soul survived bodily death. Shortly after Myers' death—he was the last to go—several ladies began, independently, to produce fragments of automatic writing, and in one or two cases of speech, which claimed to originate with the three scholars. These fragments were meaningless taken alone, but later on when they were pieced together by an outside person, they seemed to give a coherent meaning. A clue to this meaning was sometimes given beforehand in one of the scripts, and it often related to abstruse classical subjects of which few but learned scholars would ever have heard. The automatists were scattered across the world, and only two of them knew any Latin or Greek. Of these two, one, Mrs. Verrall, was the wife of Dr. Verrall, a distinguished classical scholar, and was herself a classical lecturer at Cambridge;[1] the other was their daughter Helen, who later married W. H. Salter, a life-long and highly-skilled psychical researcher. Among the rest were Dame Edith Lyttelton; Mrs. Fleming, a sister of Rudyard Kipling, who lived in India; and Mrs. Coombe-Tennant, a woman well-known in public life, who was at one time a Government representative at the League of Nations.[2,3] There was also one American, Mrs. Piper, the only professional medium in the group. She was exhaustively studied over many years by the American S.P.R., and her talent was as remarkable as Mrs. Leonard's.

The scripts containing the scattered fragments were usually signed "Myers", or "Gurney", and they went on for some time before it was noticed that they seemed to form parts of elaborate verbal jigsaw puzzles, which, in the view of the investigators, showed every sign of having been *designed* by somebody, and somebody, moreover, with an expert knowledge of the classics. And there were other unexpected items. For instance, before Mrs. Fleming in India knew that other people elsewhere were writing scripts which also purported to come

---

commentaries. Valuable studies of them can be found in the following books. *Zoar: The Evidence of Psychical Research concerning Survival*, by W. H. Salter, Sidgwick and Jackson, 1961. *Lectures on Psychical Research*, by Professor C. D. Broad, International Library of Philosophy and Scientific Method, Routledge & Kegan Paul, 1962. *The Challenge of Psychical Research*, by Professor Gardner Murphy, Harper, New York, 1961. *Evidence of Survival from the Cross Correspondences*, by H. F. Saltmarsh, Bell, 1938. The present writer has also made a shorter summary of the evidence in *The Sixth Sense*, Chatto and Windus, 1959 and Pan Books, 1966.

[1] After Dr. Verrall's death he purported to be among the communicators.

[2] Mrs. Lyttelton, Mrs. Fleming and Mrs. Coombe-Tennant used the pseudonyms Mrs. King, Mrs. Holland and Mrs. Willett respectively, as they all wished to keep secret their unpopular gift of automatic writing.

[3] A book entitled *Swan on a Black Sea*, Routledge & Kegan Paul, appeared in 1965, which consists of automatic scripts by Miss Geraldine Cummins, purporting to come from Mrs. Coombe-Tennant. It has a long and valuable analytical foreword by Professor C. D. Broad. The scripts contain material apparently unknown to Miss Cummins, and the characterisation of Mrs. Coombe-Tennant, whom she had never met, is remarkably good.

from Myers, her script itself instructed her to send it to 5 Selwyn Gardens, Cambridge. This was an address unknown, at least to her conscious mind, in a city she had never visited, but it turned out to be Mrs. Verrall's, who had been the first of the group to experiment with automatic writing in the hope that if Myers were still in existence she might thereby enable him to demonstrate this.

Once the apparent designs in the scripts were noticed, they were all sent to the S.P.R. to be pieced together by an outside person. In the view of the investigators who studied them for years in detail, chief of whom was the second Earl Balfour, himself a classical scholar, more and more scattered references were found to make wholes when fitted together. As already mentioned, most of these sets of references were to the classics, though there were a few to later writers, such as Dante and Browning. The scripts themselves insisted that the various automatists must *not* see each others' work, for they claimed that Myers, Gurney and Sidgwick had devised this method of demonstrating their continued existence and power to plan. These three had discovered during their lifetime that to demonstrate continued existence is extremely difficult. For a purported communicator merely to say, "I am Myers", is no proof at all of identity. If he says "Do you remember this or that?" the answer is "Yes, and because I do, even if the automatist has not discovered it by normal means, it is simpler to say that she got it telepathically from my living mind than from the dead." But, said the script intelligences, here we are producing evidence of design which was not in any living mind. So where would that have come from? They also said repeatedly, as do other purported communicators, that using the brain of another person to transmit messages was *extremely* difficult, because if what they caused her to write became too meaningful to her, it was liable to arouse trains of her own associations, and these would appear as misleading extraneous matter in the scripts. Hence the evidence for design had to be given in cryptic fragments. They called it "A tangle for your unravelling". Even to make contact with a living person, they said, was painfully difficult. Mrs. Fleming's (Holland's) "Myers" once wrote, "The nearest simile I can find to express the difficulties of sending a message is that I appear to be standing behind a sheet of frosted glass—which blurs sight and deadens sound—dictating feebly to a reluctant and somewhat obtuse secretary. A feeling of terrible impotence burdens me." Again, in another script "he" wrote, "It is impossible for me to know how much of what I send reaches you . . . I feel as if I had . . . reiterated the proofs of my identity in a wearisomely frequent manner—but yet I cannot feel as if I had made any true impression . . ." At the time Mrs. Fleming was writing such scripts Mrs. Piper's "Myers" wrote that "he" was "trying with all the forces to prove that I am Myers", and the same intensity is often found in Mrs. Willett's scripts. Her "Gurney" wrote: ". . . the passionate desire to drive into incarnate minds the conviction of one's own identity, the partial successes and the blank failures . . . I know the burden of it . . . to the uttermost fraction . . ."

The Palm Sunday Case[1]

Whether or not the Cross Correspondence scripts are what they claim to be, to appreciate the flavour of authenticity they convey, hundreds of them need to be read. But some idea of the type of scattered fragments which they themselves insisted would provide evidence of their design by the discarnate Myers and his friends may perhaps be given by a summary of the last reported episode, the Palm Sunday Case. This has more human interest than those solely concerned with classical legends, since its apparent purpose is to convey the abiding love of a discarnate person for one still living, a purpose seen again in recent scripts purporting to come from one of the Palm Sunday Case automatists, Mrs. Coombe-Tennant, fairly soon after her death. These express her continuing love and concern for her sons and her regrets for mistakes in relation to them which she now realises she had made during her lifetime.[2]

The background

The Palm Sunday Case stems from the little known and long past love story of a young girl, Mary Catherine Lyttelton, and Arthur, first Earl Balfour, and of its apparent continuation beyond the grave. Only the salient points are given here.

The few who can remember Arthur Balfour nowadays will think of him as an aloof philosopher or as Prime Minister of Great Britain. There is no one alive who knew him as a sociable though somewhat shy young man, who delighted in good music, good talk and the company of his friends. In 1871 he met Mary Lyttelton at a Christmas ball at Hawarden, William Gladstone's home, and straightaway fell in love with her. Although her looks were not outstanding, she had great charm and unusually beautiful hair, and she was a very good pianist. But Balfours were never precipitate, and well-brought-up young women of that time did not meet their suitors even half-way, so it was not until four years later, in 1875, that he got as far as speaking of his deep feeling for her. Even then he did not actually propose. That he intended to do at the next opportunity. But there was no next opportunity. Immediately after their talk she fell ill of typhus and died on Palm Sunday, 1875, shortly before her twenty-fifth birthday.

Though few were aware of it, for Balfour her loss turned his world to dust and ashes. He gave her sister his mother's beautiful emerald

---

[1] *The Palm Sunday Case: New Light on an Old Love Story*, by Jean Balfour, *Proceedings* S.P.R., Vol. 52, Part 189, 1960.

[2] See note on p. 236.

ring to be buried on her (Mary's) finger. He wrote to his friend, Edward Talbot, her brother-in-law, "I think—I am nearly sure—that she must have grasped my feelings towards her . . . Now perhaps, when she watches the course of those she loves who are still struggling on earth I may not be forgotten." He never married. But every year until his death, unless affairs of state prevented it, in remembrance of her he passed Palm Sunday in seclusion with her sister.

The scripts

The suggestion made in the Palm Sunday Case is that new light may be shed on this old love story by independent automatic scripts written many years later by four ladies who do not appear to have heard about the events they refer to. The scripts purport to contain evidence that Mary Lyttelton and Balfour's younger brother, Francis, who had been killed climbing in 1882, were both very much alive, and that he was helping her to convey to her lover the knowledge of her enduring devotion to him.

The four automatists were Mrs. Verrall, her daughter Helen, Mrs. Fleming and Mrs. Coombe-Tennant: women of almost ferocious integrity. None of these four appear to have known anything about the old romance. Among the investigators and interpreters of the scripts were Arthur Balfour's brother, Gerald, afterwards the second Lord Balfour, also a scholar and statesman, and their scientist sister, Mrs. Henry Sidgwick. Owing to their very personal nature the scripts were kept a strict secret at the time and were eventually bequeathed to Jean, Countess of Balfour, who only felt free to publish them in 1960 when all the people directly concerned with the story were dead. They fall into two groups. The first, from 1901 to 1912, consists of cryptic allusive fragments, written independently by Mrs. and Miss Verrall and Mrs. Fleming who was living in India. The fragments apparently referring to Mary Lyttelton were interspersed with a lot of other material, some consisting of the classical and other puzzles mentioned above, some of warnings and comments about the stormy international situation and of plans for future peace.

It was not until 1912 that Mrs. Coombe-Tennant's scripts took up the Mary Lyttelton theme and these now began to give clues which linked together the scattered and hitherto meaningless fragments written earlier by the others. She had already produced a number of scripts purporting to come from Myers and Gurney and her automatism was now taking an unusual form. Sometimes she wrote, but at others she talked alternately to the investigators and to the script intelligences. These said they were training her to do this as they did not wish her to become an ordinary trance medium, who loses normal consciousness entirely. They wanted her to learn to poise her consciousness on a knife edge, so that she could become aware of what they said, and yet retain enough contact with the exterior world to be able to report back to the investigators.

In 1912 her script insisted, against her conscious wish—she did not like strange sitters—that Arthur Balfour's brother Gerald should come and sit with her while she wrote. He came, and the script intelligences, whoever they were, showed a nice dramatic sense, for they chose Palm Sunday to begin to elucidate the mystery. The earlier scripts by the three other automatists must be gone through again, they said. This was done, and in the light of indications provided by Mrs. Coombe-Tennant's new scripts the investigators came to the conclusion that for ten years the continued love of Mary Lyttelton for Arthur Balfour had often been alluded to in symbolic fashion.

In the earlier scripts, for instance, allusions had been made to the Palm Maiden, May Blossom, the Blessed Damozel and Berenice. The first three were clear enough. Mary died on Palm Sunday, her family called her May, even in Heaven the Blessed Damozel yearned for her lover. But why Berenice? (She, it will be remembered, sacrificed her hair to the gods for her husband's safe return from war.) The scripts had also contained scattered references to a candle and candlestick, a lock of hair, something purple, a metal box and a periwinkle.

The link between all these apparently disparate items was not evident even to the investigators until 1916 when, in response to impassioned appeals by Mrs. Coombe-Tennant's script, Arthur Balfour himself came to sit with her. In July she wrote a long and moving script for him, speaking of the presence of the May Blossom and referring to the various symbols mentioned in earlier scripts and to a lock of hair. She also wrote, among other emotional passages, "And if God will I shall but love thee better after death." This script was signed, M. (Other early scripts had had her initials, and one of Mrs. Fleming's had been signed Mary L., but that, of course, had meant nothing to her.)

This long allusive script of July 1916 was full of meaning for Arthur Balfour. He now told his brother for the first time that shortly after Mary Lyttelton's death, over forty years earlier, her sister had shown him a lock of her beautiful hair, which had been cut off during her last illness, and that he had had made for it a silver box, which was lined with purple and engraved with periwinkle and other spring flowers. This lock of hair incident is a typical instance, so it seemed to the investigators, of a later event throwing light on earlier scripts, which had been written by people who knew nothing of the events referred to. Another is the frequent use of the candlestick symbol for Mary Lyttelton, by three automatists who had no idea that she had been photographed holding a candle at the foot of a staircase.

One or two apt symbols for a particular person might be discounted as due to chance, but the numbers occurring in this case try that hypothesis rather high. Nevertheless, and wisely, Arthur Balfour was slow to commit himself about so basic a matter as the authenticity of the scripts, but gradually over the years he came to accept that the messages he received did indeed come from Mary Lyttelton, and they appear to have been a great comfort to him. In 1926, when he was very old and ailing after pneumonia, he wrote an answer to an emotional script begging him to believe in her continued presence, which was to be read to Mrs. Coombe-Tennant when she was in the half dissociated state in which she wrote her scripts. Part of it read:

"The message is understood by him and deeply valued . . . Assuredly he does not require to be told that death is not the end . . . The hour of reunion cannot be long delayed . . . Through his complete deficiency in psychic gifts he has no intuition of that 'closeness beyond telling' of which the message speaks with such deep conviction and which he conceives to be of infinite value. Further messages would greatly help . . ."

In October 1929, Arthur Balfour, now eighty-one and very frail, was living with his brother, Gerald, at Fisher's Hill near Woking. Mrs. Coombe-Tennant went there for a visit and while sitting one evening quietly with the two Balfour brothers and their sister, Mrs. Sidgwick, she fell into a half-dissociated state and had an experience which moved her profoundly. Lady Betty Balfour, Gerald's wife, wrote down what she said as she was coming back to normal consciousness. Her first words were that the room was "full of presences—such light, such radiance". Lady Betty asked: "What sort of presences?" The answer was:

"One figure there—things coming out of that figure—such wonderful things . . . It was a woman's figure—quite young, dressed in an old-fashioned dress—lovely quantities of hair gathered round her head . . . every form of life you can imagine radiated from her. Her hand was upon his arm—she never took her eyes from his face . . . When you have an experience like that you *know* masses that no mere words can describe . . ."

A few months later Arthur Balfour had a stroke and died soon after it. Immediately before the stroke, his nephew's wife, (now Jean, Countess of Balfour, the compiler of *The Palm Sunday Case*) was with him. So strictly had the secret of the scripts been kept that at that time even she knew nothing of them or of the work of their interpreters. She wrote afterwards in her private diary that suddenly she had felt, as a blind person might do, that the room was full of dazzling light and that there were people clustered round his bed, "eager, loving and strong . . . I felt they were there for some purpose". Then she saw A. J. B.'s face "transfigured with satisfaction and beauty" as at a glorious vision. A moment later he had the stroke, to her great distress, but, even so, she wrote afterwards in her diary:

Q

"The extraordinary thing was that I was vividly aware that the feeling in the room had *not* changed, that the radiant joy and light still thrilled around him, that the agonising spectacle of the poor body's affliction caused no dismay whatever to those unseen who watched. As I ran for the doctor I was saying to myself over and over again, 'It was intended, it was *intended*'."

Material of this kind is liable to arouse vigorous reactions, both for and against. But the question the psychical researcher has to ask himself is not whether or not he likes it, but what is its source? Must he in honesty admit that the most plausible hypothesis to account for it is indeed the staggering claim made by the scripts that they were designed by Myers, Gurney and their friends to demonstrate their own continued existence? Or can he argue that the original investigators were misled by wishful thinking to see patterns that are not there? Or, if the patterns are there, can they all be ascribed to a fantastic series of chance coincidences? Or is it conceivable that a number of highly respected men and women got together to perpetrate a conscious fraud? If so, to what purpose? It would bring them no gain, but, on the contrary, would merely get them laughed at as cranks. Or could the whole business have originated in the subconscious mind of Mrs. Verrall? In that case, did she, an austerely upright woman, hold what might be called a subconscious class of other upright women, some of them thousands of miles away, to deceive *their own* conscious selves as well as those of their friends? There is one snag to this explanation: the patterns continued after her death and when there seemed no one left with both the classical knowledge, the close acquaintance with the dead scholars and their friends shown by the scripts, and interest enough in the subject to induce his or her subconscious to indulge in the lengthy planning such an elaborate hoax would involve.

The present position regarding the evidence for survival

In the best mediumship then, the psychical researcher is faced with facts—on occasion extremely complex facts—which need a lot of explaining. He might think it just possible that in such cases as the Macaulay one, some part of the medium's psyche did achieve the remarkable feat of collecting information about Mr. Macaulay by retrocognition, or telepathically from the living at several removes, and then presenting it as communications from a discarnate person. But when he goes on to cases as complex as the Cross Correspondences, the possibility that the mind of a person who has survived bodily death is continuing to think, plan and carry out intentions seems scarcely, if at all, more fantastic than the alternative explanations available. In other words, if there are any mediumistic phenomena which cannot be explained by some form of E.S.P. of mundane events—and this incidentally would have to be of an excellence never observed elsewhere —plus unconscious dramatisation on the medium's part, it may be necessary to postulate the survival of *something*.

From the point of view of the investigator, then, the findings of psychical research in relation to death seem to amount to something like this. On the one hand the apparent potentialities of E.S.P. make it hard to conceive what kind of evidence could give coercive proof of survival—evidence that could not at a pinch be ascribed to some combination of telepathy, clairvoyance, precognition or retrocognition in relation to events in this world. As against this, the more we learn about the range of these capacities, about man's apparent power to transcend the limitations of the known senses and of time and space as presented to him by those senses, the less inconceivable it may be that the early researchers were on the right track in surmising that there could be something in him—what Professor C. D. Broad discreetly calls some psi component—which might be able to function independently of a physical body.

In a book concerned with attitudes to death some reference should perhaps be made, not only to the attitude of the scientific researcher as regards the possibility of survival, but also to those of people who have themselves had E.S.P.-type experiences connected with death. It may be guessed that most actively religious Christians who have such experiences accept them for what they appear to be, and that a number of the non-Christians who have them join some group, such as the theosophists or spiritualists, into whose beliefs their experiences will fit, for this gives them peace of mind. But how many people are there like the flight lieutenant, who appeared to talk quite normally with his dead fellow pilot and yet had no framework of belief which would hold his experience? Judging from the many cases sent to Dr. Louisa Rhine and to other writers of seriously-intentioned books on psi, there must be an appreciable number, and owing to the present orthodox belief that death is the end, it looks as if some of them dare not mention such experiences for fear of being thought out of their minds. Some even wonder, could that perhaps be true? "Can you possibly explain this?" they write, "I have never dared ask anyone before. Do you think I could be mad?"

The experiences most often reported, incidentally, as with most of the authenticated cases in the annals of psychical research, are far removed from the headless, chain-clanking "ghosties and ghoulies" of fiction and Christmas Numbers. Apart from the apparently aimless haunting type, modern "ghosts" usually seem to want to help, or warn, or merely to appear to a loved friend or relative. And sometimes they are not distinguished from living persons until they vanish.

For those of us, then, who are conditioned by the widespread belief that mind and body die together, and who yet have apparent contacts with the purposeful discarnate, what is our rational attitude towards those contacts, especially as they are admittedly sporadic, fleeting, and not to be repeated to order? Perhaps I may be forgiven a personal summarised illustration of this dilemma, since it is not easy to describe other people's experiences as if from the inside.

In the 1950s the expected death occurred of an inventor friend, with whom, as we both accepted that death was the end, I had shortly before agreed regretfully that he would never be able to bring to fruition the many ideas still seething in his brain. About ten days after his death I was astounded and delighted to "meet", quite naturally, his apparently living personality, and to be assured with emphasis that we had been quite mistaken; he now had scope and opportunity beyond his wildest dreams. In some imageless way I seemed able to participate in his awareness of scope and opportunity and I was rejoicing in this when it flashed across my mind that I ought to ask for evidence of his splended liberation. But the reply he made was, "I can't give you any evidence. You have no concepts for these conditions.[1] I can only give you poetic images." Which he did. But quite soon I realised that I could not hold the state into which, unexpectedly, my consciousness had switched, so I said, "Goodbye, I must drop now." And I "dropped" at once to ordinary awareness of mundane surroundings.

Although this experience does not appear to be very exceptional, there is not a shred of evidence to support my account of it, and investigators will therefore—and quite rightly—feel it their duty to dismiss it as a mere anecdote. But again, what is the rational attitude for the people who have such experiences, sometimes repeatedly? Should we discard them all as illusions, in obedience to orthodoxy? Should we even suspect our own sanity? (I asked two eminent psychiatrists to check on mine and they both gave me a clean bill of health. But one did say sadly, "I'm *afraid* you're quite sane.") Or should we defy the voice of contemporary science and bet on the reality of our own experiences, however fleeting and unpredictable?

On one thing perhaps, the psi-experiencing agnostic can afford to bet—that were the whole of humanity to have experiences similar to his own, of the occasional momentary, purposeful presence of discarnate persons he had known in life, it would not occur to them, however mistaken they might be in fact, to doubt the reality of survival. As things are, however, the only place where his reason can feel at ease and honest is on the fence. And there he will at least be encouraged to find a number of distinguished scholars who have thought it worthwhile to study the evidence for survival for many years. This is how three among

---

[1] In an article in *The New Scientist* for August 30th 1962, Dr. Richard Gregory has suggested that travellers in space might be faced with a similar problem. "Suppose," he says, "we were to meet something really odd—say a new life form—could we see it properly? The perceptual system is a computer, programmed by evolutionary experience and by our own personal experience of the world. A new kind of object requires the perceptual computer to solve a new problem with an old programme, which may be neither adequate nor appropriate."

them summed up their conclusions in the 1960s. First, the well-known American psychologist, Professor Gardner Murphy.

"Where then do I stand? To this the reply is: what happens when an irresistible force strikes an immovable object? To me the evidence cannot be by-passed, nor, on the other hand, can conviction be achieved . . . Trained as a psychologist and now in my sixties, I do not actually anticipate finding myself in existence after physical death. If this is the answer the reader wants, he can have it. But if this means that in a serious philosophical argument I would plead the antisurvival case, the conclusion is erroneous. I linger because I cannot cross the stream. We need far more evidence; we need new perspectives; perhaps we need more courageous minds."[1]

Next, the doyen of British psychologists, Professor Sir Cyril Burt.

"The uncertainty leaves the matter open in *both* directions. On the one hand the theoretical psychologist (and that includes the parapsychologist) should, on this particular issue, preserve a strict agnosticism, pressing physicalistic interpretations as far as they will go, and, even if in the end he feels compelled to adopt the hypothesis of a surviving mind, he must remember that it is, like the ether of old, no more than a hypothesis. On the other hand, those who, from reasons of faith, metaphysics, or what they take to be personal revelation, still wish to believe in survival for themselves or those they love, need have no grounds for fearing scientific censure. Thus our verdict on the whole matter must be the same as that pronounced by Plato two thousand years ago—the reply he puts into the mouth of Socrates while waiting to drink the hemlock. 'I would not positively assert that I shall join the company of those good men who have already departed from this life; but I cherish a good hope.' Hope implies, not the virtual certainty of success but the possibility of success. And it is, I think, one important result of recent psychological and parapsychological investigations to have demonstrated, in the face of the confident denials of the materialists and the behaviourists, *at least the possibility* of survival in some form or other, though not necessarily in the form depicted by traditional piety or fourth century metaphysics."[2]

And finally, Professor C. D. Broad, sometime Knightbridge Professor of Moral Philosophy at Cambridge. He, incidentally, does not hide the fact that he does not want to survive.

"The position as I see it is this. In the known relevant normal and abnormal facts there is nothing to suggest and much to counter-

---

[1] *Challenge of Psychical Research*, Harpers, New York, 1961, p. 273.
[2] *Article*, "Psychology and Parapsychology" in a symposium *Science & E.S.P.*, edited by J. R. Smythies, International Library of Philosophy and Scientific Method, Routledge and Kegan Paul, p. 140.

suggest, the possibility of any kind of persistence of the psychical aspect of a human being after the death of his body. On the other hand, there are many quite well attested *paranormal* phenomena which strongly suggest such persistence, and a few which strongly suggest the fullblown survival of a human personality. Most people manage to turn a blind eye to one or other of these two relevant sets of data, but it is part of the business of a professional philosopher to try to envisage steadily both of them together. The result is naturally a state of hesitation and scepticism (in the correct as opposed to the popular sense of that word). I think I may say that for my part I should be slightly more annoyed than surprised if I should find myself in some sense persisting immediately after the death of my present body. One can only wait and see, or alternatively (which is no less likely) wait and not see."[1]

It looks then as if at the present time to step off the fence on either side as regards survival entails an act of faith. On one side we can believe—but cannot prove—that men of science already know enough about the nature of things to be able to assert with safety that it is impossible; on the other we can believe—but equally cannot prove— that certain phenomena demonstrate that it is a fact.

Personal postcript

I sent the foregoing chapters to the publishers feeling that they contained all I was entitled to say about the question of survival. Their reply was to ask me, "Can you now go on to a more speculative, personal positive assertion of your own views on the nature and extent of the life after death?" This was startling. I was not even convinced that there was a life after death. And who was I to have *personal positive* views about a mystery which has defeated all mankind?

But it made me think. Even if not convinced, perhaps one ought to try to have views as to what such a life might be like. After all, we *know* that we all must die. We do *not* know with the same certainty that the majority of contemporary scientists are right in asserting that conscious-ness must cease with the death of the body. Perhaps we should keep on reminding ourselves that the science of today is not at the end of the road and that some great scientists do not endorse the majority verdict. Schroedinger, for one, held that consciousness is inextinguishable. "In no case", he wrote, "is there a loss of personal consciousness to deplore. Nor will there ever be."[2] Here then there seemed to be a jumping off point, if not for anything so positive as views, at least for speculation about man's possible situation immediately the other side of death.

---

[1] *Lectures on Psychical Research*, International Library of Philosophy and Scientific Method Routledge and Kegan Paul, 1962, p. 430.
[2] *What is Life?*, by Erwin Schroedinger, C.U.P., 1951 edition, p. 92.

The first question to ask seemed obvious: how "bright" would be a spark of human consciousness when stripped of interaction with a physical environment *via* the senses, and of the urge to excel, to possess, to propagate, to keep the body alive? Would it range from a flickering match in the earthy-minded to a hundred watt bulb in the saint and genius? Might A be half asleep, and B, like my purported inventor, have scope and opportunity beyond his wildest dreams? Or does each spark lose its identity in a vast sea of consciousness?

Next question: if identity remains, how could the discarnate make contact with their environment? Could consciousness exist without a vehicle? Or, as many Eastern thinkers maintain and as some apparently out-of-the-body experiences hint at, do men even in this life possess one which relates them to other aspects of the universe, but is imperceptible so long as their attention is held by the insistent impacts of the senses?

To ask such questions as these was easy, but only philosophers could attempt to answer them. I soon came to the conclusion that all I could hope to contribute was a little raw material: some account of personal changes of consciousness which tally with the guess that it need not depend solely on the type of information which reaches it through the senses. It is perhaps worth reminding ourselves how specialised are these senses. Even in physical life, had men the eyes of bees, they would see unimaginable colours; were they equipped with radar instead of eyes they would see solid objects in the sky where there now seems empty space; if they were not men, but worms or snails, they could detect X-rays; if they were certain fish, magnetic fields.

I shall mention briefly three types of changed consciousness which I have experienced. (So, incidentally, have thousands of other people, but as I said earlier, the educated nowadays tend to keep quiet about it for fear of being laughed at—which they usually are, unless they happen to be poets who are not always expected to mean literally what they say.) The first change was induced to order by the psychedelic drug, mescalin. The second takes place, very seldom and quite unexpectedly, in response to the apparent presence of a dead friend; the third, again unexpectedly and all too seldom, in response to extreme natural beauty.

Although nowadays the mention of psychedelic drugs is liable to conjure up all sorts of emotions and prejudices, I still have to record that a dose of mescalin brought home to me the parochialness of sensory perception and the possibility of more vivid kinds of awareness and communication. I was fortunate enough to take it before Aldous Huxley's book, *The Doors of Perception*, came out, or psychedelic drugs became fashionable, and I did so, not for a kick—indeed I was very frightened—but because a doctor who was seeking a cure for schizophrenia needed volunteers who were willing to experience a model psychosis. I had no idea what to expect, but once thoroughly "out of my mind" it seemed clear enough that my task for the doctor was to penetrate as far as might be into the "hinterland" of consciousness. After a time my body and the outer world disappeared and my consciousness found itself in new surroundings far more vivid than mundane ones. As is now well-known, ordinary language is a useless tool to describe these surroundings; for one thing such words as then or now, here or there, near or far, did not apply. I seemed, rather, to be in a world of fluid relationships whose patterns altered in response to thought and feeling.

At the furthest point "in", when I felt on the verge of disintegration through sheer excess of glory, I appeared to be shown—I emphasise *shown*—by a celestial figure that the force holding the universe together was love, all-pervading, warm as sunlight, in a sense personal but quite unsentimental. Embarrassing as this is to write—an interesting sidelight on our culture—when "out of my mind" that love seemed a fact of nature in the same sense that the all-pervading warmth coming from the sun in the sky is a fact. Also, the more one identified oneself with it, the more alive one appeared to be. A second self-evident fact was that values are as real as St. Paul's. Also, incidentally, at that distance "in", whited sepulchres could not exist; all was only too visible for what it was.

What on earth—one can hear the irritated comment—has such drug-induced babbling to do with speculation about life after death? The answer for me is, not that a psychedelic drug conveys anything of what that life may be like—though it may do so, I cannot tell—but that it releases the imagination from a solely mundane outlook. With the physical world banished and desire dead, consciousness seemed enhanced and surroundings supremely meaningful; possibly, I have thought since, because desire *was* dead, and hence, like an artist, I was aware of all things as existing in their own right and not in relation to my own little ego. Was all this a psychotic illusion, or was it a hint that the brain, as Bergson and other philosophers have suggested, may be an organ of limitation, whose temporary malfunctioning induced by the drug released my consciousness into a wider world? (Poets, too, have faced this problem. Keats felt frustrated because "the dull brain perplexes and retards"). In either case, as I said, for me the experience has made other kinds of awareness *imaginable*. I can now wonder whether one reason why we are so little aware of the presence of the dead (on the hypothesis that they are present) may be, as my purported inventor said, that we have no concepts for their conditions and they have therefore become *unreal* to us. It also helps me to think I understand why, for many people, including myself, the apparent presence of the purposeful dead is so often an invisible one. As Mrs. Coombe-Tennant once wrote: "It is as minds and characters that they are to me." Apparitions of the dead would not be incompatible with this idea. My inventor said he could only convey something of his situation indirectly by means of mundane images. Possibly images of the dead as they had been in life might be needed to convey their presence to persons not directly aware of them as "characters".[1]

If consciousness survives the death of the body, I would guess, then, that what one calls character, individuality, can endure and that opportunity can be increased. And energy too. For example, a few days after the late Lady Rhondda's death I unexpectedly became aware of her as directing a "beam of strength" towards her friend, Theodora Bosanquet, whom she had left a heavy task to perform on her behalf. (In that curious state of consciousness a beam of strength is as actual as a beam of light in a normal one.) Lady Rhondda's vigour surprised me because she had been very worn out for some time before she died. I would also guess that to the newly dead our excessive sorrow at their apparent loss may seem pointless, indeed, distressing. I once felt positively bullied by a young friend who had been killed in an aircrash to go and stop her mother, whom I scarcely knew, from overdoing the mourning. "I'm *very* happy," she said, "and I can't *stand* it."

This attitude seems natural enough if they do not feel that their earthly links have been broken. What more trying, as the purported Myers wrote somewhat heatedly through a Cross Correspondence automatist, than to be treated as "non-existent". Incidentally, even when intellectually one cannot quite accept survival, that thought may justify feeling and behaving *as if* the dead exist and do not want to feel cut off from those on earth. If this is *not* true, if death is the end, one is merely being a fool. If it *is* true, to reject them as non-existent is to be a knave.

Two incidents have suggested to me that our lack of contact with them might be due in part to our own self-centred deafness and blindness. I once had an impression that George Tyrrell, a psychical researcher friend who had recently died, was trying to guide me to write a certain passage about the problems of communication with the dead in a certain way; but I could get no impression as to whether or not I had got it right. Then, by chance, a mutual friend, a non-professional sensitive, came to see me, and although she knew nothing of my impression, she unexpectedly "saw" him in my room, and he was signifying approval.

But why, if it was George, was I deaf and blind? Was my ego too concerned with my own little efforts? A recent change of consciousness induced by natural beauty suggests this. One summer morning I stood for some time by an estuary, enthralled by the flying clouds and gulls and the sunlight on blue water; then I turned up the sleepy village street towards an ancient church which guarded its end. Flowers were rampant in the cottage gardens, and at the sight of one splendidly

---

[1] This may not apply to apparently aimless apparitions which "haunt" a particular spot, and for which, as I mentioned earlier, several other explanations can be envisaged. Occam's razor can sometimes be made to cut too vigorously.

flaming rose bush my little consciousness broke out of its shell as a chicken breaks out of its egg, into awed awareness of a Supreme Consciousness within whose ambience all that rejoicing beauty was held in love. (None of these poor sloppy little words are any good.) I crept into the silence of the empty church to submit quietly to that tremendous Presence and then, suddenly, in Its light, I seemed to look down and see—me. I was (symbolically) a polygonal little figure, feebly well-meaning, but its every facet muddied over by mild egocentricity. Not one of them was clear, not a single one. Gradually I "stepped down" to "normal", knees shaking, tears of humility dripping. What I had been shown does not become less apparent as the years go by: one cannot expect to see anything clearly, including the departed—for the last time, *if* they exist—through muddied glass.

4. What Kind of Next World?

by H. H. PRICE

IF WE are to discuss the problem of survival intelligently, we must try to form some idea of what the life after death might conceivably be like. If we cannot form such an idea, however rough and provisional, it is pointless to discuss the factual evidence for or against the "survival hypothesis". A critic may object that there *is* no such hypothesis, on the ground that the phrase "survival of human personality after death" has no intelligible meaning at all.

When we speak of the after-life or of life after death, the "life" we have in mind is not life in the physiological sense (by definition this ceases at death). "Life" here means consciousness or experience. And consciousness has to be consciousness *of* something. Experiences must have objects of some sort. In this way, the idea of life after death is closely bound up with the idea of "The Next World" or "The Other World". This Other World is what the surviving person is supposed to be conscious *of*. It provides the objects of his after-death experiences. The idea of life after death is indeed a completely empty one unless we can form at any rate some rough conception of what "The Other World" might be like.

On the face of it, there are two different ways of conceiving of the Next World. They correspond to two different conceptions of survival itself, and something must first be said about these. On the one hand, there is what I shall call the "embodied" conception of survival. On this view personality cannot exist at all without a body of some kind. At death one loses one's physical body. So after death one must have a body of another sort, an etheric body or an astral body, composed of a "higher" kind of matter. It is generally held, by those who accept this view, that each of us does in fact possess such a "higher" body even in this present life, and that this is the explanation of what are called "out-of-the-body" experiences (experiences of being out of the *physical* body).

It is interesting to notice that this conception of survival is compatible with a new version of materialism. According to the classical version of the materialist theory, the one which philosophers call epiphenomenalism, consciousness is unilaterally dependent on processes in the physical body and could not continue once the physical body has disintegrated. But suppose it was suggested, instead, that consciousness is unilaterally dependent on processes in the "higher" body. This would be a new version of the materialist theory of human personality, and it would be compatible with survival, as the old version is not. Similarly there might be a new version of behaviourism. Instead of saying that consciousness is reducible in one way or another to the behaviour of the physical organism (a view which excludes the possibility of survival) someone might suggest that it is reducible to the behaviour of the "higher" organism. Perhaps some view of this kind—"higher body" materialism as one might call it—will be the prevailing one among the tough-minded naturalistic thinkers of the 21st century. Perhaps it is already the prevailing view among the tough-minded thinkers of the Next World, if there is one.

I turn now to the "disembodied" conception of survival. On this view what survives death is just the soul or spirit, and it is a wholly immaterial entity. Its essential attributes are consciousness, thought, memory, desire and the capacity of having emotions. In this present life the immaterial soul interacts continually with the physical organism, especially with the brain. At death, this interaction ceases; or rather, death just *is* the permanent cessation of this interaction. And thereafter the immaterial soul continues to exist in a disembodied state. Most of the thinkers who have conceived of survival in this way, Plato and Descartes for instance, have also accepted the doctrine of a substantial soul. But the disembodied conception of survival is equally compatible with the "Serial Analysis" of personality advocated by David Hume the philosopher, William James the psychologist, and in the east, by the Buddhists. We should merely have to say that the series of mental events which constitutes a person can be divided into two parts, an *ante mortem* part and a *post mortem* part; and that those in the first part are closely associated with physical events in a certain brain, whereas those in the second part are not associated with physical events of any kind. (This serial conception of personal identity is also, of course, compatible with the "embodied" conception of survival; and Buddhism, at least according to some Western interpretations of it, appears to accept both.)

The next world—two views

Corresponding to these two different conceptions of survival, there are two different conceptions of the Next World; a quasi-physical conception of it on the one hand, and a psychological conception of it on the other.

If we accept the "embodied" conception of survival, we think of the Next World as a kind of material world. It would be the environment of the etheric or astral body, and composed of the same sort of "higher" matter. Presumably this body would have sense organs of some kind, though they might be very different from our present ones, and by means of them we should be aware of our after-death environment. In this way we should be provided with objects to be conscious of, and could have desires and emotions concerning them. Among such objects there would be the "higher" bodies of other surviving human beings; and possibly we might also encounter some personalities embodied in the same manner who had never had *physical* bodies at all.

The Other World, thus conceived, must of course be a spatial one. Both the "higher" body and the objects which constitute its environment would have to have properties which are at any rate analogous to shape, size, location and mobility as we know them in this present life. But if the Other World is a spatial one, *where* is it? Is it "above the bright blue sky" perhaps (that is, in or beyond the stratosphere)? Or is it somewhere in the bowels of the earth? Could we reach it by means of a rocket, or by digging a deep enough tunnel? Anyone who accepts this conception of the Other World must hold that such questions arise from a misunderstanding. We have no *a priori* reason for assuming that the physical space with which we are now familiar is the only space there is. There might perfectly well be two worlds, each standing in no spatial relation to the other, or indeed there might be more than two. Suppose that in the Next World there is a New Jerusalem, and that it is quite literally a spatial entity, with a shape and a size and complex spatial relations between its parts, as the traditional descriptions of it imply. It does not follow the New Jerusalem stands in any spatial relation at all to the old Jerusalem in Palestine. The Next World and all that is in it might just be in a space of its own, different from the space of the physical universe. Moreover, it might be a different *sort* of space as well. Its geometry need not be even approximately Euclidian. It might have more than three dimensions. When I say that the space of the Next World "might" have some queer features, I mean that its possession of them is compatible with the "embodied" conception of survival from which this whole line of thought starts. And similarly the causal laws which prevail in it might be very different from the laws of physics. Indeed, they *must* differ to some extent from the laws of physics if such phrases as "higher" body and "higher kind of matter" are to have any meaning.

A kind of dream world

But now suppose we start from what I called the disembodied conception of survival. If the after-death personality is something wholly immaterial, can there be any sort of other world at all? It seems to me that there can. We could think of it as a kind of dream-world. To put it in another way, we could suppose that in the next life mental imagery will play the part which sense-perception plays in this one. People sometimes ask what is "the purpose" or "the point" of our present life in this world, or whether it has any. Perhaps this question is not so utterly senseless as most contemporary philosophers suppose. We might even be able to suggest an answer to it. The point of life in this present world, we might say, is to provide us with a stock of memories out of which an image world may be constructed when we are dead.

It might be objected, however, that in this present life we know—or claim to know—where dream-images are. We are inclined to say that a person's dream-images are "in his head", that is, in some region or other of his brain; and obviously they cannot occur there after the brain itself has disintegrated. But what exactly do we mean by the word "in" when we say (of a living and physically-embodied person) that his dream-images are in his head? I think we can only mean that some cerebral processes or other, which do quite literally occur in his head, are *causes* or part-causes of the dream-images he has in this present life. But the images themselves are not located in physical space at all. Suppose I dream of a wolf emerging from a dark forest. Then the wolf-image is indeed located in relation to the images of the trees. But does it make any sense at all to ask whereabouts this wolf-image is in the space of the physical world? Is it, for instance, two and a half inches to the north-west of the dreamer's left ear? So far as I can see, there is no meaning in such a question. (It is rather like asking how far away Fairyland is from London.) Dream-images are in a space of their own. They do have spatial relations to other dream-images. But so far as physical space is concerned they are not anywhere; or rather the question "where they are" does not arise.

We are also liable to think that there is something "unreal" about mental images in general and about dream-images in particular. This too seems to me to be a confusion. Mental images are non-physical, certainly, but they are as real as anything can be. They do actually exist or occur. Moreover, some mental images (visual and factual ones) are spatial entities, though they are not in physical space. But perhaps when people say that mental images are "unreal" they are using the word in a kind of evaluative sense. Perhaps they mean that mental images make no appeal to our feelings, that they are uninteresting or unexciting, that they "cut no ice" with us from the emotional point of view. But surely this is false, as anyone who has ever had a nightmare knows. Both for good and for ill, our dream experiences may be as vividly felt as any of our waking ones, or more so. And for some people, indeed for many people on some occasions, the mental images they experience when awake are more interesting—more attention-absorbing —than the physical objects they perceive. Moreover, waking mental images may be interesting in an alarming or horrifying way, as dream images can. They may force themselves on our attention when we would much rather be without them.

It is worth while to emphasise these points, because this way of conceiving life after death does enable us to answer a logically irrelevant but emotionally powerful objection to the whole idea of survival, the objection that it is "too good to be true". On the contrary, such a dream-like next world, composed of mental images, might be a very unpleasant world for some people and a rather unpleasant one for almost all of us some of the time.

It would of course be a psychological world and not a physical one. It might indeed *seem* to be physical to those who experience it. The image-objects which compose it might appear very like physical objects, as dream objects often do now; so much so that we might find it difficult at first to realise that we were dead (a point often mentioned in medium-istic communications). Nevertheless, the causal laws obeyed by these image-objects would not be the laws of physics, but something more like the laws of depth psychology which such investigators as Sigmund Freud and C. G. Jung began to explore. It is of course sometimes said that dreams are "incoherent", and this again may be part of what is meant by calling dream objects unreal. But dreams (or waking fantasies) are only incoherent if judged by the irrelevant standard of the laws of physics; and this is only another way of saying that dream objects are not physical objects, and that an image-world, as we are conceiving of it, would indeed be an "other" world, which is just what it ought to be.

To put it rather differently, the other world, according to this conception of it, would be the manifestation in image form of the memories and desires of its inhabitants, including their repressed or unconscious memories and desires. It might be every bit as detailed, as vivid and as complex as this present perceptible world which we experience now. We may note that it might well contain a vivid and persistent image of one's own body. The surviving personality, according to this conception of survival, is in actual fact an immaterial entity. But if one habitually *thinks* of oneself as embodied (as one well might, at least for a considerable time) an image of one's own body might be as it were the persistent centre of one's image world, much as the perceived physical body is the persistent centre of one's perceptible world in this present life.

It may be thought that such a Next World would be a purely private and subjective one, that each discarnate personality would experience a Next World of his own, with no access to anyone else's. But suppose we bring telepathy into the picture. It may well be that in this present life the physical brain inhibits the operation of our telepathic powers, or at any rate tends to prevent the results of their operations from reaching consciousness. In the after-life, if there is one, telepathy might well be much more extensive and continuous than it is now. If so, we might expect that A's images would manifest not only his own desires and memories, but also the desires and memories of other personalities B, C, D, etc. if these were sufficiently similar to his own. In this way, there might be a common image world for each group of sufficiently "like-minded" personalities, common to all the members of the group though private to the group as a whole. There would still be many Next Worlds and not one (a suggestion which most religious traditions would, I think, support) but none of them would be wholly private and subjective.

Physical and psychological conceptions

Let us now compare these two conceptions of the other world, the quasi-physical conception of it which goes with the "embodied" conception of survival, and the psychological conception of it which goes with the "disembodied" conception of survival. At first sight these two ways of thinking of the other world appear entirely different and indeed incompatible. If one is right, surely the other must be wrong? But perhaps they are not quite so different as they look. They do agree on several important points. In both, the Next World is a spatial one (I would remind the reader that visual and tactual images are spatial entities). In both, the space of the Next World is different from physical space. In both, the causal laws are other than the laws of physics. In the first, the discarnate personality has a body, but it is not an ordinary physical body. In the second he has a dream body or image body.

What we have really done in this discussion of the Other World is to start from two different analogies and work out their consequences.

The first analogy which we considered was a physical one, suggested by our experience of the material world. The second was a psychological one, suggested by our experience of dreams and other forms of mental imagery. Some people will feel more at home with the physical analogy; others will be more attracted by the psychological one. But perhaps the choice between them is only a choice between starting points. Both analogies have to be stretched in one way or another if we are to achieve our aim, which is to give some intelligible content to the notion of the "next life" or the "next world".

It may well be that the two lines of thought, if pushed far enough, would meet in the middle. It is at any rate an attractive speculation that there may be realities in the universe which are intermediate between the physical and the psychological realms as these are ordinarily conceived. The contents of the other world, if there is one, may be in this intermediate position, more material than ordinary dream-images, more image-like or dream-like than ordinary material objects; like material objects in possessing spatial properties of some sort, and some degree at any rate of permanence; like mental images in that the causal laws they obey are the laws of psychology rather than the laws of physics.

The Relation between Life and Death, Living and Dying

The Relation between Life and Death, Living and Dying

by Arnold Toynbee

"In the midst of life we are in death."[1] From the moment of birth there is the constant possibility that a human being may die at any moment; and inevitably this possibility is going to become an accomplished fact sooner or later. Ideally, every human being ought to live each passing moment of his life as if the next moment were going to be his last. He ought to be able to live in the constant expectation of immediate death and to live like this, not morbidly, but serenely. Perhaps this may be too much to ask of any human being. Certainly I myself have never come anywhere near to rising to this spiritual level. I have known some human beings—people who were holy and at the same time robust and courageous—who have seemed to me to have succeeded in living permanently on a level not far below the ideal one, and who have been able to rise to the ideal level on supreme occasions; but I doubt whether even they have managed to live on this topmost spiritual level more than intermittently—admirable though their performance has been. What can be said with assurance is that, the closer that a human being can come to attaining this ideal state of heart and mind, the better and happier he or she will be.

To live in the constant expectation of immediate death is not, of course, an end in itself. The reason why a human being will be better and happier in so far as he manages to live like this is that he will be to that extent the better prepared for meeting death, if death should overtake him suddenly, in the state of grace (at best, of course, imperfect) in which every human being would wish to die, whatever may be his guess about the sequel. It has been noted already that people's guesses on this point differ. Some people guess that the sequel to death is annihilation; others guess that the sequel is a re-merger in the Ultimate Spiritual Reality behind the universe from which a human soul has emanated and against which it has asserted a separate personal identity that, on this view, is certainly ephemeral and is possibly illusory; others, again, guess that the sequel to death is personal immortality. The beliefs differ widely, but the respective holders of them have one wish in common. We all wish to have, at the moment of departing from this life, as clean a bill of spiritual health as it may be possible for a human

[1] The Order for the Burial of the Dead in the Book of Common Prayer of the Episcopalian Church of England.

being to earn; and, if we take this wish seriously, it will move us to keep our spiritual condition constantly under review.

All of us, at all times, are committing all kinds of sins, and, for most of the time, we are unmindful of most of these. It is a good practice to call to mind frequently as many of our sins as we can; but each of us is more sensitive to some of his sins than he is to others. I myself—perhaps overlooking sins of mine that are more heinous—find myself uneasily sensitive to the sin of feeling uncharitableness, ill-will, hostility, or malice towards a fellow human being. "Let not the sun go down upon your wrath."[1] So long as I am conscious of feeling any animus against anyone, I am ill at ease, and, if I have not got rid of my animus already, I try to cleanse myself of it when going to bed, in case I might die in the night, still contaminated by it. I am not a believer in personal immortality; I do not believe that death is followed by judgment; yet I wish, like believing Zoroastrians, Jews, Christians, and Muslims, to be as free as I can be from this sin—and, of course, from the rest of my sins too—at the moment when death overtakes me.

Each of us, no doubt, has some particular sin (it may not be his worst sin) for which he feels special compunction. This is a matter of individual character, temperament, and experience. I have been dealing with it in terms of my own experience, and I am going to write the rest of this chapter in the same terms, because the subject of the chapter as a whole is one on which second-hand information can be no more than conjectural and must therefore be inconclusive. The key, for each one of us, to the relation, for him, between life and death is, I believe, the extent of his familiarity with death and the stage in his life at which he has become familiar with it—supposing that he has not had the misfortune to remain unfamiliar with death until he is brought up against it, perforce, by finding that he himself is *in articulo mortis*. This brings up again a theme that has been touched upon in a previous chapter.[2]

One of the first things that anyone learns about himself is the name that has been given to him by his elders. In my case, when I learned my name, I learnt at the same time the reason why I bore it. I learned that I had been called after an uncle of mine who had died six years before I had been born. I had been called after him because I had been the first male child in my uncle's and father's branch of the Toynbee family to be born after my uncle's death. In a small way, my being named "Arnold" was a memorial to my uncle. (The outstanding and enduring memorial of him was the foundation of Toynbee Hall, which was the earliest of the university "settlements" in East London.) There had been an eagerness to provide memorials of him because his death had been premature, unexpected, sudden, and tragic. At the age of thirty, he had died, already a famous man, of something which con-

---

[1] Eph., iv, 26.
[2] "Increased Longevity and the Decline of Infant Mortality", p. 155 ff.

temporary doctors called "brain fever" and which their present-day successors might perhaps have diagnosed as being meningitis. (I have no idea whether even present-day medical skill could have saved my uncle's life.) Thus, since the earliest date in my life of which I have retained any memory, I have been familiar with the fact of premature death from disease—death that the medical science of my uncle's generation had been unable to avert.

Thanks to the accelerating progress of medical science, death in the form in which it overtook my uncle has become much less common, and therefore less familiar, within my lifetime. Though my Uncle Arnold had died before I was born, so that I never had the chance of knowing him personally, my early knowledge of his death made a deep and enduring impression on me—partly because I was aware that I had inherited his name, partly because I was familiar with a medallion of him, and a number of photographs, which revealed a man with a noble and engaging countenance, and partly because his personality had evidently been so striking that something of it could be conveyed at second-hand through descriptions of him by people who had known, admired, and loved him. He was constantly being talked about by his surviving contemporaries, and this not only by members of his family but by Fellows, in his generation, of Balliol College, Oxford, of which he had been a Fellow himself. One or two of these Balliol contemporaries of his were still alive, and had not yet retired, when I came up to Oxford as a Balliol undergraduate.

In this early experience of a premature death—an experience that has been vivid in spite of its having been at second-hand—I have been participating in a relation to death which has been familiar to human beings since time immemorial. I am, in fact, in virtue of this experience, a citizen of the Ancient World. On the other hand, I am a citizen of the Modern World in being a member of a family of three children only. We are a product of family-planning. (The elder of my two sisters is eight years younger than I am.) We are also an illustration of the lengthening, within our lifetime, of the expectation of life; for all three of us are still alive, though, on the day on which I am reading these words in proof, I myself am seventy-nine years and three months old. Thus I and my sisters are modern in having had no experience, in childhood, of the death of anyone in our immediate family circle.

In this point, our parents belonged to the Ancient World, in contrast to their children. Both my grandfathers had died prematurely and suddenly, though my Toynbee grandfather had lived to be twenty-one years older than his son Arnold was when Arnold died twenty-two years later than his father. My grandmother on my mother's side had died in giving birth to my mother, and my only uncle on my mother's side died when I was still a child. I cannot remember ever having met my Uncle Ned Marshall; he was, and is, a dim figure for me by comparison with my Uncle Arnold Toynbee. I can, however, remember

R*

poignantly my mother's reception of the telegram informing her of his unexpected death. The shock that this news gave her communicated itself to me. From that time onwards, I have always felt a sinking of the heart when I have received a telegram, and if, on being opened, it has proved (as, of course, it has, much more often than not) to be not an announcement of bad news, I have always felt a sense of relief.

I have noted that the household in which I grew up belonged already to the Modern World in the point that the number of my parents' children was planned and was small and that all three of us have been long-lived. Our household belonged, however, to the Ancient World in another point. It housed not just two generations, but three. The house in which I was born and brought up and in which I lived continuously till the age of twenty-two belonged, in fact, not to my parents, but to an uncle of my father's. My Great Uncle Harry was a widower by the date of my parents' marriage, so it suited both him and them that they should come to live with him, should keep house for him, and should look after him as an old man who is a widower needs to be looked after if he is long-lived—and Uncle Harry, though he was born in 1819, was a modern in his achievement of keeping alive till he was only a few months short of reaching ninety. This was the more remarkable, considering that he had been a sailor, serving in sailing-ships that were at sea for weeks and months on end without carrying a doctor on board. Uncle Harry was, I should guess, quite unaware of modern medicine (he was his own dentist, for instance, till the end of his life), though his elder brother Joseph, my grandfather, had been a distinguished physician. Joseph Toynbee had been the first ear, nose, and throat specialist in London, and had been active in working for the improvement of the administration of public health, and the consequent reduction of the death-rate, in the new raw industrial towns that had been springing up in Great Britain, like ugly mushrooms, in my grandfather's generation.

My grandfather, born in 1815, had died in 1866; my Uncle Harry, born in 1819, was seventy years old when I was born in 1889. He lived on for another twenty years, and I remember standing with my mother, on the eve of his funeral in 1909, while we gazed together at his face, serene in death. In life, he had not been serene; he had been stern, alarming, exciting, and dynamic. In life as well as in death, he made a deep and lasting impression on me—a blend of awe and fascination. The tie between him and me is an instance of the intimate relation between members of the same family, two generations apart in age, that was normal in the Ancient World but has become less common in the Western world now.

In another context[1] I have cited my Uncle Harry as an example of an unquestioningly believing Christian who was terrified at the prospect of death, though he must have believed that, for him, the risk of going

[1] See p. 93.

to hell was slight, since he was certainly sure that he was one of the few people who had got his theology exactly right. I discovered his terror of death in my own early childhood. Since my family were members of the Episcopalian Church of England and my parents took me to church every Sunday, I soon became acquainted with the Psalms in the English version of them in the Book of Common Prayer, and—conscious, as I was, of Uncle Harry's being a very old man—the tenth verse of the Ninetieth Psalm caught my attention on account of its applicability to him. Subconsciously, I must have realised that the seventy years' difference between our ages, which gave him so awesome an advantage over me, also gave me a converse advantage over him. Anyway, I said to him one day: "You know, Uncle Harry, it says in the Bible: 'The days of our age are three-score years and ten', and you are older now than that." I said this partly in order to see what would happen. I expected a thunderbolt. To my astonishment, Uncle Harry answered never a word. Like the Suffering Servant, "as a sheep before her shearers is dumb, so he openeth not his mouth".[1] Unwittingly I, the puny imp, had dealt a knock-out blow to the mighty Olympian. I had reminded him that, according to the Bible, which he believed to be inspired by God *verbatim*, his death was already overdue. He could not bear the reminder; he was dumbfounded. As soon as my mother and I were alone (my mother had witnessed the scene), she said to me, gently as always, but in a tone that I have never forgotten: "What you said to Uncle Harry just now was very unkind." I recognised that it had been. I was contrite, but I was triumphant too.

In my next experience of death I am a man of my generation—not a typical one, because I was not a combatant in the First World War, owing to the accident of being disqualified for active military service by dysentery contracted while hiking in Greece in 1912. If this germ had not continued to plague me, as it did, for a number of years, before I succeeded in getting the better of it, the chances are that, instead of being alive, with a pen in my hand, in 1968, I should have been killed in action in 1915 or 1916. This was the fate of about half of those school-fellows and fellow-undergraduates of mine who were my intimate friends. Since that time, death has been my constant companion, for my contemporaries who were killed in the First World War have never been out of my mind from then till now. Ever since then, I have felt it strange to be still alive, and I have counted as a bonus all the years through which I have lived since 1916. (Most of my close friends who were killed in the First World War had met their deaths before the end of that year.)

The tale of my bonus years of life has now mounted up to more than half a century. This time-bonus has been particularly valuable for me, because I have been an historian, and historians, like philosophers and politicians, need more time than mathematicians, ballet-dancers, or

[1] [Deutero-] Isaiah, liii, 7.

football-players to achieve results in their particular line of work. I am now more than two and a half times as old as my Uncle Arnold was when he died. If, like him, I had died at thirty, and, *a fortiori*, if I had died in my middle twenties—the age, at death, of my contemporaries who were killed in the First World War—I should have died without leaving any memorial to speak of. The posthumous published work of my scholar contemporaries who were killed in 1915-1916 is pathetically small in amount, though some of it is high in quality and great in promise. The loss of their, and their German fellow victims', potential contribution to mankind's cumulative intellectual achievement has been a loss to the world, not just to their personal friends.

"In the midst of life we are in death." Having lived with this experience, as I now have, for more than fifty years, I am indeed familiar with death. I shall therefore have no excuse if, when my turn comes to die—and, at my age, death cannot be far off—I fail to face death readily and cheerfully. Of course I cannot be sure that I shall not fail. No one knows how he is going to take his own death till it stares him in the face.

I can, however, be certain of two things. If I do flinch and quail and repine, I shall feel deeply ashamed, because I shall be unable to forget the time-bonus that I have enjoyed. I can also be certain that death is not going to take me by surprise as an event that has not been in my mind till it has overtaken me. It has been in my mind constantly: my Uncle Arnold's death since as early in my life as I can remember; my contemporaries' deaths for more than half a century by now; and—most poignant of all my experiences of death so far—the death of my eldest son twenty-nine years ago. He was the first male child, after me, in our branch of the Toynbee family. (My father was the only one of my Toynbee grandfather's sons who had children.) My son died still more unexpectedly, suddenly, and tragically than his great-uncle Arnold, and also at a still younger age—at the age of my own contemporaries who had died in the First World War. "In the midst of life we are in death." This lesson—so harsh, yet so salutary—has been driven deep into my consciousness by a succession of hammer-strokes.

This life-long familiarity with death has reconciled me, if I am not deceiving myself, to the prospect of my own death at my present age. If one of my grandchildren were to say to me, now, what I said to my Great Uncle Harry when he was a year or two younger than I now am, I do not believe that I should take the child's pin-prick as tragically as Uncle Harry took mine. I hope that I am reconciled to the prospect of my own death *bona fide*. The test, of course, will come when I know that my own death is imminent. But to be reconciled to the prospect of one's own death—supposing that one truly is—does not mean that one is reconciled to death itself as one of the inescapable facts of our human condition. If I really am reconciled to the prospect of death for myself, this is just because I am not reconciled to the deaths of a number of other people—deaths that are now long-since-accomplished facts and that are outstanding events in my own experience.

It may be pointed out that all the deaths in question, except my Great Uncle Harry's, have been premature deaths, so it may be argued that it is their intolerable prematurity that has reconciled me—if it *has* reconciled me—to my own coming death at what will be a ripe old age. One may rebel against premature death without rebelling against death itself when it comes in the form of a natural death in the fullness of years.

Premature death may be incurred in various ways. It may be inflicted by human hands deliberately either by public enterprise (war and the execution of judicial death-sentences) or by private enterprise (murder). It may be inflicted by non-human living creatures (bacteria, sharks, man-eating tigers). It may be caused by hunger, thirst, or exposure to the elements—defeats of man by non-human nature that have been becoming less frequent in the economically "developed" minority of mankind, though the reduction of the rate of premature deaths from these causes among this minority is being offset by an increase in the rate of premature deaths caused by accidents—particularly in the form of miscarriages of our increasingly high-powered machinery which, in its application to our means of locomotion, has enabled us to "annihilate distance" at the price of a high toll of deaths in road-vehicles and in aeroplanes. (The toll taken by the now obsolescent railway-train was comparatively light.)

Since death is irretrievable, the deliberate infliction of premature death by one human being on another is surely a heinous offence—and this not only in murder and in war, but also in the execution of judicial death-sentences. Murder has been almost universally condemned—though there have been, and still are, some exceptional societies in which a youth does not qualify for being accepted as a man until he has taken another man's life. Killing in war has, till now, been almost universally regarded as being respectable—though a misgiving about its respectability is betrayed in the euphemistic use of the word "defence" to signify war and preparation for war, however aggressive the intention. For instance, the Spartan official formula for a mobilisation order with the object of invading a foreign country was "to declare a state of defence" (*phrouran phainein*); and the costs of genocidal atomic weapons are entered under the rubric "defence" in the budgets of present-day states. The infliction of premature death by process of law has been approved of still more widely and confidently than the infliction of it by act of war. When the abolition of the death-penalty has been mooted, this has usually aroused violent controversy; yet the abolition of it is now an accomplished fact in some states in the present-day world. The reason for this obstinately resisted abandonment of an age-old practice is that "while there is life there is hope". A change of heart may be experienced by even the most apparently hardened criminal.

We ought not to be reconciled to premature death when this is caused by human design or callousness or incompetence or carelessness. Yet there are cases in which even premature death is acceptable—the cases in which it has been risked and suffered voluntarily for the benefit of some fellow human being or of mankind in general. Voluntary premature death in war is the form of heroic self-sacrifice that has been both the most frequently performed and the most enthusiastically applauded; yet this is also the form of heroism that is the most ambivalent, since a man who is killed in war dies prematurely in the act of trying to inflict premature death on some of his fellow human beings. There is nothing questionable about the heroism of the premature death of someone who sacrifices his or her life in trying to save a fellow human being from meeting death by, say, drowning or burning; and we can also accept, while we lament, the premature death of pioneers and inventors who have deliberately risked their lives in the cause of making life better for mankind as a whole.

Many men have sacrificed their lives prematurely in winning for mankind, by daring and dangerous experimentation, the art of domesticating wild animals, the art of navigation, the art of aviation. (Scaling the Matterhorn, reaching the Poles, and breaking out of the earth's air-envelope into outer space do not seem to me to be objectives for which lives ought to have been risked and lost.) Many physicians have sacrificed their lives prematurely by tending the victims of deadly contagious diseases, or by experimenting perilously on themselves. My grandfather, who was a doctor, killed himself, unintentionally, when he was at the height of his powers, by experimenting on himself, in the early days of the use of anaesthetics, in order to discover what the right degree of dosage was. So there are circumstances in which premature death is not unacceptable, however grievous it may be.

What are we to say about the premature death of the spirit in a human body that still remains physically alive? I am familiar with this form of premature death too—the death-in-life of insanity and senility. I have been at very close quarters with a human being who lived on physically to a higher age than I have reached now for more than thirty years—about three-eighths of his total span of physical life—after he had suffered the death of the spirit. I have also known intimately three persons—two of them dominating personalities and the third a robust one—who have succumbed to senility in old age. This premature death of a human spirit in advance of the death of its body is more appalling than any premature death in which spirit and body die simultaneously. It is an outrage committed by nature on human dignity. "Slay us", nature or God, if you choose or if you must, but slay us "in the light".[1] Allow the light of reason—the faculty that makes a human being—to

[1] *Iliad*, Book XVII, line 647.

survive in us till the end of the life of the body. The spectacle of insanity and senility has always appalled me more than the witnessing or the hearing of a physical death. But there are two sides to this situation; there is the victim's side, as well as the spectator's; and what is harrowing for the spectator may be alleviating for the victim.

It will not, of course, be alleviation for him if the failure of his mental faculties overtakes him only gradually and then only to a degree that leaves him aware of what is happening to him. I can think of no worse fate than this, and I have seen it befall my oldest and closest friend—a man three months younger than myself. Our friendship had begun at school when we were thirteen years old and had continued for more than sixty years before he died. One could hardly suffer a greater loss than I suffered in losing him. Yet I could not and cannot regret his death, grievously though I miss him; for his death was, for him, a merciful release from a distress that was irremediable and that was becoming excruciating for him. As for those other three friends of mine, they did not suffer as my poor school-fellow suffered; for their mental eclipse was, not partial, but total—as complete as if they had been dead physically as well as mentally—and, for two of the three, this mental death, so far from being a torment, was a release from acute unhappiness. One of these two had previously been in a constant state of painful anxiety, fretfulness, and tension; and, for her, senility brought with it a serenity that she had not enjoyed since her early years. The other, who was love incarnate, had been inconsolable for the loss of her husband till she was released from her unbearable grief by oblivion— a mental death which was a merciful anticipation of the physical death that was tardy in coming to her rescue.

This two-sidedness of death is a fundamental feature of death—not only of the premature death of the spirit, but of death at any age and in any form. There are always two parties to a death; the person who dies and the survivors who are bereaved.

Death releases its prey instantly from all further suffering in this world—and from any further suffering at all, if one does not believe in personal immortality or in metempsychosis, but believes either that death spells annihilation or that it spells reabsorption into the Ultimate Spiritual Reality from which the life of a human personality is a temporary aberration.

Lucretius believed that death spells annihilation, and that it therefore confers on the dead a total and everlasting immunity from suffering, either mental or physical. He preaches this nihilist gospel of salvation with a passionate conviction and a fervent concern for the relief of his fellow mortals that make this passage of his poem[1] particularly memorable.

---

[1] Lucretius, *De Rerum Natura*, Book III, lines 830-930, minus lines 912-918, which have been misplaced in the surviving manuscripts.

Death, then is null for us—null and irrelevant—in virtue of the
conclusion that the spirit of man is mortal. We felt no ill in that
past age in which the Phoenicians were flocking to battle from all
quarters—an age in which the whole earth was rocked by the fearful
turmoil of war, rocked till it quaked horrifyingly under the lofty
ceiling of the air; an age in which the fate of all mankind was
trembling in the balance. One of the two contending powers was
going to win world-wide dominion on both land and sea, and none
could foresee which of the two would be the winner. Well, we felt no
ill in that age, and we shall feel no ill, either, when we have ceased
to exist—when once soul and body, whose union constitutes our
being, have parted company with each other. We shall have ceased
to exist; that is the point; and this means that, thenceforward,
nothing whatsoever can happen to us, that nothing can awaken any
feeling in us—no, not even if land were to fuse with sea, and sea with
sky . . .[1]

We can feel assured that, in death, there is nothing to be afraid of.
If one is non-existent, one is immune from misery. When once
immortal death has relieved us of mortal life, it is as good as if we
had never been born . . .[2]

So, when you see someone indulging indignantly in self-pity [at the
thought of his body's destiny after death], you may be sure that,
though he himself may deny that he believes that, in death, he will
retain any capacity for feeling, his profession of faith does not ring
true. It is belied by a latent emotion that is subconscious. As I see it,
he is not really conceding his premise and its basis. He is not removing
and ejecting himself from life radically. Unconsciously he is making
some vestige of himself survive . . . He is not dissociating himself
fully from his cast-away corpse; he is identifying himself with it and
is infusing into it his own capacity for feeling, under the illusion that
he is standing there beside it. This is the cause of his indignant self-
pity at having been created mortal. He fails to see that, in real death,
he will have no second self that will be still alive and capable of
lamenting to itself over its own death, or of grieving, as he stands,
in imagination, over his prostrate self, that he is being mangled by
beasts of prey or is being cremated.[3]

Lucretius goes on to put his finger on the difference between the fate
of the dead and the fate of the survivors. He pictures a dead man's wife
and children saying, as they stand by his funeral pyre:

"Poor wretch, what a wretched fate. One cruel day has deprived
you of all the blessings of life." But, in this pass, they do not go on to
say: "However, death has simultaneously released you from any

[1] Lines 830-842.
[2] Lines 866-9.
[3] Lines 870-887.

desire for these blessings." If they realised this truth clearly and matched it in what they said, they would be able to release their souls from a heavy burden of anguish and fear. "You," they would say, "are now oblivious in death, and in that state you will remain until the end of time, exempt from all pain and grief. It is we who are the sufferers; it is we who, standing by you, reduced to ashes on the appalling pyre, have mourned you to the limit of human capacity for grief, and find ourselves still inconsolable. Our sorrow is everlasting. The day will never come that will relieve our hearts of it."[1]

From this Lucretius draws the following conclusion in the lines that immediately follow.

So this man [who feels an indignant self-pity in contemplating his future after death] has to be confronted with the question: What is there that is particularly bitter in this future, if it is just a return to sleep and quiet? What is there in this prospect that should make anyone pine away in everlasting grief?[2]

This lapse of a sensitive spirit into such obtuse complacency pulls up Lucretius's reader with a jerk. Is a man who is feeling distress at the prospect of his own death going to be totally relieved by the realisation that his death will automatically bring with it an immunity from suffering for himself? Is he going to feel no concern for the grief of his bereaved wife and children? Is his certainty of "everlasting" peace and quiet for himself in death going to console him for the "everlasting" sorrow of the survivors?

It may be answered that, though the poet has used—and perhaps deliberately used—the same word "everlasting" to describe the respective states of the survivors and of the dead, the application of the word to the survivors is an exaggeration, considering that they, in their turn, are going to attain, sooner or later, "the return to sleep and quiet" that death brings to every mortal in the end. Meanwhile, they are going, on Lucretius's own showing, to experience the extreme of suffering; and Lucretius has denied himself the licence to play this suffering down on the ground that it will be only temporary; for, in a later passage,[3] he argues, eloquently and convincingly, that the fancied everlasting torments of the damned in hell after death are fabulous projections of genuine torments—mostly self-inflicted—which we experience in this life. "It is here, in this world," he sums up the argument of this passage in its last line, "that people make life hell through their own stupidity." Yet he has admitted that bereavement makes life hell, here in this world, for the bereaved. Is he prepared to write off their torment, too, as the self-inflicted penalty for a stupidity that is avoidable and reprehensible?

[1] Lines 898-908.
[2] Lines 909-911.
[3] Lines 973-1023.

The truth is that Lucretius has been preoccupied by his characteristically impetuous effort to deprive death of its sting and the grave of its victory for the person who is dreading the prospect of death for himself. He has overlooked the crucial fact that, in a death, there are two parties to the event. "For none of us liveth to himself and no man dieth to himself."[1] Man is a social creature; and a fact of capital importance about death's sting is that it is two-pronged. Lucretius may have succeeded in excising the sting for the person who dies, but he has failed to excise it for the dead's survivors. It looks, indeed, as if he has been blind to the significance of the pain of bereavement that he has described incidentally in such moving words. Euripides had been more perceptive. After asking if the experience that we call dying is not really living, and if living is not really dying,[2] he immediately goes on to observe that the spectators of a death are not saved from suffering by their awareness that the dead are exempt from all suffering and from all ills.

When, therefore, I ask myself whether I am reconciled to death, I have to distinguish, in each variant of the situation, between being reconciled to death on my own account and being reconciled to it on the account of the other party. Supposing that I am really reconciled to the prospect of my own death at a ripe old age, am I also reconciled to the prospect of the sorrow and the loneliness that death is going to bring upon my wife if she survives me? Supposing that I feel that people who have risked and suffered premature death deliberately for the sake of fellow human beings have found a satisfactory fulfilment of the possibilities of life for themselves, am I reconciled to the loss that their premature deaths have inflicted on mankind, including me? (This question is the theme of George Meredith's novel *Beauchamp's Career*.) Supposing that I feel that the oblivion conferred by senility or insanity has been a boon for someone who was suffering spiritual agony so long as he was in full possession of his mental and spiritual faculties, am I reconciled to my loss of this friend through his lapse into a death-in-life? And, apart from my personal loss, am I reconciled to the brutal affront to human dignity that nature has committed in choosing this humiliating way of releasing a human being from spiritual suffering?

Finally, am I reconciled to the prospect that I may survive my wife, even supposing that she lives to a ripe old age in full possession of her faculties and without suffering more than the minimum of physical pain that is the normal accompaniment of death even in its easiest forms, with the exception of instantaneous deaths and deaths in sleep? The hard fact is that the ways of dying that impose the lightest ordeal on the person who dies are, by their very nature, the ways that inevitably make the shock for the survivors the severest. I have mentioned an old friend of mine whose unbearable grief for the death of her husband was

---

[1] Romans, xiv, 7.
[2] Fragment from Euripides' lost play *Phrixus*, quoted on p. 182.

eventually obliterated by the oblivion of senility. The shock that she had suffered had been extreme. She had found her husband lying dead in his bed one morning. He had appeared to be in normal health the day before; but for some years his heart had been weak, and he had died from heart-failure in his sleep—peacefully and almost certainly painlessly; I myself recently had the experience of receiving a severe shock from learning of the sudden death of someone with whom my life had once been intimately bound up, though, in this case too, the death had not been a lingering one or been physically very painful, and had come at an age—six months younger than mine—at which death is to be expected.

If one truly loves a fellow human being, one ought to wish that as little as possible of the pain of his or her death shall be suffered by him or by her, and that as much of it as possible shall be borne by oneself. One ought to wish this, and one can, perhaps, succeed in willing it with one's mind. But can one genuinely desire it in one's heart? Can one genuinely long to be the survivor at the coming time when death will terminate a companionship that is more precious to one than one's own life is—a companionship without which one's own life would be a burden, not a boon? Is it possible for love to raise human nature to this height of unselfishness? I cannot answer this question for anyone except myself, and, in my own case, before the time comes, I can only guess what my reaction is likely to be. I have already avowed a boastful guess that I shall be able to meet my own death with equanimity. I have now to avow another guess that puts me to shame. I guess that if, one day, I am told by my doctor that I am going to die before my wife, I shall receive the news not only with equanimity but with relief. This relief, if I do feel it, will be involuntary. I shall be ashamed of myself for feeling it, and my relief will, no doubt, be tempered by concern and sorrow for my wife's future after I have been taken from her. All the same, I do guess that, if I am informed that I am going to die before her, a shameful sense of relief will be one element in my reaction.

My own conclusion is evident. My answer to Saint Paul's question "O death, where is thy sting?" is Saint Paul's own answer: "The sting of death is sin." The sin that I mean is the sin of selfishly failing to wish to survive the death of someone with whose life my own life is bound up. This is selfish because the sting of death is less sharp for the person who dies than it is for the bereaved survivor.

This is, as I see it, the capital fact about the relation between living and dying. There are two parties to the suffering that death inflicts; and, in the apportionment of this suffering, the survivor takes the brunt.

Index

Abraham, 61, 77, 79, 92
Absolute, divine, 102–4
Achilles, 70–1, 78
Addison, Joseph, 47
Adonis, 67
Adrian, Lord, 211
Advaita Vedanta, 101, 107
Advertising, *see* subliminal advertising
Africa, Southern, 151
After-life, 25–7, 35, 106, 110, 113, 118–19, 121, 124, 135, 137, 140, 142, 173, 191, 248, 255
Agamemnon, 76
Ahaz, King, 61
Ahriman, 88, 91
Ahura Mazdah, 88, 91
Akkadians, 85
Alexei, 79–81
Algeria, 151
Allah, 67
Allen, Warner, 200
American Revolution, 147
American Society for Psychical Research, 186, 199, 236
Amida, 99
Amitabha, 99, 107
Amoeba, 62, 68–9
Amon-Re, 66
Amphipolis, 76
Anabaptists, 120
Ancestors: cult of, 79, 87, 110, 112–13; relics of, 59
Anesaki, Professor, 84
Anglicanism, 121
Antiochus, Emperor, 78
Antoninus Pius, Emperor, 81
Apollo, 66
Apuleius, 215
Ariès, P., 46
Aristotle, 119
Arjuna, 104
Artemidorus, 72
Ashramas, 106
Ashur, 66
Assyrians, 91

Astral body, 251–2
Athena, 66
Athos, Mount, 85
Atomic weapons, 150, 154
Attis, 67
Auden, W. H., 173
Austin, J. L., 25
Australia, 73
Autopsies, 15
Avatars, 104
Avery, G., 48; Works, *Dangerous Sports, A Tale Addressed to Children Warning Them Against Wanton, Careless, Or Mischievous Exposure To Situations From Which Alarming Injuries So Often Proceed*, 48q.
Ayer, Professor A. J., 25, 210, 212; Works, *Language, Truth and Logic*, 25q.
Aztec, 62, 151

Babylonia, 88
Babylonians, 85
Bacteriological warfare, 152
Badajoz, 146
Balder, 67
Balfour, Arthur, 1st Earl of, 222, 238–41
Balfour, Francis, 239
Balfour, Gerald, 2nd Earl of, 237, 239–41
Balliol College, Oxford, 261
Barrett, Sir William, 222
Barth, Karl, 133, 143
Beausobre, Madame Julia de, 199
Beauvoir, Simone de, 162, 176; Works, *A Very Easy Death*, 162q.
Beckett, Samuel, 173; Works, *Malone Dies*, 173q.
Beecher, Dr. Henry, 23
Bennett, Arnold, 200
Bereavement, 94, 269–70
Berenson, Bernard, 200
Bergson, Henri Louis, 213, 248
Berlin, 150
Bernadette, 215

Bhagavad Gita, 104–5
Bhakti, 115
Bhang, 205, 209
Bible, The, 33, 121, 136, 143
Birth, attitude to, 32
Blackmuir, R. P., 167; Works,
   Language as Gesture, 167q.
Blake, William, 215
Bodhisattvas, 99, 110
Bonhoeffer, Dietrich, 143
Book of the Dead, 88
Bosanquet, Theodora, 249
Boswell, James, 130
Bouchet, Dr. E., 20
Brahma, 66, 95
Brasidas, 76
British Army, 146
Broad, Professor C. D., 211–13, 225,
   243, 245
Brontë, Emily, 200
Browning, Robert, 237
Bruhier-d'Ablaincourt, J. J., 15, 19
Bruno, Giordano, 126
Buchan, John, 200
Bucke, Dr. R. M., 214
Buddha, 71, 80, 83, 95–101, 104, 106,
   113–14, 181, 215
Buddhism, 66, 95–6, 98–104, 107–8,
   110–14, 123, 252
Buddhists, 62, 73, 84, 92–3, 95–6, 98,
   100–1, 105, 107, 110–12, 114, 130,
   252
Bultmann, Rudolf, 34, 134, 140
Burial, 59–60
Burt, Sir Cyril, 211, 213, 218, 225, 245
Bushido, 112

Caesarean sections, 15–16
Calvinist doctrine, 123
Cameron, Mrs., 54; Works, *History of
   Margaret Whyte, or the Life and Death of
   a Good Child*, 54q.
Camus, Albert, 174–6; Works, *The
   Outsider*, 174q., 175q.; *The Plague*, 174q.
Canaan, 61
Canaanites, 151
Cannibalism, 60–1
Carré, Claude, 15
Carroll, Lewis, 131, 160, 166
Carthage, 61

Catholicism, 142
Ch'an, 108, 111
Chardin, Teilhard de, 134, 140
Charles V, King, 16
Chemosh, 61
Cheyne, Dr. G., 16
Children: attitudes towards own death,
   53–5; ties with parents, 47; under-
   standing of death, 50–2; Victorian, 49
China, 72–3, 95, 108, 150
Chinese, 79, 147
Chitragputa, 105
Christ, 34, 67, 135
Christian radicalism, 136, 140, 143
Christian salvation, 96
Christian theology, 66
Christianity, 62, 66, 90–1, 100, 116–19,
   122, 126–7, 130, 133, 140–1, 143–4,
   147, 180
Christians, 73, 125, 146, 219, 243, 260,
   262
Christie, Agatha, 160
Chu Hsi, 111
Church of England, 141
Civille, M. Francois, 15
Clark, Dr. Stafford, 187
Cleomenes III, King, 72
Clergy, 43, 45
Clough, Arthur Hough, 157; Works, *The
   Latest Decalogue*, 157q.
Cocteau, Jean, 170; Works, *Orphée*, 170q.
Commemoration, 75–7, 79
Commodus, 81
Common Prayer, Book of, 129, 263
Communism, 32
Confucianism, 95, 108–14, 123
Confucius, 80, 108, 110–11
Congregationalism, 141
Constant, de Rebecque, Henri, 174
Contraceptives, 157
Control personality, 230, 232, 234
Coombe-Tennant, Mrs., 236, 238–41, 248
Coroner, 13
Cox, Harvey, 133; Works, *The Secular
   City*, 133q.
Cremation, 106–7
Cretans, 68
Croesus, King, 70, 221
Crookall, Dr. Robert, 200
Cross Correspondences, 235, 238, 242,
   249

Cuba, 150
Custance, John, 205; Works, *Wisdom, Madness and Folly*, 205q.

Damnation, fear of, 136
Dante, Alighieri, 85, 88, 94, 124, 170, 237; Works, *Divina Commedia*, 85q., 124q.; *Inferno*, 94q.
Darwin, Charles, 201, 224
David, 92
Death: attitudes to, 32–3, 59–60; attitudes towards the dying, 37–41; cellular, 19; comforting of patients and the dying, 40–4, 137, 142; concept of, 27; diagnosis of, 13–23; fear of, 185; premature, 265–7; realisation of, 43–5; somatic, 19; sparing patients' feelings, 40–5; sudden, 29; survival of, 25, 27, 35, 113, 116–17, 219, 230n., 242, 246, 251–2, 254–5; views of, 34; Western outlook on, 129–30
Death certificate, 13, 19, 21–2
'Death of God' theology, 140
Decapitation, 18, 21
de Fontenelle, J., 15, 126; Works, *Conversations of the Plurality of Worlds*, 126q.
Democritus, 72
Demosthenes, 72
Descartes, René, 252
Dickens, Charles, 160–1; Works, *The Old Curiosity Shop*, 160q.
Dissection, 13
Doctors, 13, 159
Dodds, Professor E. R., 234–5
Donnet, Cardinal Archbishop, 16
Dostoievski, Fyodor Milhailovich, 161
Douglas, Keith, 170–1; Works, *Vergissmeinnicht*, 170q.
Dreams, 189–90, 202, 228, 233, 254–6
Drugs, *see* Psychedelic drugs
Duke University, 200, 226
Dying, 27–33, 36–45, 131, 142, 185

East Lynne, 49
Eccles, Sir John, 211
Ecumenism, 143
Eddington, Sir Arthur, 206, 210
Ego, 189

Egypt, 74–5, 88, 90, 145
Egyptians, 69
Einstein, Albert, 125
Electrocardiogram, 23
Electroencephalogram, 22–3
Eliot, George, 200
Eliot, T. S., 171, 195, 216; Works, *Four Quartets*, 216q.; *The Waste Land*, 171q.
Elysium, 85, 87, 93
Empson, William, 160–2, 167, 172; Works, *Ignorance of Death*, 160q.
Enlil, 66
Epiphenomenalism, 251
Episcopalian Church of England, 129
Eschatology, 137, 140
E.S.P. (Extra-Sensory Perception), 223–32, 234–5, 242–3
Etruscan tombs, wall paintings in, 88
Euripides, 182–3, 270
Existentialism, 25, 32–5, 121, 134, 140
Eysenck, H. J., 225

Faithfull, Marianne, 192
Fall, the, 135, 139
Family household, composition of, 155–6
Findlay, Stephen, 199
First World War, 146, 148–9, 153, 167, 263–4
Fleming, Ian, 171
Fleming, Mrs., 236–7, 239
Flew, Anthony, 26
Fodére, F. E., 18–19
Forster, E. M., 162
Fox, Oliver, 201
France, 151
French Revolution, 127, 147
Freud, Sigmund, 160, 187–8, 226–7, 255
Freya, 66
Funerary rites, 60, 62, 106, 141–2, 173

Galapagos Islands, 201
Gandhi, Mohandas Karamchand, 104
Ganges, 107
Gannal, F., 20
Geddes, Lord, 195, 197, 201, 204, 206
Gehenna, 119
Genesis, 33, 77, 79
Genocide, 74, 153
Gerhardi, William, 191, 200

Germans, 153

Gibbon, Edward, 46, 127; Works, *The History of the Decline and Fall of the Roman Empire*, 127q.

Gilgamesh, 75

God: belief in, 25, 67–8; judgment of, 134

Gomes, Professor, 211

Gorer, Geoffrey, 141, 143, 162, 171, 187; Works, *Death, Grief and Mourning in Contemporary Britain*, 141–2q., 162q., 187q.

Gorky, Maxim, 172; Works, *My Childhood*, 172q.

Grail, the, 189

Grass, Gunter, 171; Works, *The Tin Drum*, 171q.

Gray, Thomas, 171; Works, *Elegy*, 171q.

Greeks, 62, 68, 70, 147

Green, C. E., 200

Guernica, 148–9

Gurney, Edmund, 222, 236–7, 239, 242

Hades, 78, 85, 87, 93

Hadrian, 81

Hadwen, W. R., 17

Haeckel, Ernest, 224

Hamburger, Professor, 22

Happold, Dr. F. C., 200

Hardy, Sir Alister, 210, 225

Hardy, Thomas, 167–9, 171; Works, *The Walk*, 168q.; *Titanic, The Convergence of the Twain*, 167q., 169q., 171q.; *Veteris vestigia fiammae*, 167q.

Hart, Professor Hornell, 200

Haunts, 227–8

Hawks, John, 172; Works, *Second Skin*, 172q.

Heaven, 91–6, 108, 119–20, 123, 135, 208

Hedonism, 69

Heidegger, John James, 25, 34, 109

Heisenberg, Warner, 210

Hell, 91–5, 102, 119–20, 123, 132, 135–6, 170, 208

Hellenic Age, 88

Hemingway, Ernest, 200

Henri IV, King, 127

Hera, 70

Herodotus, 69–70

Heroism, 30–1, 266

Hindu mythology, 103–4

Hinduism, 66, 71, 95, 98, 101, 103–4, 113, 122–3

Hindus, 62, 72, 79, 84, 92, 96, 101, 130, 181

Hiroshima, 150

Hitler, Adolf, 66, 73–4

Homer, 70; Works, *Illiad*, 70q., 71q., 76q.; *Odyssey*, 76q., 78q., 85q.

Honen, 112

Horace, 76

Horus, 88

House of Clay, 101

Houston, 128

Hudson, Dr., 210–11

Human sacrifice, 61

Hume, David, 252

Huxley, Aldous, 102, 205, 247; Works, *The Doors of Perception*, 205q., 247q.; *The Perennial Philosophy*, 102q.; *Hymn for Infant Minds*, 50

Icard, Dr., 20

Immortality, personal, 26, 35, 45, 67–9, 84–6, 89, 92, 96–7, 101, 107, 109–110, 116–19, 122–3, 126, 129, 133, 135–6, 158, 182, 259, 267

Incarnation, 134–5

India, 66, 83, 95, 142

Indian philosophies, 62

Infant mortality, 64

International Symposium on Brain and Consciousness, 211

Ionesco, Eugene, 170; Works, *Amédée*, 170q.; *Exit the King*, 170q.

Iouktas, Mount, 68

Iranians, 62

Iraq, 65, 145

Isaac, 61

Isis, 88, 215

Islam, 62, 66–7, 90–1, 122

Israel, 116–18

Ixion, 88, 94

Jainism, 62, 95, 100–1, 103–4, 107, 114

James, William, 191, 194–5, 214, 252; Works, *The Varieties of Religious Experience*, 214q.

Japan, 73, 95, 144

Japanese, 149
Jarrell, Randall, 170; Works, *The Death of a Ball Turret Gunner*, 170q.
Jastrow, Professor Joseph, 225
Jean, Countess of Balfour, 239, 241-2
Jeans, Sir James, 210
Jeffries, Richard, 206
Jephthah, 61
Jerusalem, 78
Jesus, 80-1, 89-90, 117, 125, 134
Jews, 73, 78, 92, 123, 125, 153, 260
Jivanmukti, 106
Johnson, Dr., 130
Johnson, Dr. Rayner, 200
Jones, Dr. Ernest, 187
Joyce, James, 165-6, 170; Works, *The Dead*, 165q.; *Ulysses*, 166q.
Judah, Kingdom of, 91-2
Judaism, 62, 66-7, 78, 88, 90-1, 122
Juggernaut, 72
Jung, Carl G., 188-91, 208, 219-20, 255

'Ka', 86
Kali, 105
Karma, 71, 83, 99-100, 102, 104-7, 109, 114, 183
Keats, John, 164, 170, 248; Works, *Hyperion*, 170q.
Kesselring, Joseph, 173; Works, *Arsenic and Old Lace*, 173q.
Kir-haraseth, 61
Klein, Melanie, 168
Koestler, Arthur, 192, 200, 203-4, 209, 214-15
Korea, 150
Krishna, 104, 205
Kwan Yin, 215
Kyoto, 84

Lampedusa, Giuseppe di, 164; Works, *The Leopard*, 164q.
Lancet, 16, 24
Lao-Tse, 108-9
Larkin, Lieutenant J. J., 220
Larkin, Philip, 161
Laski, Marghanita, 200
Last Judgment, 89
Last Trump, 89, 91, 93

Lawrence, D. H., 165, 200; Works, *Sons and Lovers*, 165q.
Leavis, F. R., 161
Lenk, Timur, 153
Leonard, Mrs. Osborn, 220-1, 234-5
Life, artificial prolongation of, 21-3
Linguistic analysis, 25, 34
Literature, children's, 48
Logical positivism, 204
Louis, Professor A., 16, 18
Lucian, 72
Lucretius, 72, 94, 122, 267-70; Works, *De Rerum Natura*, 94q., 122q.
Luther, Martin, 112
Lycians, 73
Lyttelton, Dame Edith, 236
Lyttelton, Mary Catherine, 238-41

Macaulay, Mr., 234, 242
Macedonians, 91
Madhva, 102
Mahakalpa, 95
Mahavira, 106
Mahayana, 98-101, 107-8
Maitreya, 100
Manasseh, King, 61
Mann, Thomas, 176; Works, *Doctor Faustus*, 176q.
Mara, 98-9, 113
Marcion, 183
Marconi, Guglielmo, 214
Marcus Aurelius, 81
Marduk, 66
Marihuana, 205
Mariolatry, 164
Marshall, Dr. T. K., 17
Marx, Karl, 80, 160
Marxism, Catholic, 140
Mayhew, Christopher, 206
Maze, Dr., 20
M'Connel, Lieutenant David, 220, 226
McGlashan, Dr. Colin, 190-1
Medina, 80
Mediums, 220-1, 230-5
Mediumship, 230-1
Meiji, 113
Meredith, George, 200, 270; Works, *Beauchamp's Career*, 270q.
Mescalin, 205-6, 208, 212, 247
Mesha, King, 61

Messiah, The, 91–2
Metempsychosis, 62, 83, 267
Methodism, 141
Mexico City, 128
Middle Kingdom, 75
Milarepa, 203
Mongols, 153
Monks, 129–30
Montaigne, M. de, 46
Moravians, 120
Mosaic Law, 78
Moses, 120
Mourning, 51, 53, 55, 142–3, 166, 168–9, 173
Muhammad, 80, 184
Muldoon, Sylvan, 201
Mummification, 75, 89
Murder, 65, 145, 147, 152, 265
Murphy, Professor Gardner, 216, 245
Muslims, 260
Mutilation of dead enemies, 60–1
Mycerinus, 69
Myers, Frederic, 222, 236–9, 242, 249

Nagasaki, 150
Napalm bombs, 153
Napoleon I, Bonaparte, 148
Nazis, 153, 233
Neanderthal Man, 59
Newton, Sir Isaac, 215, 222
Nichiren, 112
Neo-Confucianism, 111–12, 114
Nerva, 81
Nirvana, 66, 71, 83–4, 93, 95–9, 101, 108, 111, 114, 130, 181–3
Numaa Pompilius, law of, 16
Nysten, Pierre Hubert, 18

'Oceanic feeling', 204
Occultists, 213
Odin, 66
Odysseus, 70–1, 85
Old Kingdom, 75, 87–8
One Reality, 102
Organ transplantation, 19, 21
Origen, 120
Orphic tablets, 88
Orphics, 86
Osiris, 87–8, 90

Otto, Rudolf, 193
Ouspensky, Peter Demianovich, 216
Owen, Wilfred, 170; Works, Strange Meeting, 170q.
Oxford University, 200

Palaeolithic Age, 82
Palaeolithic paintings, 76
Palestine, 88, 253
Pantheon, 66
Paradise, 110, 113
Parapsychology, 185, 219, 222, 224, 228
Parsees, 107
Path, the, 97–8
Pascal, Blaise, 124, 126, 180
Pasternak, Boris, 172
Pausanias, 61
Pearce-Higgins, Canon John, 186
Pearson, Gabriel, 160; Works, Dickens and the Twentieth Century, 160q.
Penfield, Dr. Wilder, 211
Pensions, 156
Pentateuch, 80
Peregrinus, 72
Pericles, 76
Persian Empire, 88
Persians, 91
Persephone, 67
Personal identity, 26
Peru, 74
Pessimism, 69–72
Peter the Great, 79–81
Peu, P., 16
Pharisees, 78, 117
Philip II, King, 16
Phoenicians, 73
Piper, Mrs., 236–7
Plato, 245, 252
Plomer, William, 173
Plotinus, 183, 203, 215
Poe, Edgar Allen, 167
Polanyi, Professor Michael, 214
Posterity, 80, 82
Poteat, W. H., 35
Predestination, 123
Premature burial, fear and execution of, 13, 15, 17–19, 21, 24
Price, Professor H. H., 213, 216, 225, 233
Prix Dusgate, 20
Protestantism, 120–1, 138–9

Proust, Marcel, 168
Prussian state, 148
Psalms, 63, 263
Psi-component and phenomena, 213, 221, 223, 226, 228, 243–4
Psyche, see Souls
Psychedelic drugs, 208, 247–8
Psychical research, see Parapsychology
Psychology, 179, 181–2
Puebla, 128
Pure Land, 112–13, 115
Purgatory, 119–20, 132
Pyramid texts, 88
Pythagoreans, 86

Qualified Non-Dualism, 102, 104
Qur'an, 80

Rahner, Karl, 34, 134–5
Raine, Dr. J. B., 223
Ramanuja, 102, 107, 115
Rayleigh, Lord, 222
Reincarnation, 103
Rebirth, doctrine of, 106–7, 109–10, 114
Redgrove, Peter, 171; Works, Corposant, 171q.
Relativity, 179–80
'Religionless Christianity', 143–4
Resurrection, 35, 78, 89–93, 117–19, 134–5, 140
Retrocognition, 235, 242–3
Reverence towards dead, 60, 113
Rhadakrishnan, ex-President, 102
Rhadamanthus, 88
Rhine, Dr. Louisa, 200, 226, 243; Works, ESP in Life and Lab, 226q.
Rhondda, Lady, 249
Robinson, John, 133; Works, Honest to God, 133q.
Roman Catholic Church, 127–9
Roman Empire, 82
Romans, 147
Rosenberg, Isaac, 169–71; Works, Dead Man's Dump, 169q.
Rousseau, Jean Jacques, 46; Works, Emile, 46q.
Royal Medical Society, 195
Royal Society, 124
Russell, Lord, 82

Ryan, M., 19
Ryle, Gilbert, 210

Sadducees, 78
Saint Augustine, 215
Saint John of the Cross, 216
Saint Mark, 81
Saint Paul, 33, 64, 80, 89–90, 120, 135, 193, 203, 215, 271
Saint Teresa of Avila, 215
Saint Thomas Aquinas, 119
Salter, W. H., 228–9, 236
Salvation, 105, 117–18, 135
Samkara, 101–4, 107–8
Samsara, 114
Samurai, 112
Sartre, Jean-Paul, 34, 175; Works, La Nausée, 175q.
Sati, 72
Schipa, Tito, 229–30
Schleiermacher, Friedrich, 120
Schroedinger, Erwin, 246
Second World War, 74, 148–50, 153, 226, 233
Segal, Dr. Hannah, 168; Works, A Psychoanalytic approach to Aesthetics, 168q.
Self, 189
Selkirk, Alexander, 180
Senility, 157–8, 266–7, 270–1
Separations, 201
Seth, 88
Shakespeare, William, 161; Works, Henry IV, Part II, 18q.; King Lear, 18q., 163q.; Romeo and Juliet, 14q.
Shem, 77
Sheol, 78, 85, 87, 93, 116, 118
Sherrington, Sir Charles, 211
Shinran, 112
Shinto, 113
Shintoism, 95, 113
Shiva, 66, 101, 103–5, 107
Sidgwick, Professor Henry, 222, 224–5, 236–7
Sidgwick, Mrs. Henry, 239, 241
Sikhism, 95
Simpson, Professor K., 14, 21
Sisyphus, 88, 94
Smith, J. G., 15; Works, Principles of Forensic Medicine, 15q.
Smith, Miss Susy, 206–7

Soal, Dr. S. G., 233–4
Society of Friends, 146
Society for Psychical Research (British), 199, 220, 222–3, 237
Socinians, 120
Solon, 70
Sophocles, 64, 70
Souls (psyche): conception of, 224; correlation with brain as instrument, 180–1; disinclination to accept beliefs in, 140; eternity of, 86–7, 96, 103–5, 252; hidden regions of, 230; individuality of, 188; judgment of, 87–90, 140–1; transmigration of, 86
Southampton University, 200
Soviet Union, 150–1
Spark, Muriel, 173
Spartan, 71
Sperry, Professor, 211
Spillane, Mickey, 171
Sravana Belgola, 101
Sri Anandamai, 205, 208
Stace, Professor W. T., 200, 216
Stevens, Wallace, 172–3; Works, *The Emperor of Ice-Cream*, 172q., 173q.
Stoppard, Tom, 161; Works, *Rosencrantz and Guildenstern are Dead*, 161q.
Strabo, 72
Stratton, Professor F. J. M., 198
Strauss, Dr. Eric, 232
Struldburgs, 158
Subliminal advertising, 213
Suffering, fear of, 42–3
Suicide, 72–3, 100, 112, 158, 172, 208
Sumer, 145
Sumerian civilisation, 65, 75, 85, 147: city states, 150; cuneiform script, 76
Supreme Ultimate, 111
Suspended animation, 14–15
Suzuki, D. T., 109
Svevo, Italo, 173; Works, *The Confessions of Zeno*, 173q.
Swift, Jonathan, 158
Syria, 88

Talbot, Mrs. Hugh, 221
Tammuz, 67
Tantalus, 88, 94
Tao-te-ching, 108–10
Taoism, 95, 108–11, 114

Taylor, Alfred, 14; Works, *Principles of Medical Jurisprudence*, 14q.
Technological progress, 64, 82, 124, 130, 143, 147
Telepathy, 224–5, 227–8, 235, 242–3, 255
Temple, 78
Tennyson, Alfred, Lord, 192, 200
Testaments, Old and New, 33, 61, 116–17, 119, 121, 133–5, 140
Theology, Protestant, 25, 34
Theodosius I, Emperor, 76
Theosophists, 219, 243
Thetis, 70
Thomas, Drayton, 234
Thor, 66
Thorpe, Professor, W. H., 211
Thucydides, 76
Thugs, 105
Tibet, 100
Tibetan Book of the Dead, 100, 105, 114
Tillich, Paul, 134, 140
Tityus, 88
Tolstoy, Alexei, 162–4; Works, *The Death of Ivan Ilyich*, 162q., 164q.
Tombs, 74
Townsend, Colonel, 15–16
Toynbee, Arnold (uncle), 260–1, 264
Toynbee, Captain Henry, 130
Toynbee, Philip, 212
Trajan, 81
Trinity, 67–8, 81
Turnbull, Colin, 205, 209
Tut-ankh-amen, 74
Tyrrell, George, 249

Ultimate Spiritual Reality, 67, 82–4, 92, 100–1, 114, 130, 147, 181–4, 259, 267
Unbelief, 126
Unconsciousness, 179, 181, 188, 191
United Nations Vital Statistics, 20, 23
United States, 127–9, 131, 138, 140, 142, 144, 148–52, 154–5
Upanishads, 101, 203
Ussher, Archbishop J., 125

Vaikuntha, 102
Valhalla, 85, 87, 93
van Buren, Paul, 133–4; Works, *The Secular Meaning of the Gospel*, 133q.

Vatican 11, 136, 139
Vaughan, Henry, 182–3; Works, *The Retreat*, 182q.
Vedanta, 102
Verney, Mary, 47
Verrall, Dr., 236
Verrall, Mrs., 236, 239, 242
Victorians, 52
Vietnam war, 14, 72, 149, 151, 153, 187
Vishnu, 66, 101–2, 104–5, 107
Vivekananda, Swami, 102
Voigt, Dr. J., 20–1, 23
von Balthasar, Hans Urs, 134
Voodoo, 230

War, 65, 145–52, 265–6
Ward, R. H., 207–8
Watts, Isaac, 49
Waugh, Evelyn, 173
Wells, H. G., 173
Weyl, Hermann, 210, 212
Whiteman, Professor J. H. M., 192, 201–4, 215
Wilkinson, Professor Denys, 194
Wisdom, John, 26

Wittgenstein, Ludwig, 25, 35, 162; Works, *Tractatus Logico-Philosophus*, 35q., 162q.
Woolf, Virginia, 164, 200; Works, *The Waves*, 164q.
Woolwich, Bishop of, 140
Wordsworth, William, 182–4, 200; Works, *Intimations of Immortality*, 182q., 183q.

Yahweh, 61, 67, 74, 77–9, 81, 92
Yama, 105
Yamantaka, 105
Yang, 111
Yin, 111
Yoga, 103, 107, 112
Yram, 201

Zaehner, Professor R. C., 200
Zarathustra, 87–8
Zarmanochegas, 72
Zen Buddhism, 108–9, 112–14
Zeus, 66, 68
Zeus Lykaius, 61
Zoroastrianism, 66, 74, 78, 88, 90–2, 100, 117, 123, 125, 260